STRESS AND ANXIETY

Volume 11

Series Editors
Charles D. Spielberger
University of South Florida

Irwin G. Sarason
University of Washington

Guest Editor of this Volume
Peter B. Defares
University of Amsterdam

⬤HEMISPHERE PUBLISHING CORPORATION, Washington
A subsidiary of Harper & Row, Publishers, Inc.

Cambridge   New York   Philadelphia   San Francisco
London   Mexico City   São Paulo   Singapore   Sydney

STRESS AND ANXIETY: Volume 11

1 2 3 4 5 6 7 8 9 0   B C B C   8 9 8

This book was set in Times Roman by Hemisphere Publishing Corporation. The editor was Diane Stuart, the production supervisor was Miriam Gonzalez, and the typesetter was Sandi Stancil.
BookCrafters, Inc. was printer and binder.

Library of Congress Cataloging-in-Publication Data

Advanced Study Institute on Stress and Anxiety in Modern Life,
Murnau, Ger., 1973.

Stress and anxiety: [proceedings] /edited by Charles D. Spielberger,
Irwin G. Sarason. Washington: Hemisphere Pub. Corp.
  v. :ill.: 24 cm. (v. 1–2: The series in clinical psychology
  v. 3–5: The series in clinical and community psychology)

  Includes bibliographies and indexes.
  1. Stress (Psychology)—Congresses. 2. Anxiety—Congresses.
I. Sarason, Irwin G., ed. II. Spielberger, Charles Donald, date, ed.
III. North Atlantic Treaty Organization. Division of Scientific Affairs.
IV. Title. [DNLM: 1. Anxiety. 2. Stress, Psychological. WM 1 72 S755a]

BF575.S75A38   1973   616.8'522   74-28292
                               MARC
ISBN 0-89116-312-3
ISSN 0146-0846
ISSN 0364-1112

Contents

II
PSYCHOPHYSIOLOGY OF STRESS AND ANXIETY

STRESS AND ANXIETY

THE SERIES IN CLINICAL AND COMMUNITY PSYCHOLOGY

CONSULTING EDITORS

Charles D. Spielberger and Irwin G. Sarason

IN PREPARATION

Contributors

A. APPELS, Department of Medical Psychology, University of Limburg, Maastricht, The Netherlands

M. BELLATERRA, Instituto de Psychiatria, Universita de Roma, Italy

W. R. BOWERMAN, Bureau of Child Research, University of Kansas, Lawrence, KS, USA

S. BREZNITZ, Ray D. Wolfe Centre for the Study of Psychological Stress, University of Haifa, Israel

P. B. DEFARES, Institute of Education, University of Amsterdam, The Netherlands

N. VAN DIJKHUIZEN, Zuidema Management Consultants, The Netherlands

P. R. J. FALGER, Faculty of Medicine, University of Limburg, Maastricht, The Netherlands

A. FIGA-TALAMANCA, Instituto de Psychiatria, Universita de Roma, Italy

B. W. FRIJLING, Department of Psychology, University of Leiden, The Netherlands

A. W. K. GAILLARD, Institute for Perception (TNO), Soesterberg, The Netherlands

E. M. GOUDSMIT, National Association for Premenstrual Syndrome, Teddington, Middlesex, England

P. GROSSMAN, Department of Psychology, Agricultural University, and Foundation for Stress Research, Wageningen, The Netherlands

W. VAN DEN HEUVEL, Study Center of Social Oncology, Erasmus University, Rotterdam, The Netherlands

K. JANSSEN, Institute of Psychology, University of Tilberg, The Netherlands

R. D. de JONG, Department of Clinical Psychology, University of Utrecht, The Netherlands

P. G. A. M. JORNA, Institute for Perception (TNO), Soesterberg, The Netherlands

A. A. KAPTEIN, Institute of Social Medicine, University of Leiden, The Netherlands

J. L. M. KREMER-NASS, Department of Psychology, University of Leiden, The Netherlands

K. C. LINDNER, Department of Psychology, University of Washington, Seattle, WA, USA

S. MATTEOLI, Instituto de Psychiatria, Universita de Roma, Italy

S. MOSTICONI, Instituto de Psychiatria, Universita de Roma, Italy

P. PANCHERI, Instituto de Psychiatria, Universita de Roma, Italy

J. PRUYN, Study Center of Social Oncology, Erasmus University, Rotterdam, The Netherlands

G. PUGLIESE, Instituto de Psychiatria, Universita de Roma, Italy

G. REDA, Instituto de Psychiatria, Universita de Roma, Italy

E. SANTARELLI, Instituto de Psychiatria, Universita de Roma, Italy

B. R. SARASON, Department of Psychology, University of Washington, Seattle, WA, USA

I. G. SARASON, Department of Psychology, University of Washington, Seattle, WA, USA

W. SCHÖNPFLUG, Institute of Psychology, Free University of Berlin, FRG

P. SCHULZ, Institute of Psychology, University of Trier, FRG

J. SNEL, Institute of Psychology, University of Amsterdam, The Netherlands

T. SOSNOWSKI, Instytut Psychologie, Uniwersytet Warszawski, Poland

J. STRELAU, Instytut Psychologie, Uniwersytet Warszawski, Poland

A. Ph. VISSER, Department of Social Psychology, University of Limburg, Maastricht, The Netherlands

J. A. M. WINNUBST, Department of Psychology, University of Utrecht, The Netherlands

Preface

In the 1980s the research literature on stress and anxiety has continued to expand at an accelerated rate. Because investigators from diverse disciplines and different countries are making significant contributions to our understanding of stress phenomena, keeping up with this burgeoning literature imposes tremendous demands on researchers. These demands have been met in part by an increasing number of international conferences and by the establishment of specialized journals on human stress, stress medicine, anxiety disorders, and anxiety research.

The Stress and Anxiety series was initiated in 1975 to facilitate the dissemination of research findings presented at international scientific conferences and advanced study institutes organized by the editors. In 1982, with the publication of Volume 8, the goals of the series were broadened. Professor Norman A. Milgram of Tel Aviv University served as guest editor of that volume, which comprised papers presented in Israel at international conferences on psychological stress in times of war and peace.

Professor Peter B. Defares of the University of Amsterdam has served as guest editor of Volume 9 and the present volume, which are based on international conferences held at The Netherlands Institute for Advanced Study in the Humanities and Social Science (NIAS). These conferences focused on stress research in western Europe and reflected various approaches to a wide range of stress phenomena. These conferences were supported in part by grants from the Dutch Ministry of Education, The Netherlands Heart Foundation, and The Netherlands Institute for Stress Research. The research reported in 18 of the 20 chapters in this volume, and in 12 of the 19 chapters in Volume 9, was carried out in Israel and six European countries.

This volume is divided into four parts, each dealing with a major area of research on stress and anxiety. Part I examines a wide range of theoretical issues that pertain to stress, coping, and performance. A common theme in these six chapters is the importance of cognitive processes as mediators and moderators of emotional reactions to stress. Part II reports the findings of investigations into the psychophysiology of stress and anxiety in both humans and animals.

Parts III and IV are concerned with the effects of stress and anxiety in the etiology and treatment of medical and surgical conditions. The chapters in Part III examine psychosocial factors, physical and emotional symptoms, and correlates of cardiovascular disease. The effects of stress and anxiety on a variety of medical and surgical conditions, ranging from infertility and the premenstrual syndrome to severe asthma and cancer, are examined in Part IV.

The editors of the series would like to express our appreciation to Professor Defares for his invaluable contributions in arranging the NIAS Stress and Anxiety conferences and his dedicated work in reviewing the manuscripts for this volume. We are also indebted to the director and the staff of NIAS for placing the resources of the Institute at our disposal during the planning and execution of the conferences as well as for their unstinting support. Finally, we thank Katherine Murphy and Diane Gregg for their help in the administrative arrangements for the conferences and Virginia Berch for her expert assistance in preparing the manuscript for publication.

Charles D. Spielberger
Irwin G. Sarason

I

STRESS, COPING, AND PERFORMANCE

1

Anxiety as a Motivating Factor and Stressing Agent

Peter Schulz and Wolfgang Schönpflug
Free University of Berlin

The role of anxiety as a motivating factor and as a stressing agent must be incorporated into an adequate theory of anxiety (Eysenck, 1979). While anxiety motivates task-related behavior, it also inevitably produces various forms of stress. The focus of this chapter is to analyze the reciprocal relationship between these two aspects of anxiety and to examine the theoretical implications of this relationship in light of the results of recent experimental studies.

ANXIETY AS A MOTIVATING FACTOR

Among the various factors that motivate people to cope with task requirements, anxiety appears to be one of the most important (Heckhausen, 1980; Seligman, 1975). Anxiety has been defined by Spielberger (1972) as an organismic emotional state, consisting of "unpleasant, consciously perceived feelings of tension and apprehension, with associated activation or arousal of the autonomic nervous system" (p. 20). Since feelings of tension and apprehension are also frequently observed in states of uncertainty (Epstein & Roupenian, 1970; Schulz & Schönpflug, 1982), it is reasonable to assume that anxiety motivates activities which serve to reduce uncertainty (Atkinson, 1964; Epstein, 1976). Moreover, given the fact that uncertainty can be produced by either internal or external demands associated with ambiguous outcomes, state anxiety is likely to intervene between such demands and task-related behavior.

It will be argued in this chapter that the "drive characteristics of anxiety" (Gaudry & Spielberger, 1971; Mandler & Sarason, 1952; Spielberger, 1966, 1972), as well as the "emotionality component of anxiety" (Liebert & Morris, 1967), are motivating factors that result from uncertainty in goal-oriented behavior. The question of why anxiety as a motivating factor is more dominant in some people than others will also be examined.

The research reported in this paper was supported by a grant to Dr. Wolfgang Schönpflug from the Government of the Federal Republic of Germany (Bundesministerium des Inneren/ Umweltbundesamt). Dr. Schulz is now at the University of Trier. Thanks are due Dr. Charles D. Spielberger for improving the final version of this chapter.

Since the outcomes of ongoing actions are often fed back as ambiguous information, they are generally open to a number of possible interpretations. Thus, individuals can develop a bias of attributing failure to their own actions. Moreover, it has been shown in a number of studies that high-anxious people tend to attribute their failures to internal factors (Kukla, 1972; Schulz & Schönpflug, 1982; Weiner & Potepan, 1970). This inevitably leads to negative self-evaluations or, as Wine (1980) pointed out, to "evaluative anxiety." Consequently, outcome feedback has greater significance for persons with high anxiety than those with low anxiety.

If external demands are imposed on persons disposed to attribute failure to personal limitations, it follows that anxious persons must try to avoid failure altogether in order to maintain self-esteem. If it is not possible to prevent failure, demotivating effects occur (Schulz & Schönpflug, 1982; Seligman, 1975). Evidence for this comes from a number of experimental studies. For example, in order to prevent failure high-anxious persons generally spend more time on assigned tasks in order to perform properly on the primary tasks (Schulz & Schönpflug, 1982), and they may resign from subsidiary tasks (Schulz, 1979). Anxious persons also tend to exert more effort during task performance than nonanxious persons (Eysenck, 1979). Moreover, failure feedback generally has greater adverse effects on high- than low-anxiety persons (Gaudry & Spielberger, 1971; Morris & Liebert, 1973).

ANXIETY AS A STRESSING AGENT

Performing an action continually changes the environment. Therefore, action outcomes must be continuously appraised because the resulting evaluations enable a person to adjust future actions in accordance with superior goals. Since appraisals depend on the subjective needs underlying the actions, the changed environment is appraised with regard to a variety of goals: social, achievement-related, affiliation-related, power-related, control-related, and so forth.

As previously noted, it is especially important for anxious people to reduce threats to self-esteem by avoiding failure. For anxious individuals, outcomes are typically appraised in terms of threats to self-esteem, which lead to more frequent appraisals concerning the correspondence between outcome and this dominant goal (Liebert & Morris, 1967) and to an increase in emotional load (Schulz, 1980). If task demands produce a high level of anxiety, this indicates that the outcome of a required action is of considerable importance. The hypothesis is that the increased significance of an outcome leads to a number of detrimental effects on ongoing task-related behavior.

In human affairs, especially those involving social relationships, outcome feedback is often unclear or insufficient. In such cases feedback appraisals evoke "worries" (Liebert & Morris, 1967) and other task-irrelevant cognitive activities (Sarason, 1975). Moreover, these task-irrelevant cognitions may cause interruptions of ongoing behavior (Mandler, 1979), which serve to "amplify" the anxiety drive (Tomkins, 1963) and produce or maintain a high level of anxiety (Mandler & Watson, 1966).

Anxiety-related interruptions of ongoing goal-directed actions are often associated with adverse effects on task-relevant cognitive procedures; more frequent and longer-lasting interruptions generally cause more anxiety and have greater detrimental effects on performance and retention (Mandler & Watson, 1966). The changed environment resulting from a previous action may also trigger appraisal processes and outcome feedback that cause anxiety and other interfering cognitive activities. Moreover, difficult tasks produce more negative outcomes and "worry interruptions" in high-anxiety persons (Liebert & Morris, 1967). It follows that negative outcome feedback during and after ongoing action is a crucial factor leading to anxiety. Thus, anxiety becomes a stressing agent that has adverse effects on performance and retention.

In the context of the general theoretical position outlined above, three questions with regard to mediating processes and mechanisms are investigated in this chapter:

1. What are the major consequences of anxiety as a motivating factor in determining how people cope with task requirements?
2. Are the same activities that are performed in coping with task demands also effective in reducing anxiety?
3. Assuming individual differences in the activity structures associated with anxiety level, what are the long-term effects on performance of high anxiety experienced while working on a task?

These questions were addressed in an experimental study in which the processes that mediate coping with task requirements over time were analyzed in persons who differed in level of state anxiety.

METHOD

Sixty subjects were each given 64 tasks designed to be analogous to problems encountered in administrative work. The subjects sat facing a keyboard and a visual display screen, divided into two fields. A problem was presented on the left side of the display field, for example, a calculation to be checked, an application to be evaluated, and so forth. By pressing button TB on the keyboard (Figure 1), the subject selected a problem, which remained visible in the left field until the task was completed.

The right side of the screen was used to display documents needed to resolve the problem, e.g., price lists, allowances, statements of account, etc. By pressing buttons 1 to 15, the various documents could be ordered, which then appeared on the right side of the screen. The subjects were free to order and use each document as frequently and for as long as they wanted, but only one document could be displayed at a time. A directory, which also appeared in the right field of the screen when subjects pressed button DB (Figure 1), listed the available documents and their respective numbers on the keyboard. Only a small number of the documents were relevant to the task solution, and these had to be identified, selected, and processed.

After completing the task, by pressing button DA the subjects could examine five alternative solutions, which appeared in the right field. One of these alternatives could then be chosen by pressing a button (SB 1 to 5). Only one alternative was correct. After each solution, the display was cleared and the

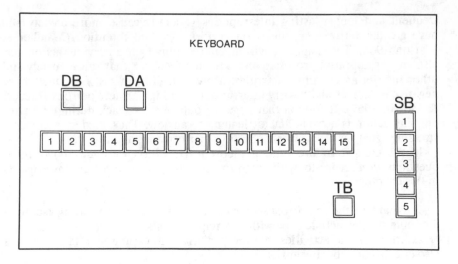

Figure 1 Keyboard for the experimental task.

subject could either rest or begin the next task by pressing the button labeled TB.

Procedure and Design

The 64 tasks were grouped in six blocks, each consisting of either 10 or 12 similar tasks. In order to be able to compare performance parameters at the beginning and at the end of the study, the first and sixth block of tasks were constructed as equivalent sets. No time limits were imposed. The tasks were executed in the same order by all subjects, as indicated below:

Block 1 (MT1): 12 mixed tasks
Block 2 (ChC): 10 tasks (checking calculations)
Block 3 (CC): 10 tasks (computing calculations)
Block 4 (DA): 10 tasks (deciding applications)
Block 5 (EC): 10 tasks (examining checks)
Block 6 (MT2): 12 mixed tasks

The trait-state approach has shown that the influence of trait anxiety on task-related behavior seems to be mediated by state anxiety (Spielberger, 1966, 1972). Therefore, state anxiety was measured at the beginning of the experiment, using a German adaptation (Laux, Schaffner, & Glanzmann, 1979) of the State-Trait Anxiety Inventory (Spielberger, Gorsuch, & Lushene, 1970). On the basis of the subjects' state anxiety scores, they were placed in low-, medium-, or high-anxiety groups whose scores were between 28 and 32, 33 to 42, and 43 to 63, respectively, with 20 subjects in each group. Noise and outcome feedback were experimentally manipulated, but only the feedback factor is considered in this chapter.

Dependent Variables

Overt task operations, physiological activity, and introspective reports were evaluated as dependent variables. In order to obtain a comprehensive pattern of achievement, five performance parameters were measured: (1) Type of information selected (directories, documents); (2) Number of times the directories and documents were ordered; (3) Sequence of operations; (4) Amount of time spent examining the various documents; and (5) Quality of task solution. After working on each block of tasks, the subjects responded to 11 questions: 8 on attributions of success or failure and 1 each on attentional lapses, changes in achievement motivation, and satisfaction with performance. These questions were answered by pressing buttons on the keyboard. On completing the experiment, the subjects were asked to describe their feelings and their strategies while working on the tasks, by responding to a special inventory constructed for this purpose.

All behavioral activities, including time parameters, introspective reports between blocks of tasks, and the three physiological measures (skin resistance, heart rate, pulse amplitude) were processed on-line* and stored by a DEC PDP 11/40 laboratory processor. The type of cognitive activity employed during each time period was inferred from the type of the documents ordered. For instance, if a subject ordered documents that could only be used in checking specifications, the operation was classified as a "checking operation." Three types of cognitive operations were differentiated:

1. Search operations: Search operations serve the purpose of selecting task-related documents from a pool of 15 items. Search operations were further differentiated into two categories: (a) number of times the directory was ordered; and (b) number of calls for task-irrelevant documents.
2. Checking operations: If subjects used documents which only allowed them to check the specifications of a task, these cognitive operations were classified as checking operations.
3. Processing operations: If subjects used documents which provided data for further processing, this was taken as an indication of processing operations.

RESULTS

Effort Expenditure

The high-anxious subjects used a significantly greater number of mental operations and spent more time on the tasks, but this result was obtained only for the first two blocks of tasks. Table 1 shows the mean effort expenditure, averaged for the 10 tasks, of the high-, medium-, and low-anxiety groups on the second block of tasks (checking calculations). This block was selected for comparison because all three types of cognitive operations were required for an optimal solution.

*The computer program was written by Rainer Klima and Wolfgang Battmann.

Table 1 Performance parameters for subjects in high, medium, and low state-anxiety groups on the second block of tasks

Performance parameters	Anxiety Level		
	High	Medium	Low
Mean time spent per task on searching needed documents (in seconds)	15.6	11.8	9.0
Mean time spent per task on checking specifications (in seconds)	46.9	35.8	27.4
Mean time spent per task on processing specifications (in seconds)	78.5	66.2	73.0
Mean time spent on one whole task (in seconds)	207	165	164
Mean error rate	0.26	0.28	0.41
Mean performance efficiency (ratio between correct solutions and time spent on tasks)	3.85	4.70	4.27

The following relationships between performance and state anxiety were found, as can be noted in Table 1: (a) the higher the level of anxiety, the more time spent on searching for documents ($p < .05$); (b) the higher the anxiety level, the more time spent on checking operations ($p < .05$); (c) as a consequence of spending more time on searching and checking operations, high-anxious subjects spent significantly more total time working on the tasks ($p < .01$); (d) high-, medium-, and low-anxiety groups did not differ in time spent on processing operations; (e) low-anxiety subjects had a significantly higher mean error rate ($p < .01$); (f) the performance efficiency index, computed as the ratio between correct solutions and time expenditure, showed that subjects with medium anxiety were most efficient. Thus, although the high-anxious subjects had the lowest error rate, their performance was less efficient.

The prolonged amount of time that high-anxious subjects spent in searching for documents and checking specifications does not reveal whether the execution of these cognitive operations required more time, or whether high-anxiety subjects selected more unnecessary documents. Further analyses revealed that the latter was the case: High-anxious subjects consulted the directory significantly more often ($p < .05$) and ordered significantly more unnecessary documents ($p < .05$). This increased effort expended by high-anxious subjects was especially evident when they were working without external outcome feedback.

Improvement of Activity Structures by Learning

The high-anxious subjects invested more time and effort working on the first two blocks of tasks, but they also acquired more task-specific information than low-anxious subjects, such as learning the association between needed documents and button numbers. Consequently, on later trials the high-anxiety subjects were more likely to call for documents without first consulting the directory and were thus able to reduce their mental load by saving on subsequent operations.

In order to determine how activity structures improved over time as a function of anxiety, performance on the last block of tasks was compared with performance on the first parallel block. Between these blocks, the subjects worked on 40 tasks which were similar in type. Since the associations between the documents listed in the directory and their numbered buttons were the same for all 64 tasks, these associations should have been easier for the high-anxiety subjects during the final block of tasks. Consistent with this expectation, as may be noted in Figure 2, the high-anxiety subjects selected the directory more often than the low-anxiety subjects on the first block of tasks, but less often during the last block. The values reported in Figure 2 are the average number of times the directory was called for per task; the observed Anxiety by Repeated Measures interaction was significant ($p < .01$).

The time spent in searching the directory documents decreased for all three anxiety groups, as can be seen in Figure 3. The high-anxiety subjects showed the largest decrease in searching time; low-anxiety subjects showed the smallest decrease. However, these results do not necessarily demonstrate that the high-anxiety subjects learned the association better, because mental effort could also have decreased as a result of demotivating factors.

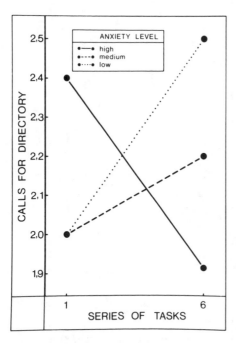

Figure 2 Mean number of directory consultations per task during the first and sixth block of tasks for subjects with high, medium, or low anxiety.

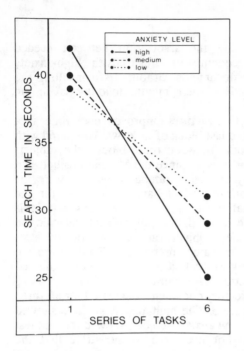

Figure 3 Mean time spent on searching task-related documents per task during the first and sixth block of tasks for subjects with high, medium, or low anxiety.

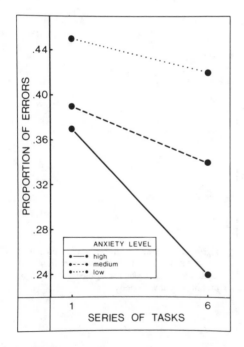

Figure 4 Mean error rate during the first and sixth block of tasks for subjects with high, medium, or low anxiety.

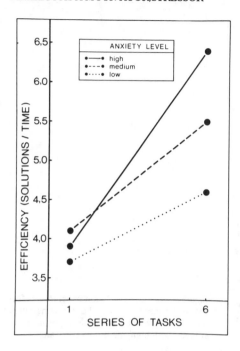

Figure 5 Mean performance efficiency during the first and sixth block of tasks for subjects with high, medium, or low anxiety.

Error rate and performance efficiency are compared in Figures 4 and 5. Two results concerning error rate that are especially relevant to the hypotheses of this study should be noted: (a) overall, error rate was lowest for high-anxious subjects and highest for low-anxious subjects ($p < .02$), when averaged over all 64 tasks; (b) the decrease in error rate from the first to the sixth block of tasks was greatest for the high-anxiety subjects. As a consequence of the decrease in working time and error rate (Figures 3 and 4), performance efficiency increased for all subjects from the first to the last block of tasks, as can be seen in Figure 5. The improvement in efficiency was greatest for the high-anxiety subjects, as reflected in the significant ($p < .05$) Anxiety by Repeated Measures interaction for this analysis.

Adaptation in Arousal Level

Since higher state anxiety was associated with a greater investment of mental effort, as reflected in more time spent in searching and checking operations (Table 1), it was expected that this increased effort would be accompanied by a higher level of arousal. Arousal was measured by skin resistance before the beginning of the experiment, at the fifth task of each block, and after termination of work on the experimental tasks. Figure 6 shows the variation in skin resistance for high-, medium-, and low-anxious subjects while they were working on the experimental tasks. As can be seen, most of the drop in skin resistance occurs during the first three blocks of tasks. Of particular interest, skin resistance for high-anxious subjects compared to subjects with low or medium anxiety decreased to an asymptotically lower level. The highly

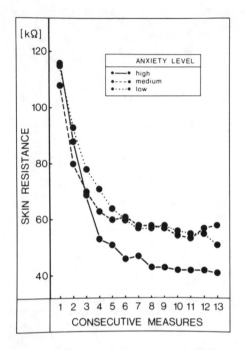

Figure 6 Mean level of skin resistance before the experiment, during the six consecutive blocks of tasks, and after the experiment for subjects with high, medium, or low anxiety.

significant ($p < .01$) Anxiety by Repeated Measures interaction for this analysis indicated that the high-anxiety subjects adapted at a higher arousal level.

The Experience of Stress

During and after the experiment, the subjects answered a number of questions concerning their experience of stress while working on the tasks. Responses to the stress questions were especially important in clarifying the relationship between state anxiety and: (a) the experience of time pressure, (b) attributions of failure, (c) effects of failure on well-being, and (d) recreational activity.

Experience of Time Pressure

The following question concerning time pressure was answered after each series of tasks: "How often during work on the tasks was self-imposed time pressure responsible for failures?" Subjects responded on a 5-point rating scale (1 = never; 5 = always). Self-imposed time pressure was reported more often by high-anxious subjects. Differences between the high-, and the low-, and medium-anxiety groups, which were significant ($p < .05$) for all six blocks of tasks, can be seen in Figure 7. The high-anxiety subjects also reported experiencing more time pressure in responding to the postexperimental questionnaire item ($p < .01$).

Attributions of Failure

The subjects responded after each block of tasks to questions concerning attributions of failure to insufficient intelligence. High-anxious subjects attributed failure to this internal, stable factor more often than low-anxious subjects, even during the last part of the experiment when their performance was actually superior ($p < .05$).

Effects of Failure on Well-Being

A number of items in the postexperimental questionnaire asked subjects to assess the effects of failure on well-being. After failures, the high-anxious subjects reported that they (a) felt more nervous ($p < .01$) and more despondent ($p = .06$); (b) became more uncertain ($p < .01$); and (c) were more impatient.

Effects of Task Activity on Recreational Behavior

The postexperimental introspective reports indicated that high-anxious subjects were not as successful as low-anxious subjects in relaxing during rest periods ($p < .01$).

Coping with Anxiety

Since high-anxious subjects expended more effort in attempting to cope with task demands, it is reasonable to ask whether this additional effort reduced anxiety. To evaluate this possibility, state anxiety was measured before and after subjects worked on the experimental tasks. State anxiety scores were evaluated as a function of two factors: (1) quality of outcome (error rate), and (2) whether or not the subjects obtained external feedback about the outcome.

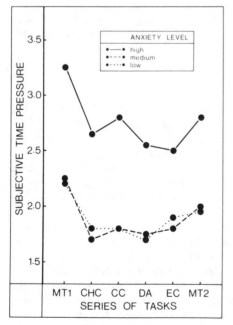

Figure 7 Reported experience of time pressure in six consecutive blocks of tasks for subjects with high, medium, or low anxiety.

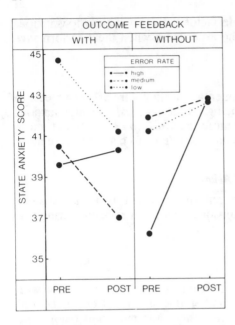

Figure 8 Mean state anxiety before and after working on the experimental tasks as a function of external feedback for subjects with high, medium, or low error rates.

The results are presented in Figure 8, in which mean state-anxiety scores are reported as a function of external feedback for subjects grouped according to error rate. The analysis of variance yielded a significant Feedback by Repeated Measures interaction ($p < .05$), reflecting the finding that anxiety increased for all groups in the no feedback condition, and decreased in the feedback condition for subjects with low and medium error rates. The configuration of the data reported in Figure 8 suggests that positive external feedback generally leads to a reduction in state anxiety.

DISCUSSION

In examining the results of this study it should be emphasized that state (and not trait) anxiety, measured before the subjects began to work on the experimental tasks, was used to select the anxiety groups. The unpleasant emotional state of tension and apprehension, indicated by high scores on the STAI state-anxiety scale, appears to have been evoked by fear of being unable to cope effectively with task demands. This kind of anxiety is often referred to as "test anxiety" (Mandler & Sarason, 1952) or "evaluative anxiety" (Wine, 1980).

Our findings are consistent with a number of experimental studies in which anxiety served as a motivating factor (see Eysenck, 1979). Subjects were free to execute task-related operations for as long and as frequently as they wanted, and performance degradation of high-anxiety subjects was obtained only when the ratio between correct responses and time expenditure was computed (Table 1). However, we believe that these results were obtained because time pressure and threat to self-esteem were *not* imposed by the instructions.

Introspective reports concerning attributions of failure, as well as reports of the effects of failures on well-being, were consistent with the explanatory mechanisms hypothesized to account for the motivating properties of anxiety. The results would seem to indicate that the motivating properties of anxiety dominate if state anxiety is measured as a reaction to situational factors. In contrast, when trait anxiety is measured independent of specific situational stressors, the properties of anxiety as a stressing agent will dominate. Evidence for this conclusion comes from the results presented in Table 1, Figures 2–4, and the superior performance of the high-anxious subjects reported in Figure 5.

The findings reported in Figures 2–5 suggest that the increased mental effort of the high-anxious subjects during the first blocks of tasks resulted in a higher gain in learning. This is an important, long-term beneficial effect of the motivating properties of anxiety on performance for consecutive tasks that are similar in type. Further, if we take into consideration the finding that high-anxiety subjects had lower error rates, then it would seem that interfering cognitive activities (e.g., worries) were also reduced. While the adverse effects of anxiety were minimized by increasing work time, in our view these results hold only for state anxiety. We believe the distinction between state and trait anxiety is valid and has important theoretical and practical implications.

The adaptation of arousal at a higher level for the high-anxiety subjects (Figure 6) was consistent with the hypothesis that state anxiety has strong motivating properties. Moreover, the stronger motivation of the high-anxious subjects resulted in superior performance (Figure 5), but this required an investment of "extra costs" during task execution to compensate for task-irrelevant cognitive activities (Hamilton, 1975). The increased mental effort exerted by the high-anxiety subjects was also accompanied by a higher amount of stress, as indicated by the results reported in Figure 7 and the subjects' responses in postexperimental introspective reports. Taken as a whole, the results indicated that anxiety was an important motivating agent underlying goal-directed action and that increased emotional load or strain (feelings of time pressure, reduced ability to relax during resting periods, feelings of distress after failure) was associated with this increased motivation.

A conflicting issue concerning subjective time pressure remains. Why did high-anxious subjects, as compared with the middle- and low-anxiety subjects, report greater time pressure in the latter part of the experiment when the time they spent on the tasks was objectively shorter? We assume that high-anxious persons experience subjective time pressure whenever they are confronted with task demands, and that they attempt to compensate by means of increased mental effort for their reduced effectiveness. Since the subjects in our study were free to execute mental operations as frequently and as long as they wanted, the detrimental effects of anxiety were reduced by employing time-consuming operations, but these compensatory activities also produced feelings of time pressure (Schulz & Schönpflug, 1982),particularly when the subjects were given no external feedback.

The finding that the high-anxious subjects initially performed a greater number of operations which led them to feel more time pressure is understandable, but the fact remains surprising that these feelings persisted even after the unnecessary additional operations were discontinued. Apparently, the feelings of time pressure, once developed, continued until the tasks at hand were completed. We believe the higher arousal level observed in high-anxious subjects (Figure 6) was due to the prevalent feelings of time pressure. Since these feelings were not in keeping with reality, arousal level was obviously not optimal.

Our findings concerning the reduction of anxiety during the experimental task (Figure 8) suggested that successful coping with state anxiety depends on two factors: (1) achieving a satisfactory outcome, and (2) the verification of such by external feedback. Apparently, superior performance in the absence of feedback does not reduce state anxiety in achievement situations. On the other hand, external feedback of a satisfactory outcome seems to be both necessary *and* sufficient for reducing state anxiety. In contrast, failure feedback generally serves to *increase* state anxiety, especially in persons who are high in trait anxiety (Gaudry, 1977; Spielberger, 1966, 1972). Thus, to reduce state anxiety, high-anxious persons need positive outcome feedback, but failure feedback increases their anxiety. The demotivating effects of failure feedback on high-anxious subjects can be explained by these potentially conflicting circumstances, which also provide insight into the reasons why outcome feedback is much more relevant for high-anxiety persons.

The conclusion that external feedback is necessary to reduce state anxiety is well in line with the theoretical position advocated in this chapter. State anxiety occurs when a person is confronted with task demands and is maintained at a high level until the uncertainty associated with task performance is removed through positive external feedback. This is especially true of high-anxious persons with low ability who may not be able to evaluate their actions reliably. Such persons may allow task-irrelevant processing activities (e.g., worries) to interfere with ongoing work, even when their performance is superior. Uncertainty concerning outcome which is not reduced by positive external feedback may not only lead to increased state anxiety, but also to diffuse long-term feelings of tension and apprehension and to neurotic behavior.

REFERENCES

Atkinson, J. W. (1964). A theory of achievement motivation. In J. W. Atkinson (Ed.), *An introduction to motivation.* Princeton: Van Nostrand.

Epstein, S. (1976). Anxiety, arousal and the self-concept. In I. G. Sarason & C. D. Spielberger (Eds.), *Stress and anxiety* (Vol. 3). Washington: Hemisphere.

Epstein, S., & Roupenian, A. (1970). Heart rate and skin conductance during experimentally induced anxiety: The effect of uncertainty about receiving a noxious stimulus. *Journal of Personality and Social Psychology, 16,* 20–28.

Eysenck, M. W. (1979). Anxiety, learning and memory: A reconceptualization. *Journal of Research in Personality, 13,* 363–385.

Gaudry, E. (1977). Studies of the effects of experimentally induced experiences of success or failure. In C. D. Spielberger & I. G. Sarason (Eds.), *Stress and anxiety* (Vol. 4). Washington: Hemisphere.

Gaudry, E., & Spielberger, C. D. (1971). *Anxiety and educational achievement.* Sidney: Wiley.

Hamilton, V. (1975). Socialization anxiety and information processing: A capacity model of anxiety-induced performance deficits. In I. G. Sarason & C. D. Spielberger (Eds.), *Stress and anxiety* (Vol. 2). Washington: Hemisphere.

Heckhausen, H. (1980). *Motivation und Handeln.* Berlin: Springer.

Krohne, H. W. (1980). Angsttheorie: Vom mechanistischen zum kognitiven Ansatz. *Psychologische Rundschau, 31,* 12–30.

Kukla, A. (1972). Cognitive determinants of achieving behavior. *Journal of Personality and Social Psychology, 21,* 166–174.

Laux, L., Schaffner, P., & Glanzmann, P. (1979). *Manual fur den Fragebogen zur Erfassung von State und Trait-Angst (STAI-G).* Weinheim: Beltz.

Liebert, R. M., & Morris, L. W. (1967). Cognitive and emotional components of test anxiety: A distinction and some initial data. *Psychological Reports, 20,* 975–978.

Mandler, G. (1979). Thought processes, consciousness, and stress. In V. Hamilton & D. M. Warburton (Eds.), *Human stress and cognition.* New York: Wiley.

Mandler, G., & Sarason, S. B. (1952). A study of anxiety and learning. *Journal of Abnormal and Social Psychology, 47,* 166–173.

Mandler, G., & Watson, D. L. (1966). Anxiety and the interruption of behavior. In C. D. Spielberger (Ed.), *Anxiety and behavior.* New York: Academic Press.

Morris, L. W., & Liebert, R. M. (1973). Effects of negative feedback, threat of shock, and level of trait anxiety on the arousal of two components of anxiety. *Journal of Counseling Psychology, 20,* 321–326.

Sarason, I. G. (1975). Anxiety and self-preoccupation. In I. G. Sarason & C. D. Spielberger (Eds.), *Stress and anxiety,* (Vol. 2). Washington: Hemisphere.

Schulz, P. (1979). Regulation und Fehlregulation im Verhalten: II. Stress durch Fehlregulation. *Psychologische Beitrage, 21,* 597–621.

Schulz, P. (1980). Regulation und Fehlregulation im Verhalten: V. Die wechselseitige Beeinflussung von mentaler und emotionaler Beanspruchung. *Psychologische Beitrage, 22,* 633–656.

Schulz, P., & Schönpflug, W. (1982). Regulatory activity during states of stress. In H. W. Krohne & L. Laux (Eds.), *Achievement, stress, and anxiety.* Washington: Hemisphere.

Seligman, M. E. P. (1975). *Helplessness.* San Francisco: Freeman.

Spielberger, C. D. (1966). The effects of anxiety on complex learning and academic achievement. In C. D. Spielberger (Ed.), *Anxiety and behavior.* New York: Academic Press.

Spielberger, C. D. (1972). Anxiety as an emotional state. In C. D. Spielberger (Ed.), *Anxiety: Current trends in theory and research* (Vol. 1). New York: Academic Press.

Spielberger, C. D., Gorsuch, R. L., & Lushene, R. E. (1970). *Manual for the state-trait anxiety inventory.* Palo Alto: Consulting Psychologists Press.

Tomkins, S. S. (1963). Simulation of personality: The interrelationships between affect, memory, thinking, perception and action. In S. S. Tomkins & S. Messick (Eds.), *Computer simulation of personality.* New York: Wiley.

Weiner, B., & Potepan, P. A. (1970). Personality correlates and affective reactions towards exams of succeeding and failing college students. *Journal of Educational Psychology, 61,* 144–151.

Wine, J. (1980). Evaluation anxiety: A cognitive-attentional construct. In H. W. Krohne & L. Laux (Eds.), *Achievement, stress, and anxiety.* Washington: Hemisphere.

2

Toward a Sequential Model of Organizational Stress

Nico van Dijkhuizen
Zuidema Management Consultants

No organization can function properly without some stimulation, tension, or stress. Since tension is inherent in achieving a certain end with a limited number of people, with limited means, or within a limited amount of time, stress is not always noxious. It may act positively and be instructive and motivating. We may learn to recognize, and if necessary, avoid stress situations by dealing with mild forms of stress. Indeed, coping effectively with stress may protect us from many dangers. The negative consequences (called strains) are usually the result of chronic exposure, often over the years.

What then do we mean by "stress?" In the context of this chapter, stress comprises those characteristics or stimuli in the work environment that, in relation to an individual's personality, are threatening to the person. In being threatening, these stimuli may generate harmful consequences, that is, strains, not only for the person but also for the social environment (the family, the organization). It may be useful, however, to speak of positive stress, or "eustress," when we deal with the tension necessary to achieve at an acceptable level for the person as well as for the organization. The converse, negative stress or "distress," may be observed when tensions are either too low, leading to understimulation, or too high, giving rise to overstimulation. Distress will be the type of stress referred to in the following pages.

PERSON VERSUS ORGANIZATION

Not all people will interpret a given job situation as stressful, nor will a given individual perceive all job situations as equally stressful. Rather, stress occurs when the abilities of a person are incongruent with the demands of the work environment, or when there are obstacles to fulfilling strong needs or values. In such situations there is a "bad fit" between individuals and their environment.

A "good fit" exists to the extent that a person's motives for working are matched by supplies for these motives in the job environment, and/or to the extent that job demands (or job requirements) are met by the relevant abilities of the person. This idea may be represented by Figure 1, adapted from Lofquist

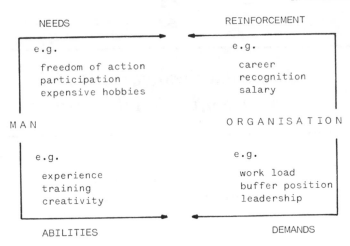

Figure 1 A model of fit and misfit between worker and organization.
Adapted from Lofquist and Dawis (1969).

and Dawis (1969). From this figure, it can be seen that, on the one hand, the organization makes demands on the person, for example, by giving him or her a high work load and demanding a high degree of creativity. At the same time it offers reinforcement in the form of an autonomous job and recognition. The person, on the other hand, possesses certain abilities which may (or may not) meet the demands of the organization. Moreover, the person brings with him certain needs the organization may or may not meet. If the organization meets the person's needs (by providing career opportunities, a salary, recognition), and the person's abilities are useful to the organization, there will be minimal stress, and the person will experience satisfaction.

If the person meets the organization's demands, one could state metaphorically that the organization is satisfied with the person. However, if the organization's demands and/or opportunities deviate to an important degree from the person's abilities and needs, the person may experience these circumstances as stressful. The greater the discrepancy, the more the stress.

Discrepancies in the transactions between organizations and employees may arise in various ways. Having insufficient skills and abilities may be threatening, because this may lead, for instance, to qualitative work overload: The work is beyond a person's abilities, knowledge, and expertise. Having more abilities than may be required to do a job may result in the underutilization of skills, which may subsequently give rise to the "big fish in a small pond" syndrome. One's needs may also exceed the organization's opportunities, for example, a desire for greater responsibility in a higher level job after a person has reached a ceiling in his present job. Or, as we observe quite frequently nowadays, a person may desire to join the Navy, but without having to sail too much.

The situations described above are only part of the picture. In reality the situation is almost inevitably much more complex. It is likely, over a period of time, that changes occur in both the demands and the supplies of the job, as well as in the values and the abilities of the employee. Take again, as an example, the problem of Navy jobs: A young bachelor, having problems with his parents, cannot be away from home long enough. Once he is married and has family responsibilities, a new sailing assignment, or even a long trip might motivate him to leave the organization and look for a job ashore. In general, we may conclude that the greater the discrepancy between the organization's demands and the person's abilities, and between the organization's opportunities or reinforcements and the person's needs, the more stress will result from the job.

Integration of Stress Research Models

In coping with organizational stress, the goal is to reduce stress by trying to attune the organization's demands to the individual's skills and abilities, and the organization's opportunities and reinforcements to the individual's needs. We must not aim at total elimination of stress in an organization; it simply is not possible nor even desirable. Some stress is necessary to perform well.

A reasonable goal for organizations is to reduce the amount of stress to an optimal level in relation to the tolerances and needs of exposed individuals. In order to cope with stress in the most appropriate manner, it is important to look for stress "centers" in a particular organization. It is irresponsible to offer a prefabricated coping program, just as it is useless, and sometimes dangerous, to administer medicine to a patient without first diagnosing the disease.

Stressors and strains may be diagnosed with the aid of the VOS, a questionnaire designed to assess organizational stress, which was translated, elaborated, and validated by Reiche and myself (van Dijkhuizen, 1980; Reiche & van Dijkhuizen, 1980). This questionnaire measures stressors, strains, and personality characteristics present in a particular situation. It is based on an integration of the stress model of French and Caplan (1972) and the role set model of Kahn, Wolfe, Quinn, Snoek, and Rosenthal (1964), described below.

The French and Caplan Model

The French and Caplan model is presented in Figure 2. The lower left box, labeled "occupational stresses," contains stressors in the work situation, such as role ambiguity, role conflict, role overload, responsibility for people, and so forth. If people experience one or more of these stressors, they may begin to experience the "psychological and physiological strains" listed in the adjoining box, for example, job dissatisfaction, job-related threat, and/or increased smoking, blood pressure, cholesterol level, and so forth.

If the influence of the stressors persists with sufficient intensity, the person may eventually develop coronary heart disease. In later versions of the model, French and Caplan have replaced coronary heart disease with the concept of a health-illness continuum. The vertical arrow from the box "personality" to the arrow between "occupational stresses" and "psychological and physiological strains" indicates the influence on the experience of strains of personality characteristics, for example, abilities and needs, and the Type A Behavior Pattern.

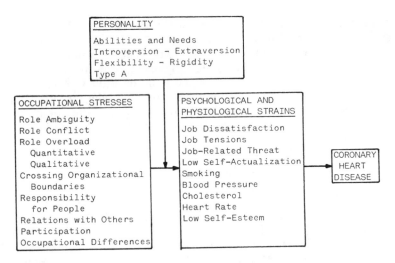

Figure 2 Stress model of French and Caplan (1972). From *The Failure of Success,* edited by A. J. Marrow, p. 31 © 1972 by AMACOM, a division of American Managem Associations, New York.

The Kahn Model

Kahn et al. (1964) use a "role set" model in their studies of groups of people within, or outside, an organization (Figure 3). The center of this group is the "focal person," the core of the study. The focal person's role conceptions, and, thus, much of his or her role behavior, is partly determined by "role senders." These role senders, that is, other relevant persons for the focal person, transmit their role expectations, which are partly determined by the senders'

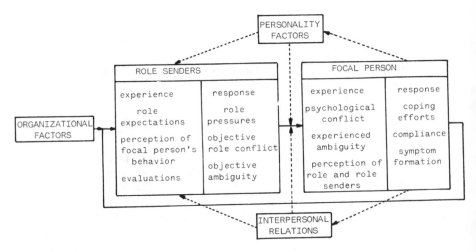

Figure 3 Role set model of Kahn et al. (1964). Reprinted with permission from John Wiley & Sons, Inc., © 1964.

perceptions of the focal person's role behavior. The interactions between role senders and a focal person are called role episodes.

The role senders are influenced by "organizational" and "personality" factors, and by their "interpersonal relations" with the focal person. Organizational factors consist of two kinds of variables. First, there are significant characteristics of the organization, such as size, number of status levels, output, and so on. The second type of variable is ecological in nature, representing the relation of a particular position (or person) with an organization, for example, the person's rank, responsibilities in the organization, or the number and the positions of others immediately related to his actions.

By interpersonal relations, Kahn et al. (1964) refer to the more or less stable patterns of interaction between a focal person and his role senders and their attitudes toward each other. The patterns of interaction may be formal or informal. Role senders transmit their role expectations by exerting role pressure on the focal person. The latter perceives these expectations and responds to them. This reaction, the role behavior, may then influence the role expectations of the role senders.

An Integrative Model

In integrating the Kahn et al. (1964) model with French and Caplan's model (1972), the role senders are located in the objective environment, together with organizational factors and functions (Figure 4). The relations of role senders with middle managers, the focal persons in the study for which this integration model was developed, are influenced by the personality characteristics of the

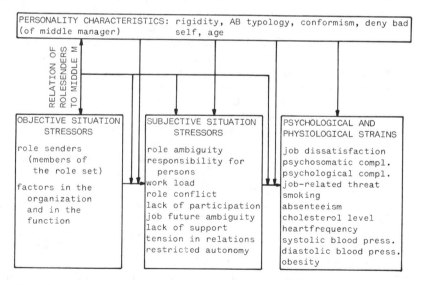

Figure 4 Structure diagram of the integration model of van Dijkhuizen and Reiche (1976) and van Vucht Tijssen, van den Broecke, van Dijkhuizen, Reiche, & de Wolff (1978). Reprinted with permission.

managers. These relations also influence how the objective environment is experienced, and the manner in which the subjective environment (the perception of the objective environment) may lead to psychological and physiological strains and illness. The relations between role senders and focal persons may be studied along the lines Kahn et al. (1964) investigated in their "intensive" study.

The VOS questionnaire for organizational stress was developed on the basis of Figure 4. It measures 16 stressors, each of which is related to a different aspect of the work situation. We were able to show relationships with the 13 strains for each of these stressors. However, if one attempted to assess these relations in order to be able to recommend strategies to eliminate or reduce one or more of the stressors, this would indeed be a very difficult job. With 16 stressors and 13 strains, there are 208 possible relationships. Thus, we attempted to reduce the stressors to a workable number by grouping them together into stress factors by means of a principal components factor analysis with varimax rotation; the number of factors to be extracted was determined by the scree test.

KEY STRESS FACTORS

The stress factors found to underlie most work situations were ambiguity, work load, and poor relations with other people.

Ambiguity

For middle managers, the stress factor eliciting the most negative consequences was ambiguity with regard to how they fulfill their jobs and the way they are going to function in the future. The managers often feel uncertain about their tasks and responsibilities and are continuously concerned about what others may think of them and their work. They are also worried about their future career opportunities and whether they will be able to continue their jobs until retirement. The middle manager's ambiguous frame of reference and uncertainty about the expectations of others, the content of the job, and future career appears to be closely related to the fact that his immediate superior gives him little social support. Ambiguity also arises when people with whom the middle managers cooperate hold different opinions about what they should do or how they should do it.

About 40 percent of the middle managers reported that their knowledge and experience fall short of what they feel is required to do the job. Leadership and social skills are high on their lists in this context. They also realize that present knowledge is made obsolete even faster by rapid technological changes. Moreover, social influences on organizations have brought new types of subordinates who are better educated, take orders less easily, and want more participation, while the age of the middle managers, as well as their very busy jobs, prevents them from getting additional education and training.

The stressors associated with the ambiguity factor include role ambiguity, lack of support from the immediate superior, tensions in relations with superiors and subordinates, and ambiguity with regard to career prospects. This stress factor shows significant correlations with psychosomatic complaints

($r = .52$); high blood cholesterol level ($r = .48$); psychological complaints ($r = .46$); more absenteeism ($r = .43$); high blood pressure ($r = .41$); and more job dissatisfaction ($r = .32$). All of these correlations were statistically significant ($p < .01$).

Work Load

The respondents reported that a lot of work was expected from them. They often have to work on several tasks at the same time and must work rapidly; there is little time to rest or to reflect on the work. About 50 percent report they have so much work to do that this adversely influences the quality of their work. A further source of conflict in this context is that immediate superiors often have different priorities than the middle managers: the latter emphasizing concentration on the social aspects of their jobs, the former insisting that they must focus their attention on the output of their subordinates.

Role conflict is often associated with work load. When superiors give orders that are incompatible with other work which has to be done, or when persons of equal rank and authority give conflicting assignments, these conflicts add significantly to the total work load. In investigating the consequences of a high work load, the following relations with specific strains were found: high work load was correlated with psychological complaints (r .32); psychosomatic complaints ($r = .26$); and high blood pressure ($r = .29$); but also, though to a lesser degree, with job satisfaction, higher self-esteem, and less absenteeism.

Poor Relations with Others

Relationships between middle managers and their colleagues, superiors, and subordinates are generally good. The respondents did complain, however, of lack of support from their colleagues and from others at work, especially when things get tough at work or when readiness to listen to and talk about personal problems is concerned. Moreover, contacts with other departments are not always without troubles, and disagreements are often denied or suppressed.

Many respondents complained about the fact that their role senders were often unclear about what they expected them to do, and a number of role senders agreed with this view. Poor communication and a lack of understanding of the problems of middle managers are important sources of stress. Communication problems with others due to lack of opportunity to participate in making decisions about how the work will be done and who will do what part of the job are also problems that are frequently encountered.

Being responsible for others is another important source of stress, especially when this responsibility relates to the future careers of subordinates, their job security, morale, and social and economic welfare. It is notable, however, that many respondents reported that they wanted more responsibility for other persons than they presently have. In terms of specific stressors, this factor was made up of lack of support from colleagues and others at work, lack of participation, responsibility for others, tensions in relations with other departments, and, to a lesser degree, job future ambiguity and underutilization of skills and abilities. The consequences of being exposed to this stress factor were greater job-related threat $(r = .63)$; more job dissatisfaction $(r = .28)$; more psychological complaints $(r = .28)$; but also lower blood pressure $(r = .44)$; and less absenteeism $(r = .31)$.

EFFECTS OF POSITION IN THE HIERARCHY

Secondary analyses showed that occupying certain positions in an organizational hierarchy has important consequences for the experience of certain stressors and strains. Therefore, treating the total sample as a whole would result in overlooking much interesting information. In general, the findings showed that the higher one is placed in the organizational hierarchy, the more one is likely to report: (a) *greater quantitative work load:* one has more to do and more complex assignments and therefore less chance to rest; (b) *more responsibility for persons:* in the higher positions, a manager feels more responsibility to control work climate to optimize the welfare, safety and job security of others; (c) *more role conflict:* in our study, role conflict originated from a condition in which simultaneous conflicting expectations were perceived from superiors; (d) *less support from colleagues:* the higher the position, the less social support is experienced regarding job-related problems, and colleagues are less willing to talk and listen; and (e) *more role ambiguity:* the higher the position, the less clear it becomes as to precisely what others expect of the individual.

A number of stressors were reported less frequently by managers in higher hierarchical positions. These included (a) *lack of participation:* in the upper reaches of a hierarchy one can clearly exert more influence on those decisions which concern oneself; and (b) *job future ambiguity:* one becomes more certain regarding career opportunities, responsibilities to be carried out in the future, and the value of one's own knowledge and experience.

Strains likewise show differences related to hierarchical position. The higher the position, the more one is likely to experience or manifest the following strains to a greater extent: (a) *obesity:* one tends to be heavier for a given body length; (b) *job-related threat:* greater doubt is experienced concerning whether one is able to meet the job demands or whether one will be accepted by others; (c) *blood cholesterol level:* and (d) *psychological complaints:* persons higher in the hierarchy tend to be more anxious, depressed, or irritable. They also report: (a) *more job satisfaction:* the work is more interesting, less monotonous, and provides greater opportunities for learning; (b) *less absenteeism:* people are in fact ill less frequently or, in the cases of minor illnesses, more inclined to carry on regardless; and (c) *less smoking.*

A SEQUENCE IN THE STRAINS

Keeping these differences in mind, let us now look at a possible sequence in the strains. A number of authors have classified strains into four categories: cognitive, affective or psychological, behavioral, and physiological (see, for example, Caplan, Cobb, French, Van Harrison, & Pinneau, 1975; French, 1976; House, 1974; Kahn & French, 1970). Among these four classes of strains, a certain sequence is hypothesized. French et al. (1972), for instance, contend that psychological strains lead to an elevated cholesterol level, and thus, by way of physiological strains, to illness. They also assume that among the physiological strains, raised heart rate may lead to an elevation of blood pressure. However, relatively little research has been done to verify the occurrence of a sequence in the strains.

The research data reported in this chapter are based on a cross-sectional analysis that, in relation to identifying a possible strain sequence, is not as powerful as longitudinal data. Inspection of eta matrices indicated, however, that very clear critical paths could be identified, leading to the conclusion that even cross-sectional data may reveal interesting results (The η was used instead of a Pearson product-moment coefficient because of presumed, and in many cases proven, curvilinearity).

Given the differences between function groups or positions in the hierarchy that were previously reported, each group was incorporated in the research design, rather than using the total sample. Strains were initially classified into affective or psychological, behavioral, and physiological categories. It was soon recognized, however, that the psychological strain category, which initially included job dissatisfaction, anxiety, and somatic complaints, appeared to be too broad. Therefore, this category was divided into "job-related" and "general" psychological strains, with "somatic complaints" as a third category. The resulting classification was partly in accord with that of Caplan et al. (1975).

A general model for testing the sequence of strains among middle managers is presented in Figure 5. In this study, "job-related psychological strains" were defined as job dissatisfaction, job-related threat, and, due to the content of the items, loss of self-esteem. The "general psychological affects" included anxiety, depression, and irritation. "Psychosomatic complaints" consisted of complaints concerning general health, and the heart in particular. The "behavioral strains" were comprised of absenteeism, smoking, and obesity; while the "physiological strains" were systolic and diastolic blood pressure, cholesterol level, and heart rate.

A particular problem arose in establishing the most likely sequence within the class of physiological strains. Since no data were available on this problem, it was arbitrarily hypothesized that if any systematic sequence existed it would most likely lead from cholesterol level by way of systolic and diastolic blood pressure to heart rate. It might be argued, however, that there is no sequence within this class of variables and that they all depend on other variables, such as catecholamines.

MULTIPLE AND SINGLE MODELS

Two kinds of models were designed for the various subsamples: "multiple models," consisting of the most significant relationships between variables and "single models," where only the highest significant relationship for each

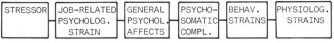

Figure 5 General sequence model (van Dijkhuizen, 1980). Reprinted with permission.

variable was taken into account, constructed to simplify the picture. Multiple models thus give a more comprehensive insight into the relationships revealed by the data, while the single models emphasize the most important or "core" relationships.

In order to illustrate the analytic procedures of this study, we will report the multiple and single models for one of the subsamples, the first line supervisors. Each eta is significant at the level of $p < .05$. Let us first consider the rather complicated picture of the multiple model which is presented in Figure 6.

The highest significant relationships in this model between stressors and strains are in the region of job-related and general psychological strains and psychosomatic complaints. A few relationships, such as those between underutilization of skills and abilities and job dissatisfaction ($n = .39$), lack of support from colleagues, and job-related threat (.41), and between job future ambiguity and loss of self-esteem (.38), follow the sequential model, in that the highest eta(s) for these stressors are associated with job-related psychological strains. Job-related threat has its highest associations with role ambiguity (.51) and role conflict (.45); and loss of self-esteem is most strongly associated with role ambiguity (.38) and job future ambiguity (.38).

Anxiety and depression, comprising the next sequence of strains in the chain, are highly associated with role ambiguity (.55 and .63, respectively), responsibility for persons (.59 and .49), role conflict (.42 and .49), lack of support from others at work (.54 and .48), and, in accordance with "theory," with job-related threat (.45 and .50). Psychosomatic complaints about health and heart problems have their strongest relationship with anxiety (.84 and .81, respectively), which is also in accordance with the theory, and health shows an important relation with depression (.76). Other associations in this field, some surprisingly strong, are those with role ambiguity (.74 and .70), responsibility for persons (.74 and .69), lack of support from others at work (.48 and .50), and with job-related threat (.48 and .40). It should be noted that this is the same set of variables that was associated with anxiety and depression.

Of the behavioral strains, smoking is significantly associated with lack of participation (.42), and health (.33); absenteeism with loss of self-esteem (.29), health (.30), and heart (.29); and obesity with heart (.58). The physiological strains are best "predicted" by "heart" as far as systolic (.36) and diastolic (.33) blood pressures are concerned, by "obesity" for cholesterol level (.52), and by "heart" for heart frequency (.31). There are also very high interrelationships among the physiological variables themselves.

In summary it can be seen that a number of variables follow the sequence as predicted in the general model presented earlier. In this context, it is especially interesting to note, for example, the chain: Role ambiguity – job-related threat – depression – health – absenteeism (also linked by way of anxiety instead of depression). This same chain is also linked by way of heart instead of health, and there is, additionally, a link from heart (by way of obesity) to cholesterol level, blood pressure, and heart frequency (heart rate).

Simplifying the multiple model into a related single model, in which only the highest significant relationship for each variable is incorporated, leads to the model shown in Figure 7. We see here that anxiety has its strongest relationship with responsibility for persons, but this relationship is a negative

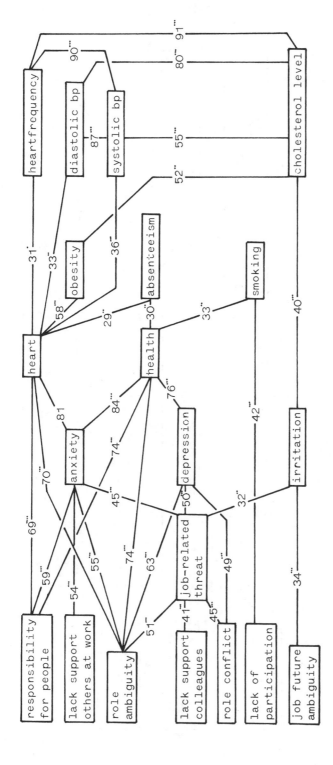

Figure 6 Multiple model for supervisors (van Dijkhuizen, 1980). Reprinted with permission.

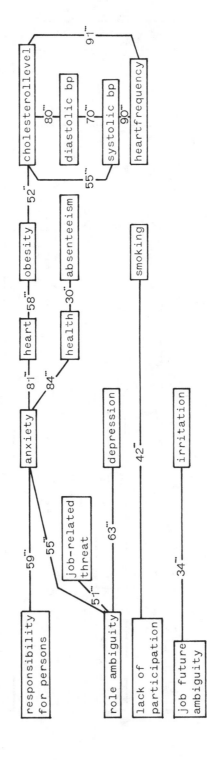

Figure 7 Single model for supervisors (van Dijkhuizen, 1980). Reprinted with permission.

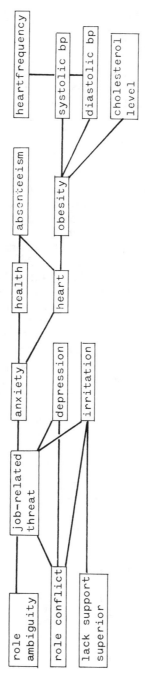

Figure 8   Combination model (van Dijkhuizen, 1980). Reprinted with permission.

one, that is, more responsibility goes with less anxiety. Therefore, we chose the next highest eta, which was with role ambiguity.

Multiple and single models were formulated for each of the five subsamples and were compared in two ways: (1) by producing models for the total sample in which, however, differences between subsamples were lost; and (2) by constructing a "combination model," in which only relations which appeared in at least four of the five subsamples were used. With regard to the association of psychosomatic complaints and behavioral strains with physiological strains, a less rigorous criterion was used, according to which a minimum of three of the five subsamples showed significant relationships. This yielded the combination model presented in Figure 8.

The combination model provides an example of a full sequence, running from either role ambiguity or role conflict by way of job-related threat to anxiety, heart complaints, and obesity on to the physiological variables. In addition, some of the variables (job-related threat, depression, irritation, and absenteeism) are linked to more than one preceding variable, which reflects the fact that none of these relationships were the strongest in all five subsamples.

When the various models for the five subsamples and the combination model are considered, some of the 13 stressors and 16 strains measured by the VOS questionnaire for organizational stress (van Dijkhuizen & Reiche, 1976) seem to be less important than others. Either they do not appear in most models, or they have no links to the strains in the sequence. The most important stressors seem to be job future ambiguity, role conflict, and role ambiguity, and to a lesser degree, lack of support from one's superiors and from others at work, work load, and tension in relations with other departments of the organization.

The strains found to be of the greatest significance in a sequential analysis, apart from the physiological variables (which are, of course, at the end of the chain) were: job-related threat, anxiety, health, heart complaints, and obesity, and to a lesser degree, depression, irritation, absenteeism, and smoking. With

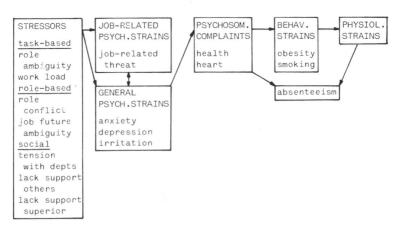

Figure 9 Empirical general sequence model (van Dijkhuizen, 1980). Reprinted with permission.

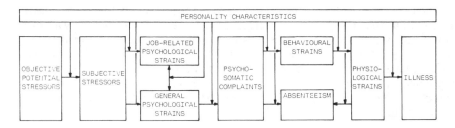

Figure 10 Theoretical general sequence model (van Dijkhuizen, 1980). Reprinted with permission.

these variables in mind, let us now return to the *general* sequence model presented earlier.

Examining the various models, we notice that the stressors often link with both job-related psychological strains (i.e., job-related threat) and general psychological strains (e.g., anxiety, depression), but are less strongly associated with psychosomatic complaints. In our opinion, this means that the sequence from stressor to general psychological strains or affects does not necessarily involve job-related psychological strains. The results, in fact, suggest an either/or relationship in which stressors are linked to either job-related psychological strains or to general psychological strains. But these two classes are closely connected and mutually influence each other.

The general psychological strains (i.e., mainly anxiety, but to a lesser degree, depression and irritation) lead to psychosomatic complaints. These, in turn, give rise to behavioral strains, which lead to the physiological strains that are here conceived of as indicators of risk factors for illness.

Some caution is warranted with regard to the behavioral strain *absenteeism,* which was used in the various models as an intermediate between psychosomatic complaints and physiological strains. Although absenteeism due to psychological or psychosomatic discomforts might eventually lead, for instance, to higher blood pressure, it is equally plausible that high blood pressure due to obesity might result in absenteeism. As Aldridge (1970) has stated: "Measures of absenteeism can be most helpful in following broad trends of sickness behavior in various working groups, but are notoriously inaccurate when it comes to the diagnostic cause of the absence" (p. 614).

These considerations lead us to conclude that the general sequence model should be replaced by the empirical general sequence model presented in Figure 9. For each class of variables, the most important are listed in the boxes. From this figure, it can be inferred that future research with the VOS might be reduced considerably in length. In fact, the most important variables in the stressor-strain chain could be assessed by measuring only those variables in the empirical general sequence model and ignoring the other variables.

Another important issue in longitudinal research is that organization developmentlike processes of restructuring the work environment can be left out if the main focus is on the effects of stressors and strains on illness. In such cases, one can start at a later point in the sequence, for instance, with general psychological strains or with psychosomatic complaints, proceeding from these to actual illness.

The empirical general sequence model requires further testing, preferably in longitudinal research. In such an endeavor the effects of intervening variables not included in this study, such as personality characteristics and interpersonal relationships, should be included. A revised general sequence theoretical model that incorporates subjective stressors and personality characteristics is presented in Figure 10. The Stress Research Group at Nijmegen has recently launched a research program to provide empirical validation for the latest version of this model.

REFERENCES

Aldridge, J. F. L. (1970). Emotional illness and the working environment. *Ergonomics, 13,* 613–621.

Caplan, R. D., Cobb, S., French, J. R. P., Jr., Harrison, R. van, & Pinneau, S. R. P. (1975). *Job demands and worker health.* HEW publication (NIOSH), 75–160.

Dijkhuizen, N. van. (1980). *From stressors to strains: Research into their interrelationships.* Lisse: Swets and Zeitlinger.

Dijkhuizen, N. van, & Reiche, H. M. J. K. I. (1976). *Het meten van organisatiestress: Over de bewerking van een vragenlijst.* Leiden: Rijksuniversiteit (internal report A and O 001–76, 002–76 and 003–76).

French, J. R. P., Jr. (1976). *Job demands and worker health: An introduction.* A symposium presented at the 84th Annual Convention of the APA.

French, J. R. P., Jr., & Caplan, R. D. (1972). Organizational stress and individual strain. In A. J. Marrow (Ed.), *The failure of success.* New York: AMACOM.

House, J. S. (1974). Occupational stress and coronary heart disease: A review and theoretical integration. *Journal of Health and Social Behavior, 14,* 12–27.

Kahn, R. L., & French, J. R. P., Jr. (1970). Status and conflict: Two themes in the study of stress. In J. E. McGrath (Ed.), *Social and psychological factors in stress.* New York: Holt, Rinehart & Winston.

Kahn, R. L., Wolfe, D. M., Quinn, R. P., Snoek, J. D., & Rosenthal, R. A. (1964). *Organizational stress: Studies in role conflict and ambiguity.* New York: Wiley.

Lofquist, L. H., & Dawis, R. V. (1969). *Adjustment to work: A psychological view of man's problems in a work-oriented society.* New York: Appleton-Century-Crofts.

Reiche, H. M. J. K. I., & Dijkhuizen, N. van. (1980). *Vragenlijst organisatiestress: Handleiding voor testafname* (internal report Nijmegen University).

Vucht Tijssen, J. van, Broeke, A. J. J. van, Dijkhuizen, N. van, Reiche, H. M. J. K. I., & Wolff, Ch. J. de. (1978). *Middenkader en stress.* 's-Gravenhage: COP/SER.

3

Causal Cognitions and Self-Evaluations: Implications for Stress Management

William R. Bowerman
University of Kansas

Individuals are engaged continually in transactions with environments, going through cycles of planning, acting, observing, revising knowledge and expectations, making new or modified plans, acting again, seeing results, comparing results with expected results, and so on. All during these cycles, one evaluates positive and negative features of the transactions and of oneself as an origin of these transactions. These evaluations are not just cognitive events. They generate emotional experience, too, the nature of which is conditioned by the cognitions involved.

This broad conception is consistent with Lazarus' (1975) theoretical position that "the various emotions arise from and reflect the nature of a person or animal's ongoing adaptive commerce or transactions with his environment" (p. 554) and that "[t]he quality and intensity of the emotion and its action impulse all depend upon a particular kind of cognitive appraisal of the present or anticipated significance of the transaction for the person's well-being" (p. 554).

This paper will deal with a special case of emotion, that of stress and anxiety arising from negative or problematic self-evaluations. Relevant issues, then, will be those arising because of conceptions people have of themselves as originating negative or problematic transactions with their environment(s), past, present, and/or future. Other approaches at least broadly related to the framework to be developed below include Defares (1979), Epstein (1973), Janis and Mann (1977), Kelman and Baron (1968), Lazarus and Launier (1978); chapters by French, Rodgers, and Cobb (1974), Goldschmidt (1974), and Mechanic (1974) in Coelho, Hamburg, and Adams (1974); and chapters by Kahn and French (1970), McGrath (1970a), and Mechanic (1970) in McGrath (1970b). Many of these approaches link stress and anxiety to social factors. This is an important theme of the present framework, too, but not one to be developed here.

I wish to thank The Netherlands Institute for Advanced Study in the Humanities and Social Sciences and the Bureau of Child Research, University of Kansas, for support during the planning and writing of this paper.

A central theoretical task is to develop a way of representing details of a person's conception of ongoing transactions with environments, and of their self-evaluations arising from these transactions. This paper presents one way of doing this, starting with Figure 1. The circle on the left of Figure 1 represents a person at a given point in time: the circle on the right, an environment, which is part social, part nonsocial. The flow-of-control arrows on the top of the figure represent the person acting on an environment and the flow-of-control arrows going from the environment to the person represent effects of the environment on the person. These paths connect, representing a continual cycle of transactions between a person and the environment.

The "cognitive map" shown within the person in Figure 1 is a representation of the person's causal cognitions of causes and effects involved in transactions with the environment. Three kinds of causal cognitions (i.e., cognitions, or combinations of cognitions, about cause and effect) are distinguished: (1) Causal cognitions that represent events in the past, such as observations, explanations, and/or causal attributions about causes of past effects, (2) Causal cognitions that represent events in the future, such as plans, intentions, expectations, and hopes and fears, and (3) Causal cognitions that are about events, features of entities, and relationships that extend over time, such as schemata, prototypes, scripts, and dispositions. These distinctions will be further considered in the discussions to follow on stress and stress management.

Figure 1 does not bear directly on the issue of what kinds or combinations of causal cognitions would be negative or problematic (i.e., lead to stress). To do this we need to combine the broad concept of transaction cycles with a more fine-grained level of analysis, involving specific features of a person's conception of actions that they are tied to and the consequences of those actions. This is done below, by introducing and applying a theory of subjective competence, which deals extensively with causal cognitions, self-evaluation, and motivation. Intellectual antecedents of this approach include Heider (1958), with special reference to attribution processes, White's concepts of

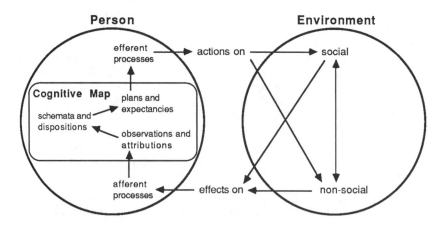

Figure 1 Causal cognitions and person-environment transactions.

effectance motivation and competence (1974), and Allport's classic work on the importance of the self (1943).

The goals of the following presentation are: (a) to delineate the underlying structure of causal cognitions that generate feelings of being ineffective, harmful, stupid, immoral, thoughtless, or otherwise negative in past, present, and/or future physical and social environments; (b) to use this conception to identify sources of stress arising from various self-referent causal cognitions; and, by extending the same framework, (c) to identify possibilities for managing the stress that problematic self-evaluations produce.

CAUSAL COGNITIONS AND SELF–EVALUATION

Subjective competence theory (Bowerman, 1978, 1979, 1981) starts with the claim that peoples' feelings about themselves (e.g., sense of competence, worth, self-esteem) are determined by combinations of beliefs about causal relationships connecting themselves, by their actions, to affectively significant consequences in the environment. Further, it claims that people are motivated to seek positive self-evaluations and to avoid negative self-evaluations. This is where stress and stress reduction enter the picture. Stress is seen here as resulting from problematic self-evaluations, and stress management as efforts to avoid the same.

Figure 2a gives an example of one particular combination of beliefs about actions and consequences that would, according to the theory, generate a positive feeling of competence. The figure represents the actor's belief that he is responsible for eating a good diet. So the first causal cognition in this belief structure is the person's belief about an *action* he has chosen, eating a good diet. A second causal cognition, linked with the first, is a belief about the *effects* of this action of eating a good diet. The perceived effects of healthy eating are that one will be thin and agile. The next causal cognition is the person's belief about the ultimate *affective* consequences of his actions: He attributes his own feeling of well-being to being thin and agile, and as represented on the bottom right of Figure 2a, he believes that being thin and agile has the good consequence of increasing a person's ability to protect his family (positively valued), by fighting better. This second affective consequence of the diet is used here to illustrate that causal structures can be complex (e.g., actions can be seen as having multiple consequences). This point will not be considered immediately, but will reemerge later.

Three kinds of causal cognitions are involved here: an *action* attribution, that "I am responsible for having a good diet," and *effect* attribution, that "a good diet makes one thin and agile," and an *affect* attribution, that "being thin and agile leads one to have a feeling of well-being." According to subjective competence theory, the *combination* of these three beliefs about oneself, as the origin of the resulting causal structure, generates a feeling of positive transaction with the environment, called *positive subjective competence.* See Bowerman (1978, 1981) for a formal definition of subjective competence and a typology of positive structures generated by that definition.

The other side of self-evaluation involves *negative subjective competence.* According to the theory, certain combinations of beliefs about one's actions and about the results of those actions generate negative feelings about oneself.

A. Positive structure

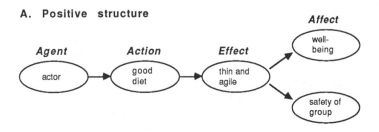

B. Negative structure

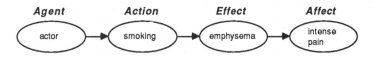

Figure 2 Subjective competence structures.

A brief example, shown in Figure 2b, illustrates this. Consider a person who smokes cigarettes while also believing that cigarette smoking may cause emphysema and that this lung disease leads to pain. To believe that one's freely chosen act of smoking will bring oneself the pain of emphysema will, it is predicted, generate a feeling of incompetence, called *negative subjective competence*. The same definition of subjective competence that generates a typology of positive structures, noted above, generates a typology of negative subjective competence structures. More will be said about these later.

The motivational claim of the theory is that people seek, in their actions and thought processes, to maximize their subjective competence. One prediction that follows is that people will seek to reach and maintain positive views of themselves; subjective competence theory provides a formal account of what constitutes a positive self-evaluation (e.g., holding positive subjective competence structures about oneself). It is important here to understand that seeking positive states is a central aspect of motivation and that some sources of stress and anxiety can be understood as being due to threats to this motivation. Similarly, some approaches to stress management involve the seeking of positive states, not just the avoidance of negative ones.

The broad point that people seek to maximize subjective competence leads to a second prediction about motivation: People try to *avoid* holding beliefs about themselves that imply *negative* subjective competence. This is presumed to be due to the fact that negative structures generate negative affect (e.g., stress and anxiety) and that people are motivated to reduce such negative affect by altering the causal structures that produce it.

Subjective competence theory can now be used in two ways to deal with stress and anxiety arising from problems in transactions with social and nonsocial environments. First, a number of conceptually possible sources of stress and anxiety (i.e., threats to subjective competence) are outlined. Then a number of stress management possibilities are presented. These are seen as ways to reduce threats to subjective competence.

STRESS PRODUCED BY SELF–REFERENT CAUSAL COGNITIONS

Four different sorts of problematic causal cognitions concerning the self will be discussed briefly in this section. Each is tied directly to the preceding treatment of self-referent causal cognitions. It will be assumed here that each of these kinds of structures, being problematic in its implications about the merits of particular transaction(s) with environments, will generate some sort of negative affective experience, call it stress and anxiety. The first two kinds of problematic structures produce stress because they involve subjective competence structures that are negative and/or changing in a negative direction. The last two sources of stress are ambiguities, uncertainties, or conflicts in representations of significant (or potentially significant) transactions with the environment.

Negative Structures

Subjective competence theory, as noted, generates a typology of structures, similar to that illustrated in Figure 2b, that imply negative evaluations of the (perceived) originator of actions that have affectively significant consequences. For example, seeing oneself as freely performing an action that prevents a pleasant event from occurring is a negative causal attribution structure, which generates a negative self-evaluation and, hence, is stressful. Another negative sequence would be to see oneself as *not* acting in a situation where acting would cause something good to happen (or something bad not to happen). See Bowerman (1978) for the formal definition that generates these structures and examples of them.

For present purposes, it should be noted that structures that are negative are expected to generate a high level of stress because each negative structure is a direct representation of an ineffective, incompetent, and/or immoral transaction with some environment. The stress from this basic representation of negative subjective competence is a direct message, a signal, to the organism that something will be, has been, or is being done wrong. This is the basic "alarm" that the system seeks to avoid, or turn off when it occurs. The problematic structures discussed below can be seen as producing stress of a sort that serves as an early warning that a basic negative structure *could* occur, in view of certain potential changes in the cognitions represented.

Negative structures can deal with anything a person does (or does not do), so long as it is represented in the cognitive system. Further, as suggested earlier, negative structures can be elicited about the future, the past, and/or the present. They can involve social cognitions of various sorts; for example, as actors influencing one's own outcomes, as "targets" of one's own actions, and as holders of views about oneself. This rich variety of possible negative structures suggests many possible sources of stress. The same points could be made about the following kinds of structures.

Deteriorating Structures

A second kind of stress is produced by *changes* in a negative direction in the subjective competence value of a salient structure. An initially *positive* structure can become less positive in three broad ways: (1) A new origin is assigned to one of the elements on the original positive sequence, resulting in the initial positive implications to the actor being "drained" or "shifted" off to this new origin (e.g., someone else is given credit for a successful plan we actually proposed), (2) The value of one of the elements on the positive sequence is reduced or reversed (e.g., from action to inaction) in a way such that the value of the sequence is lower than it had been (e.g., our pride in choosing to help a friend in need is lowered when we discover that anyone would have done the same thing in the same situation), and (3) A new affective consequence is added to the initial structure and in such a manner that the combined implications of new and old sequences is less positive than was the old sequence (e.g., we win a big tennis match by using a physically taxing backspin serve, but in the process we tear a shoulder ligament we knew was weak).

An initially negative structure can also become even more negative, by one of three kinds of changes in causal cognitions: (1) The salience/value of an external origin for one of the elements on the initial negative sequence is reduced, so blame passes more directly to you as the origin of a negative sequence (e.g., a smoker is told she can't realistically blame her smoking behavior on an "addiction"), (2) The value of one of the elements on the original structure changes such that the whole structure becomes more negative (e.g., you get a closer look at a person you have hurt), and (3) A new consequence has been added to one of the original elements and it produces a new negative structure that adds more negative evaluation onto the original negative structure (e.g., you recognize new, positive qualities in a person you have harmed).

Incomplete Structures

A subjective competence structure is incomplete to the extent that it has some, but not all, of the elements necessary to generate a subjective competence evaluation. A *significant* subjective competence structure is one that is highly positive or highly negative. A gap in a potentially significant structure, therefore, is a place where the addition of a cognitive element (of a given value) would make the structure significant (i.e., highly positive or negative in subjective competence implications).

A gap on a potentially positive structure should generate stress to the extent that it is seen as potentially "fillable," but in fact not being filled (e.g., frustration). Conversely, a perceived gap on a potentially negative self-referent structure will generate more stress the more likely it is seen as being fillable and/or being filled (e.g., fear). Note that these are some of the many testable predictions about stress (and stress management) that can be generated by the theory.

The topic of incomplete structures and negative affect could be related to many content areas where ambiguity or uncertainty can arise with respect to important matters for a person. For example, learned helplessness (Abramson, Seligman, & Teasdale, 1978) seems related to the feeling (veridical or not) that actions one can perform have no consequences of note, or that one cannot produce the actions that would lead to affectively significant outcomes. Much social comparison literature in social psychology involves gaps in subjects' knowledge about important information about themselves and/or other people. And, as Taft (1977) argues, the experience of being in a "foreign" culture is loaded with ambiguity and uncertainty, leading to stress. These topics are listed briefly here to stimulate further research and to suggest the range of topics that is potentially relevant to the present conception of self-evaluation and stress.

Conflicting Structures

A major source of stress is the existence of multiple versions of the same causal sequence, when one (some) of the versions is (are) less favorable than the other(s). If the subjective competence value of each version of the sequence is computed, and the values differ markedly, then the awareness of multiple possibilities, it is predicted, will generate stress. This situation presumably produces stress because of the possibility that the less favorable version might be accepted, which would lead to a deteriorating and/or negative structure. Note that if trivial events made up the different versions of a given transaction, there would not be implications for stress. The subjective competence implications do not vary as a function of which version (if any) is accepted. All versions of the transaction will have values at or near zero, for example, if an action in a causal structure has no consequences or if it has affective consequences that are neutral in tone.

One sort of conflict between versions of sequences that is stressful is the conflict between expected outcomes and observed outcomes. If one achieves more *or* less than one expected in a significant transaction with the environment, this suggests that some important assumption(s) about oneself and/or the environment may be wrong and in need of change. If the threatened change is negative (e.g., one fails to reach goals a number of times and begins to suspect that one's beliefs about one's abilities are too high), this produces stress due to the threat of a deteriorating structure and/or a negative structure.

If the threatened change is positive (e.g., one may be more talented than one had thought), this produces stress because accepting this change (which might be tempting from an immediate ego-enhancing point of view) leads to the risk of stress in future transactions in which goals are set higher, due to the new assumption of higher ability. Some of the possible problems are that new conflicts with other people can be created, new conflicts with old belief structures can arise, potentially significant structures with gaps in them can emerge because of being in new, uncharted territory, and of course, one can fail (i.e., experience negative subjective competence due to the nonoccurrence of an intended outcome), for example, if the original task on which one had "succeeded" was actually just an easier task than one had thought. This latter possibility is especially threatening if other people are around to see it.

Another frequent source of conflicting structures involves clashes between two peoples' views of one's own transaction(s) with some environment(s). One's own view is often different than another person's and this is a source of stress to the extent that the conflicting views are about significant causal structures. This broad topic will not be developed here, but it is clearly of extreme importance to a full understanding of sources of stress tied to self-evaluation.

The goal in this section was to delineate major kinds of stress-producing structures relating to self-referent causal cognitions. The next section, on stress management possibilities, uses these problematic structures of causal cognitions as the starting point.

MANAGING STRESS ARISING FROM SELF–EVALUATION

The theme in this section is that stress management involves a motivation to avoid, undo, compensate for, or otherwise react to sources of stress, in this case, stress arising from negative or problematic self-evaluation(s). In the interest of brevity, several points can be made now, to apply with little or no further comment to all the following points about stress management: (a) ways to avoid negative or problematic subjective competence structures can involve general beliefs, expectations, and/or observations; (b) ways to avoid negative or problematic structures can involve cognitive changes, action changes, and/or environment changes; and (c) all stress management efforts can involve other people as actors, others as experiencers, others as observers, and/or others as objects.

The first case considered is the simple one where the initial threatening structure is, itself, one of the negative structures described above and illustrated in Figure 2b. Other, more complex, cases of stress and stress management are seen as being motivated by efforts to stave off situations that could lead the person to have to accept one or more of such negative structures.

Negative Structure

A central figure of subjective competence theory, not emphasized thus far, is its account of change possibilities, cognitive processes through which an initial cognitive structure can be changed to another structure. The theory delineates a number of ways of changing an initially negative structure to make it less negative. These theoretically derived possibilities for making negative structures less negative can be seen as ways to reduce stress.

Kinds of changes available, briefly noted and illustrated with examples from the belief-deployment repertoire of an imaginary heavy smoker, are to find a new cause, other than oneself, for some element(s) in the initial belief structure (e.g., "The cause of my smoking is not me, but an addiction"), to reevaluate some feature(s) on the original negative belief structure (e.g., "It has not been proven that smoking leads to disease"), and to see or think about new positive consequences of some feature(s) of the initial structure (e.g., "Smoking gives me great pleasure"). These are called Type A (i.e., new origin), Type B (i.e., change value), and Type C (i.e., new consequences) changes in

Figure 3, which illustrates 21 ways of reducing the initial stress created by the negative belief structure illustrated in Figure 2. This typology of ways to reduce stress is generated by performing Type A, B, and C changes on each of the seven elements in the initial structure.

There is substantial empirical evidence in the areas of self-serving causal attributions (Greenwald, 1980, on benefectance) and cognitive dissonance (Bowerman, 1979) that people do use at least some of these conceptually possible reactions to threats to self-evaluation. However, the topic is ripe for much more research.

Deteriorating Structure

There are a number of ways, noted above, that the value of a given structure can be lowered. The overview point here is that one major class of stress management strategies involves efforts to protect against such possibilities, or to undo them if they occur. The theory suggests a number of ways this may be done. The case of a threat to a positive structure can serve by implication (with appropriate changes, parallel to the discussions in the stress section of the chapter) as also illustrating ways to protect a negative structure from further deterioration. Consider a politician who has taken pride in originating a tax policy that he believes will bring benefits by creating more business, and ultimately, more jobs. If this source of pride is threatened, in any of a number of possible ways, there is a set of cognitive maneuvers that could be used to protect the initial positive structure. Possibilities (parallel to the "21 ways" noted in Figure 3) run from reasserting personal credit for the plan (especially relevant, clearly, when a challenge to "ownership" is what produces the threat), to believing more strongly than before that the tax policy will create more jobs, and to seeing new and different benefits of the tax policy.

The immediate reaction to a threat to self-evaluation is often to increase effort or belief in the merits of one's plans. Fox and Staw (1979), in a framework involving self-justification as a motivation, explore conditions that lead administrators to redouble effort to get a "failing" action to stop failing (often with disastrous results in the long run, since "reality" is indifferent to efforts at self-justification that are "unrealistic").

Lowering general beliefs about one's abilities, reliability, sensitivity, and so forth, is especially threatening, since such a change would have implications for a wide range of future transactions with environments (as well as past ones, given the restructuring of memory). So many stress management possibilities involve controlling the implications individual events have for general beliefs about the self. For example, the occurrence of a single failure can be attributed to chance, or to task difficulty, rather than to an enduring, personal disposition, so inferences about one's future are not lowered because of one's failure (Heider, 1958; Kelley, 1967; Weiner, 1974). Or, as noted by Jones and Berglas (1978), one can avoid such threats by establishing expectations beforehand, through such "handicapping" strategies as drinking and/or not trying very hard, so the behavioral "failure," when it happens (and it will), can be attributed plausibly to something other than one's ability, indeed something that hampers one's ability. Procrastinating is a pretty good handicapping strategy, too. Complications arise, of course, when these become self-conscious, or when

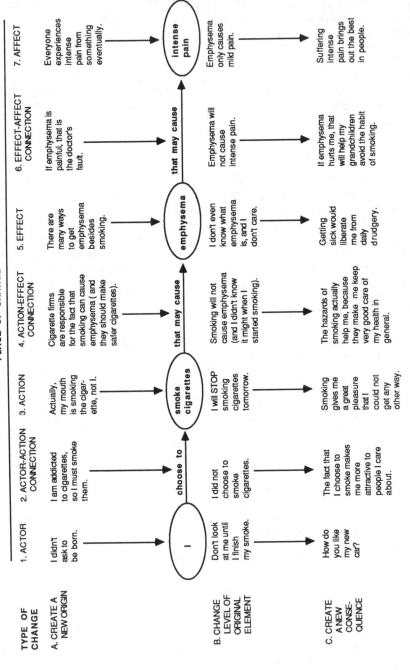

Figure 3 Illustrations of 21 ways to reduce a threat to subjective competence.

44

attributions are made about oneself as the origin of the ultimately self-limiting or even self-destructive strategies that have been used. One of the goals of stress management efforts is to make it easier to avoid such short-term stress-reduction strategies, and replace them with long-term strategies that are preferable both pragmatically and morally.

Incomplete Structure

If people are motivated to seek positive structures and to avoid negative structures, then it follows that they will be motivated to fill in gaps in potentially positive structures and to avoid filling in (indeed, to widen) gaps in potentially negative structures. The theory makes a number of detailed predictions about when and how people will be motivated to fill gaps in incomplete structures, or to avoid the filling of a gap. When? When it makes a big difference in self-evaluation. How? Using the changes illustrated in Figure 3, with cognitive and environmental factors dictating which possibilities are available.

There are many directions to go to pursue this point. One is to link it to the information processing side of stress and stress management (Miller, 1981) and to White's work on effectance motivation (1974). Clearly a person is often interested in gaining new information, and the present approach suggests some reasons why and also some cases where one seeks ignorance in order to keep gaps in knowledge *open*. Bandura's (1977) work on self-efficacy is central here, too, as it deals with the importance of providing a person with skills to move from current to desired states, by learning how to perform actions and what the consequences of actions will be.

Conflicting Structures

When two (or more) versions of the same subjective competence structure are being considered at once, any differences in the self-evaluations implied by the versions will produce stress (the more so, the more the differences). The two basic responses to this sort of threat are to try to change the lower-valued version of the structure so it moves up to the level of the most favorable version and to try to remove the lower-valued structure from consideration entirely. Choices or oscillations between these conflicting responses (i.e., to improve the worst version or to remove it) cause some of life's least pleasant moments.

There are a number of sources of conflict, as noted above, but two especially important cases will be discussed briefly. During transactions with the environment there is always the possibility of conflicts between generalizations and expectations, between expectations and observations, and between observations and generalizations. Details are beyond the scope of this paper, but ways to avoid conflicts in versions of transactions include keeping aspirations low (so results are not less than expected), misremembering past hopes (so one thinks one got what one had been expecting), and attributing unfavorable outcomes to external factors (so abilities do not come into question). A second large class of conflicts in versions of transactions involves differences between one's own conception of oneself and one's beliefs about someone else's beliefs about oneself. Ways to deal with the stress produced by this kind of conflict are many and are especially problematic, both pragmatically and morally. They include acting in ways that others will like and then accepting the new behavior (i.e., bringing oneself into line with another person's standards), making the other accept one's own version, forgetting one's own version, and avoiding holding the other person's version, either by ignoring the person, by removing him/her, or by denigrating the validity of the other's contact with reality.

This concludes a brief outline of broad kinds of stress management possibilities suggested by the present framework as following from a motivation to avoid negative or problematic self-evaluations. It is clear that there are many ways that self-evaluations, as generated by causal cognitions tied to oneself as an actor, are related to stress management. This discussion has raised a number of empirical, theoretical, applied, and normative issues that could be pursued in future work.

CONCLUSION

The main points of the paper can be summarized briefly. The starting point is the assumption that stress is a signal to the organism that something is wrong, and that the cause of stress connected to self-evaluation involves beliefs about oneself as engaged in negative or problematic transactions with some environment. To pursue this point fruitfully, to make testable and useful claims about stress and stress management arising from negative or problematic self-evaluations, it is necessary to have a conception of what kinds of causal cognitions about the self produce stress and how these could be changed to reduce and/or manage stress. The subjective competence theory is claimed to offer a conceptual apparatus to do this. It is described and used to make a number of points about different kinds of stress arising from negative or problematic self-evaluations, and to outline points about how stress from these sources might be reduced.

There are a number of directions one could go from here. Certainly, the information processing approach (Miller, 1981) should be brought in, with benefits to be expected in each direction when the present, more motivational approach is combined with greater detail on just how information is processed before, during, and after stressful events. Social factors, mentioned frequently in passing, are of central importance in many, if not most, real-life cases of stress and stress management, so the topic should be explored fully and systematically. While the present approach does not offer a morally "right" solution to any given problem, it does suggest variables that are involved and indicates what the major options are. Four social/moral dimensions that run through much of the topic of stress and stress management are the role of others as actors, others as authorities who "demand" to be obeyed (Milgram, 1974), others as "victims" of our actions (Glover, 1977), and others as standard setters, judges, observers of our interactions with the physical and social world. Descriptive and normative issues need to be explored, both with respect to pragmatic matters (e.g., long-range vs. short-range solutions; conservative vs. innovative reactions to novelty) and social/moral issues (e.g., hedonism vs. altruism; obedience vs. deviance).

In conclusion, it should be emphasized that this is only an introduction to the range of ways in which self-referent causal cognitions, and resulting self-evaluations, may be related to stress and stress reduction. Much theoretical and empirical research, basic and applied, is necessary to fully explore this approach to stress and emotion. Also, the present orientation clearly needs to be tied, ultimately, to approaches that focus on other cognitive factors and/or physiological factors, which are obviously of great significance for a comprehensive understanding of stress and emotion.

REFERENCES

Abramson, L. Y., Seligman, M. E. P., & Teasdale, J. D. (1978). Learned helplessness in humans: Critique and reformulation. *Journal of Abnormal Psychology, 87*, 49–74.

Allport, G. W. (1943). The ego in contemporary psychology. *Psychological Review, 50*, 451–478.

Bandura, A. (1977). Self-efficacy: Toward a unifying theory of behavior change. *Psychological Review, 84*, 191–215.

Bowerman, W. R. (1978). Subjective competence: The structure, process, and function of self-referent causal attributions. *Journal for the Theory of Social Behaviour, 8*, 45–75.

Bowerman, W. R. (1979). Subjective competence theory applied to cognitive dissonance phenomena: Reactions to negative self-referent causal attributions. Unpublished manuscript, Netherlands Institute for Advanced Study in the Humanities and Social Sciences.

Bowerman, W. R. (1981). Applications of a social psychological theory of motivation to the language of defensiveness and self-justification. In M. M. T. Henderson (Ed.), *1980 Mid-America Linguistics Conference Papers*. Lawrence: University of Kansas Linguistics Department.

Coelho, G. V., Hamburg, D. A., & Adams, J. E. (Eds.). (1979). *Coping and adaptation*. New York: Basic Books.

Defares, P. B. (1979). Social perception and environmental quality. *Urban Ecology, 4*, 119–137.

Epstein, S. (1973). The self-concept revisited. *American Psychologist, 28*, 404–416.

Fox, F. F., & Staw, B. M. (1979). The trapped administrator: Effects of job insecurity and policy resistance upon commitment to a course of action. *Administrative Science Quarterly, 24*, 449–471.

French, J. R. P., Jr., Rodgers, W., & Cobb, I. (1974). Adjustment as person-environment fit. In G. V. Coelho, D. A. Hamburg, & J. E. Adams (Eds.), *Coping and adaptation*. New York: Basic Books.

Glover, J. (1977). *Causing death and saving lives*. Harmondsworth, England: Penguin Books Ltd.

Goldschmidt, W. (1974). Ethology, ecology, and ethological realities. In G. V. Coelho, D. A. Hamburg, & J. E. Adams (Eds.), *Coping and adaptation*. New York: Basic Books.

Greenwald, A. G. (1980). The totalitarian ego: Fabrication and revision of personal history. *American Psychologist, 35*, 603–618.

Heider, F. (1958). *The psychology of interpersonal relations*. New York: Wiley.

Janis, I. L., & Mann, L. (1977). *Decision making*. New York: The Free Press.

Jones, E. E., & Berglas, S. (1978). Control of attributions about the self through self-handicapping strategies: The appeal of alcohol and the role of underachievement. *Personality and Social Psychology Bulletin, 4*, 200–206.

Kahn, R. L., & French, J. R. P., Jr. (1970). Status and conflict: Two themes in the study of stress. In J. E. McGrath (Ed.), *Social and psychological factors in stress*. New York: Holt, Rinehart and Winston.

Kelley, H. H. (1967). Attribution in social psychology. In D. Levine (Ed.), *Nebraska symposium on motivation*. Lincoln: University of Nebraska Press.

Kelman, H. C., & Baron, R. M. (1968). Inconsistency as a psychological signal. In R. P. Abelson, E. Aronson, W. J. McGuire, T. M. Newcomb, M. J. Rosenberg, & P. H. Tannenbaum (Eds.), *Theories of cognitive consistency: A sourcebook*. Chicago: Rand-McNally.

Lazarus, R. S. (1975). A cognitively oriented psychologist looks at biofeedback. *American Psychologist, 30*, 553–561.

Lazarus, R. S., & Launier, R. (1978). Stress-related transactions between person and environment. In L. A. Pervin, & M. Lewis (Eds.), *Perspectives in interactional psychology*. New York: Plenum Press.

McGrath, J. E. (Ed.), (1970a). *Social and psychological factors in stress*. New York: Holt, Rinehart and Winston.

McGrath, J. E. (1970b). Some strategic considerations for future research on social-psychological stress. In J. E. McGrath (Ed.), *Social and psychological factors in stress.* New York: Holt, Rinehart and Winston.

Mechanic, D. (1970). Some problems in developing a social psychology of adaptation to stress. In J. E. McGrath (Ed.), *Social and psychological factors in stress.* New York: Holt, Rinehart and Winston.

Mechanic, D. (1974). Social structure and personal adaptation: Some neglected dimensions. In G. V. Coelho, D. A. Hamburg, & J. E. Adams (Eds.), *Coping and adaptation.* New York: Basic Books.

Milgram, S. (1974). *Obedience to authority.* New York: Harper & Row.

Miller, S. M. (1981). Predictability and human stress: Toward a clarification of evidence and theory. In L. Berkowitz (Ed.), *Advances in experimental social psychology* (Vol. 14). New York: Academic Press.

Taft, R. (1977). Coping with unfamiliar cultures. In N. Warren (Ed.), *Studies in cross-cultural psychology.* London: Academic Press.

Weiner, B. (1974). *Achievement motivation and attribution theory.* Morristown, New Jersey: General Learning Press.

White, R. W. (1974). Strategies of adaptation: An attempt at systematic description. In G. V. Coelho, D. A. Hamburg, & J. E. Adams (Eds.), *Coping and adaptation.* New York: Basic Books.

4

Experience, Stress, and Information Processing Underwater

P. G. A. M. Jorna and A. W. K. Gaillard
Institute for Perception, Soesterberg

INTRODUCTION

Divers in open sea have to cope not only with high pressure and its effects on their physiological systems but also with effects of cold, fatigue, and anxieties which are bound to occur when they are fully aware of the possible dangers in their working environment. These combined stresses may reach the point where it is impossible to maintain performance at optimal levels as has been shown by studies on diver performance. Baddeley (1966) found that it was not possible to explain performance decrements in open sea diving by the mere effects of increased pressure. A later study by Baddeley and Flemming (1967) revealed a similar difference between open sea and hyperbaric chamber diving. No such discrepancy was found when diving conditions were ideal (Baddeley, De Figueredo, Hawkswell-Curtis, & William, 1968). Psychological factors such as anxiety could interact with the effects of increased pressure, thus resulting in a performance decrement larger than predicted by the effects of pressure alone as measured during hyperbaric chamber diving. This was supported by the studies of Davis, Osborne, Baddeley, & Graham (1972), where divers classified as anxious performed worse than non-anxious divers.

Experience with the underwater situation however can improve performance as shown by Weltman, Christianson, and Egstrom (1970), who found differences in performance as well as in physiological parameters for inexperienced and experienced divers while working on a pipe construction in open sea. This was also thought to be related to mental load during open ocean diving, since both groups were quite comparable during relatively safe hyperbaric chamber diving. A specific underwater situation can have different effects on performance depending on the experience a diver has with that situation.

In order to make a safe dive, the diver is required to process information relevant for diving. For instance, depth, course, air supply, possible dangerous obstacles and decompression limits have to be monitored. Additionally, the diver has to cope with the emotional reactions to diving in a hostile environment. A distinction between the effects of these components of stress is not always clear. Hamilton (1977) has argued that anxiety is essentially information that may require attentional processes and thus can compete for space and time with the processing of other information. In this view, a diver is forced to actively process the information from the environment and the information concerning his own emotional reactions. Coping with the underwater situation can result in a reduced demand made by the diving due to a more efficient processing of information and/or a reduction in emotional load. The aim of this study was to evaluate the extent to which it is possible to process information underwater at different levels of experience with that situation. We assumed that the more experienced a diver, the more he or she will be able to cope with the underwater situation, and thus become better able to time-share the dive with the processing of additional task relevant information. By adding a demanding mental task that requires active information processing to the underwater situation and measuring task performance at different levels of experience, it will be possible to gain more insight into the effects of coping on performance underwater.

In addition to behavioral measures, physiological measures can contribute to evaluating the coping process. Some of the most widely applied physiological measures are heart rate and heart rate variability. Under laboratory conditions, it has been shown that increased task demands (mental load) caused a decrease in the variability of the cardiac interval signal (Kalsbeek & Ettema, 1963; Mulder & van der Meulen, 1973). However, recent work has revealed three major frequency components in the cardiac interval signal which determined about 95 percent of the variability (Hyndman & Gregory, 1975; Mulder, 1980; Sayers, 1975). The first component, located at about 0.03 Hz is believed to originate from thermo regulatory vasomotor activity. The second component at about 0.10 Hz is originated by oscillations in the blood pressure control system and the last component reflected respiratory linked activity usually located between 0.25 and 0.40 Hz. It was found that the suppression of heart rate variability was mainly due to a reduction or even a loss of the 0.10 Hz component and this reduction was accompanied by an increase in blood pressure. Mulder (1980) found that the energy of the 0.10 Hz component was not only influenced by mental task load but also by emotional load. It did not matter whether a subject was submitted to dental treatment or to a mental task, in both conditions a decrease in energy of the 0.10 Hz component was found. The application of this technique to cardiac interval signals obtained from inexperienced and experienced divers can provide information on the effects of experience on the physiological reactions to the diving. Physical load however can affect these measures (Boyce, 1974; Opmeer, 1969). It is therefore necessary to control the physical load needed for a particular dive, in order to obtain results that can be correctly interpreted.

To evaluate effects of experience with the underwater situation on task performance and physiological measures, test dives were made by inexperienced (novice) divers at different time points in their training program and their performances were compared with results obtained from a control group of experienced divers. If it is correct that divers with more experience are better able to cope with the underwater situation than less experienced divers, then performance should reveal differences underwater, but not in a dry control situation. Due to training, performance should improve for inexperienced divers while experienced divers should show no such improvement with task replications underwater, because their coping is already near optimal levels. To control for pure task learning, performance in dry control situations should show no improvement due to replications for both groups of divers. To inspect the energy in the 0.10 Hz component (blood pressure component), heart rate was recorded underwater for each dive.

METHOD

Subjects

Two groups of male subjects, 12 novice and 6 experienced divers participated in the study. The experienced group had approximately 75 diving hours, ranging from 50 to 100 hours and consisted of divers stationed at the training center for Dutch Naval divers located at Den Oever in The Netherlands. All divers in this group had completed the basic training course for "ship divers." Two frogmen and an instructor with far more experience (800 hours) were included. The average age of this group was 25 years. The novice divers were Naval personnel selected after psychological and medical testing for training to become ship divers. These divers were randomly selected out of the available novice divers. The average age of this group was 22 years.

Diving

Dives were made at the training center in shallow (3–5 m) water with no visibility. The temperature of the water ranged from 4°–8° C. Dives were made singly and the diver was connected with the surface by means of a signal line. Underwater a bottom line (yackstay) was placed, to guide the diver while swimming on a standard underwater trajectory. The divers used a dry suit assembly (AVON) and were equipped with Loosco Scuba gear. Full face masks (Dräger) were used during the study.

Task

The diver was required to memorize a set of letters denoted as the positive set. The set size was either two or four letters. After memorization, letters were presented auditorily to the diver with intervals of 2200 msec. The diver had to decide, on each presentation of a test letter, whether it belonged to the memorized positive set. If it was decided that the test letter belonged to the positive set (i.e., it was a target letter), a response was given by pressing a button located in the left hand of the diver. If the test letter was a nontarget, no response was emitted. In addition, the diver had to set a counter in memory for each letter in the positive set. Whenever a target letter was detected the corresponding counter value had to be incremented by one. The updated values of the counters had to be rehearsed in order to keep them in memory. The final counter values were reported at the end of the task.

Twelve letters (consonants) were selected from the Dutch alphabet in such a way that the discriminability of the specific letters used was optimized. The selected letters were spoken on tape and digitized by way of a PDP-11 computer. With this material, the computer generated randomized series of letters with fixed intervals. Each task (4 target–2 target) contained about 25 percent letters designated as targets. The total number of targets varied between 33 and 38 and the specific target letters differed in probability of occurrence. Targets were presented with a set of six nontargets. The total series contained 141–146 letters and task duration was about five minutes. The target letters were changed each dive, and during a dive letters designated as targets in one task were not used as nontargets in the other task.

Apparatus

The presentation of stimuli and recording of responses and physiological signals were controlled by a Diver Applied Telemetry and Recording system (DATAR), developed especially for this purpose (Eernst and Jorna, 1980). The DATAR system was placed into a compact underwater housing and was attached to the air cylinders of the diver. The hinderance for the diver was minimal and a realistic dive was possible. The system was equipped with waterproof inlets for biological signals (heart rate, respiration) and responses made by a response button operating with magnetic switches.

Stimuli were presented to the diver by means of a bone-conductor system connected to a cassette recorder in the housing. Stimuli, responses, and biological signals were sent to the surface for on-line monitoring. Additionally, all information was multiplexed and recorded on cassette in the housing.

Procedure

The training course for shipdivers takes nearly 8 weeks of intensive training. In the first week of training, inexperienced divers were trained in a swimming pool for familiarization with the breathing apparatus. During this week they were informed about the procedures of the experiment, and were trained on the task. The inexperienced group divers made three test dives, one in the first week of diving in open water (Period I) one in the fourth week (Period II) and one near the end of the training course (seventh week—Period III). The experienced group divers made two test dives, at Periods I and III. Both groups also performed the tasks in a dry control condition at the same periods (Periods I and III). These dry tests were taken in the diving raft where the experimental equipment was housed.

Each dive, divers were instructed which target letters were to be used; consecutively, they were given a test trial to determine the best place for the bone conductor (usually mastoid). Divers were instructed to react as quickly as possible whenever a target letter was detected. They were also informed that the experimenter could check the responses at the surface. The counting of the targets was done covertly and the final counts were noted underwater on a note panel attached to the divers arm. The diver was informed in which order the two tasks (2 target–4 target) would be presented. The order of presentation was balanced between subjects.

After attachments of the ECG electrodes (left–right chest, sternum), final preparations for diving were made. The diver started the DATAR system underwater by pressing his response button and commenced swimming in a calmly regular fashion along the bottom line (length ± 20 m). The tasks were presented with five minute intervals. The diver was not allowed to stop swimming, unless in case of emergency. The signalman controlled the dive and reported any deviations in swimming speed. Divers received no feedback on their performance or physiological signals at the end of the dives.

Scoring and Analysis of Data

Task performance was based on the reported final counts at the end of a task and expressed as a percentage deviation from the correct target numbers (deviation from correct). Also, the percentage of detected target letters, that is target letters with a response, was calculated to inspect if inexperienced and experienced divers differed in their ability to distinguish the target letters in the presented series of letters.

The analysis of heart rate was based on the R-peaks (the most pronounced peak in the ECG). The Interbeat intervals (IBI) were calculated by a PDP-8 computer with an accuracy of one msec. For each dive, power spectra were computed for this time series of IBIs (Mulder et al., 1973; Mulder, 1979; Mulder, 1980). The mean power or energy between 0.06 and 0.14 Hz was used as an index for the energy in the 0.10 Hz component. In addition, the mean IBI and respiratory rate were calculated.

Due to the scoring method used for assessing task performance (percentages, inhomogeneous data) and the relative low number of subjects involved, it was decided to analyze the data with nonparametric statistics.

The Wilcoxon test was used for two related samples; the Friedman analysis of variance for differences between repeated measures and the Mann Whitney-U test for differences between the groups of divers participating in the study. The same statistics were applied to the physiological measures. The procedures used were those described by Siegel (1956).

Two inexperienced divers were dropped from the analysis due to technical failures during diving. Also, the second dry control condition for the experienced divers was dropped since three divers were not able to complete this condition as they were stationed elsewhere at that time.

RESULTS

Task Performance

The percentage deviation from correct was calculated for both groups of divers to inspect performance at different time points in training and to compare inexperienced and experienced divers under wet and dry conditions. In Figure 1, we have depicted this score for the inexperienced and experienced divers for the four target tasks.

For the inexperienced divers, a significant ($p < 0.01$) decrease in deviations from correct was found when they had more training in diving. No such decrease was found under dry control conditions. This ensured that the observed improvement in performance was not due to an artefact of task learning. Moreover, no differences in performance were found for the experienced divers when tested again underwater. Note that the inexperienced divers reached the same level of performance as the experienced divers at the

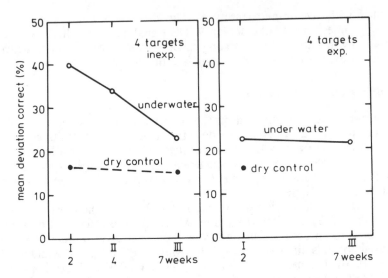

Figure 1 Percentage deviation from correct in the 4-target task for inexperienced divers at different training periods, compared to experienced divers under wet and dry conditions.

end of the training course and that both groups did not differ in performance under dry conditions. However, it was observed that even for the more experienced diver (including divers at the end of the training course) wet conditions produced a significant ($p < 0.01$) increase in deviations from correct as compared to dry control conditions.

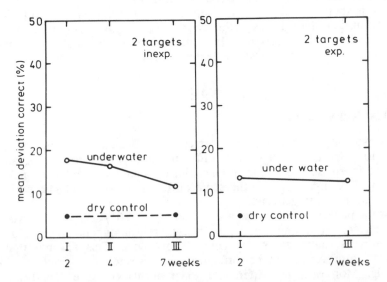

Figure 2 Percentage deviation from correct in the 2-target task for inexperienced divers at different training periods, compared to experienced divers under wet and dry conditions.

In Figure 2 we depicted the deviation from correct for both groups for the two target task. The decrease in this score was only marginally present and in fact not significant for the inexperienced divers. Again, no decrease was found under dry control conditions. For the experienced divers, performance underwater was stable, and both groups were similar under dry control conditions. For this two target task then, only marginal effects of training were found, but again wet conditions produced a significant ($p < 0.01$) increase in deviations from correct as compared to dry control conditions.

Inspection of the percentage detected targets revealed no differences for inexperienced and experienced divers. The number of false alarms, that is a non-target taken for a target, was negligible. This assures that both groups of divers received the same information with identical quality.

Physiological Data

For each diver, mean heart rates of inexperienced divers was calculated and expressed as the average IBI. The inexperienced divers decreased their heart rate significantly ($p < 0.01$) during the training course, whereas for experienced divers no changes were observed. However, heart rate of inexperienced divers decreased to even lower levels than heart rate for the experienced divers, as illustrated in Figure 3. This decrease resulted in a significant ($p < 0.02$) difference in heart rate between the groups of divers at the end of the training course.

For a possible clarification of these findings, we also inspected heart rate under the dry conditions, as shown in the right panel of Figure 3. The training course resulted in a significant ($p < 0.02$) decrease in heart rate for the inexperienced divers. Inspection of the available data for the experienced divers (three subjects) indicated that no such dramatic decrease was present for this

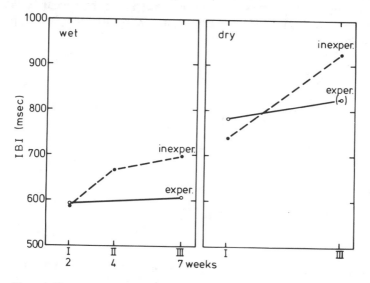

Figure 3 Heart rate (IBI) for inexperienced and experienced divers under wet and dry conditions.

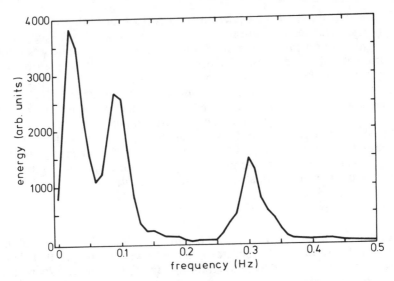

Figure 4 Spectrum for a swimming diver at a depth of five meters. Three components can be identified at 0.03 Hz, 0.10 Hz, and 0.30 Hz.

group. The specific training that the inexperienced divers received during their training course must have induced this difference, as both groups were quite comparable during the first part of the experiment.

The cardiac interval signals were frequency analyzed, to inspect the blood pressure component (0.10 Hz). The spectrum obtained from a diver swimming underwater revealed the same major frequency components as found in the laboratory studies. From these spectra, as shown in Figure 4, we used the mean energy between 0.06 and 0.14 Hz as an index for the blood pressure component.

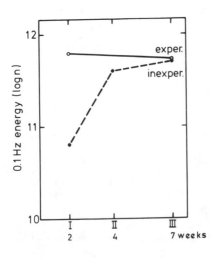

Figure 5 0.10 Hz energy for inexperienced divers at different training periods compared to experienced divers underwater.

The inexperienced divers revealed a low energy in this component at the first period of training, but this energy was increased significantly ($p < 0.01$) during the later parts of the training course as presented in Figure 5.

The experienced divers revealed an energy significantly ($p < 0.04$) higher than the inexperienced divers during the first period and no change was observed when these divers were tested again underwater. Note that in contrast with heart rate, inexperienced and experienced divers have similar energy values in their blood pressure components at the last period of training.

Inspection of the respiratory measurements revealed that the breathing frequency of the inexperienced divers decreased from 0.24 Hz to 0.20 Hz and 0.17 Hz for the respective training periods, while the experienced group breathed at an average frequency of 0.14 Hz.

DISCUSSION

The aim of this study was to evaluate effects of experience with the stressful underwater situation on the performance capabilities of the diver. It was stated that due to coping with this initial stress, increased experience should result in a more effective performance. A main result of increased experience was the improved underwater performance for the initially inexperienced divers as reflected in a decrease in deviations from correct for the four target tasks. The dry controls indicated that we succeeded in diminishing unwanted effects of task learning. Impaired sound quality underwater cannot account for the obtained data since no improvement in performance was found in the two target task, while the same total number of target letters was presented to the diver. The results indicate that it is possible for an inexperienced diver to maintain a performance level equal to more experienced divers, as long as the task is not highly loading. The data confirmed the notion that experienced divers should have a stable performance underwater as coping is already near optimal levels. Both groups differed only in the underwater conditions and not in the dry control conditions, so it can be concluded that the observed performance differences were induced by the interaction of the divers' experience and the underwater environment. Coping with this environment will improve diver performance, although performance was found to be less optimal then under dry conditions.

Coping is not only reflected in task performance, but also in the physiological reactions underwater. The heart rate of inexperienced divers decreased as a function of training, although the blood pressure component data were more convincing. Respiration is not the main determinator for these results as the respiration frequencies in the last two periods of training would predict a substantial increase in energy, because the frequency is then most close to the blood pressure component. However, the main increase in the blood pressure component was observed in the first and not the last parts of training.

The remarkable difference for both groups as observed in heart rate, can be explained by an artifact of diving training. The physical training to become a diver is very harsh. Medical examinations showed that physical fitness is improved remarkably by this training, thus resulting in a general lower heart rate at the end of training. Because the experienced divers were far less involved in physical exercise during the training period, a difference in heart rate underwater can develop. If so, then the results obtained for the blood pressure components would suggest a relative independency for physical fitness, which would make it an excellent tool for studies in which physical training is involved. Further studies will be needed to test this hypothesis. The general results of the spectral analyses were quite similar to the performance data in that large improvements as a function of training can be found, whereas no such change is evident in already experienced divers.

The results of this study were obtained in what we think was a stressful situation for the subjects who had to learn how to dive. Studying stress in training situations like this seems to be an ethical way of collecting real-life data. The diving situation involved in this study was a very simple one in that the environmental information presented to diver was generally low (no marine life, sandy bottom, etc.). Coping with this environment, therefore, most likely resulted in a major reduction of the emotional load involved in diving with absolutely no visibility. This reduction then could result in a better processing of task relevant information and reduce the physiological response to that environment. This study was limited to one specific diving situation, so diving in a new, different situation could impose new demands on the diver. Is the diver who became experienced in our training situation also "experienced" for diving in the North Sea at extended depths, or is additional coping required? Further studies will be needed to clarify the relation between coping with a stressful situation and the concept of "experience" as used in diving. The methods outlined in this paper can be useful in answering these questions. The techniques are now well applicable to the underwater situation and do not interrupt a realistic dive. Research in more complicated and dangerous diving situations is envisaged.

REFERENCES

Baddeley, A. A. (1966). Influence of depth on the manual dexterity of free divers: A comparison between open sea and pressure chamber testing. *Journal of Applied Psychology, 50,* 81–85.

Baddeley, A. D., De Figueredo, J. W., Hawkswell-Curtis, J. W., & William, A. N. (1968). Nitrogen narcosis and performance underwater. *Ergonomics, 11,* 157–164.

Baddeley, A. D., & Flemming, N. C. (1967). The efficiency of divers breathing oxy-helium. *Ergonomics, 10,* 311–319.

Boyce, P. R. (1974). Sinus arrhythmia as a measure of mental load. *Ergonomics, 17,* 177–183.

Davis, F. M., Osborne, J. P., Baddeley, A. D., & Graham, M. F. (1972). Diver performance: Nitrogen narcosis and anxiety. *Aerospace Medicine, 10,* 1079–1082.

Eernst, J. T., & Jorna, P. G. A. M. (1980). DATAR: A diver applied telemetry and recording system for the measurement of diver responses underwater. *Institute for Perception TNO,* The Netherlands.

Hamilton, V. (1977). Cognitive development in the neuroses and schizophrenias. In V. Hamilton and M. D. Vernon (Eds.), *The development of cognitive processes.* London: Academic Press.

Hyndman, B. W., & Gregory, J. R. (1975). Spectral analysis of sinus arrhythmia during mental loading. *Ergonomics, 18,* 255–270.

Kalsbeek, J. W. H., & Ettema, J. H. (1963). Scored regularity of the heart rate pattern and the measurement of perceptual or mental load. *Ergonomics, 6,* 306–307.

Mulder, G. (1979). Coping with mental workload. In H. Ursin & S. Levine (Eds.), *Coping and health.* New York: Plenum Press.

Mulder, G. (1980). The heart of mental effort: Studies in the cardio-vascular psychophysiology of mental work. Unpublished doctoral dissertation, University of Groningen (The Netherlands).

Mulder, G., & Mulder-Hajonides van der Meulen, W. R. E. H. (1973). Mental load and the measurement of heart rate variability. *Ergonomics, 16,* 69–84.

Opmeer, C. H. J. M. (1969). Sinusaritmie als maat van mentale belasting bij verschillende niveau's van de hartfrequentie. *Report Laboratory of Ergonomic Psychology TNO.* Amsterdam: The Netherlands.

Sayers, B. M. A. (1975). Physiological consequences of information load and overload. In P. H. Venables, & M. J. Christie (Eds.), *Research in psychophysiology.* London: Wiley.

Siegel, S. (1956). *Non-parametric statistics for the behavioral sciences.* New York: McGraw-Hill.

Weltman, G., Christianson, R. A., & Egstrom, G. H. (1970). Effects of environment and experience on underwater work performance. *Human Factors, 12,* 587–598.

5

Time Anxiety
and Type A Behavior

J. A. M. Winnubst
University of Utrecht

For many persons living in industrialized countries, time has become a scarce commodity. Consequently, the ability to accurately budget time, especially as one's position rises on the social scale, has great importance for individual adjustment. The growing use of planning aids such as calendars, memorandum books, diaries, and clocks supports the assumption that many individuals are anxious about the flow of time, whereas others consider time relatively unimportant. Ironically, some high-status persons (e.g., corporate executives, medical doctors, professors) seem to regard it as their prerogative to let people wait for their appointments, while they themselves experience considerable irritation when inconvenienced by others' lack of punctuality. This brief sketch of the role of time in everyday life brings us to the theme of this paper: the relation of time attitude and anxiety to psychoanalytic theory and Type A coronary-prone behavior.

Time attitude encompasses the physical and psychological reality of time, and the various procedures and devices employed to accurately describe and measure it. A major assumption in this paper is that people differ substantially in their time attitude. In the course of the following discussion, I will also contend that the emphasis on time urgency in the A/B typology has corresponding roots in psychoanalytic theory.

THE ANAL CHARACTER
IN PSYCHOANALYTIC THEORY

Considering time as a scarce commodity is related to the psychoanalytic conceptions of the anal personality and obsessive-compulsive neurosis. The concept of anal character refers to a set of personality traits that Freud (1908, 1941) observed in his patients, which always seemed to occur together: orderliness, obstinacy, and parsimony. Jones (1918), Pettit (1969), and Kline (1972) have specifically linked these so-called anal character traits to time attitudes. In research on the relation of attitude toward time and the theory of anality, two questions are of prime importance: (1) What are the origins and constituent elements of the anal syndrome? (2) What is the relation between anality and attitude toward time?

Freud noted that the anal character syndrome appeared primarily in persons who were late in toilet training, especially those who tended to postpone bowel movements. Consistent with his theory of psychosexual stages, Freud (1905, 1942) believed that such persons derived sexual pleasure from this behavior. Experiencing sexual gratification through bowel motion was assumed to reflect an anal-erotic preoccupation in childhood which, in the course of libidinal development, provided the impulsive drive that formed the anal personality. Since this interest often completely disappeared in later life, Freud reasoned that anal eroticism was prohibited by a strict taboo in Western culture. Consequently, in the sexual latency period (between 5 and 11 years of age), anal preoccupation was displaced from its original objective and deflected into sublimations or reaction formations. The process of expressing libidinal energy in accordance with moral values of anal-erotic origin ultimately resulted in the typical anal triad—orderliness, obstinacy, and parsimony.

Freud considered orderliness, cleanliness, and dependability as a reaction formation to the child's original interest in the unclean, the dirty, and whatever was alien to the body (in this context Freud quotes an English proverb: "Dirt is matter in the wrong place"). With regard to obstinacy, Freud held the opinion that in toilet training the small children for the first time in their lives produce a product of their own will that is valued by their parents and is, therefore, used to intimidate them. According to Freud, the relationship between bowel motions, the concept of parsimony, and intense interest in money is well documented. He observed, for example, that constant constipation was often a symptom in neurotics who were obsessed with money. Freud also noted a strong tie between money (also gold) and excrement in primitive thought (e.g., myth, fairy tales, superstition, dreams), and in neurosis.

Freud (1913, 1943) attributed both the origin of the anal personality and the dynamics of compulsive neurosis to the anal stage of psychosocial development. In compulsive neurosis, Freud theorized that the patient regressed to the pregenital, auto-erotic stage because of an early fixation in this developmental period. This explanation was based on his observation that expressions of petulance, hate (obstinacy), and anal sexuality frequently occurred together in compulsive neurosis. Furthermore, the neurosis was often manifested in meticulous behaviors, such as cleanliness compulsions and cleansing rituals characterized by repetition and a fixed rhythmic pattern. These behaviors were interpreted by Freud as reflecting sublimation and reaction formation against anal-erotic stimuli.

In summary, compulsive neuroses and anal character structure appear to have the same origin, though Freud himself hardly associated the two concepts. After describing and interpreting the three fundamental traits of the anal personality, Freud did not further elaborate on his initial insights, but a number of authors have subsequently refined and extended Freud's original ideas. Among the earlier contributors were Abraham (1921), Ferenczi (1914), Jones (1918), Menninger (1943), and Sadger (1910). More recent contributions include studies by Gottheil (1965), Heimann (1962), and Kline (1972).

EMPIRICAL RESEARCH
ON THE ANAL PERSONALITY

A central question in research on the anal personality syndrome is whether there is, in fact, a constellation of personality traits in which orderliness, obstinacy, and parsimony are predominant. In other words, does an anal syndrome exist? And if so, can it be established that the anal personality is related to toilet training and infantile sexuality?

One of the earliest studies of anal personality was conducted shortly after the Second World War. Barnes (1952) had subjects respond to a number of questionnaire items related to different psychosexual stages, including the anal stage, and then factor analyzed their responses. His hypothesis that fixations at different stages of psychosexual development would yield separate factors was not confirmed, but the first factor he extracted was consistent nevertheless with the concept of anality. The specific traits that defined this factor included meticulousness, orderliness, neatness, trustworthiness, and a sense of duty.

In a study of the origins and structure of the anal personality, Beloff (1957) hypothesized: ". . . a psychological, functional entity exists, corresponding to the anal character, as described by psychoanalysis" (p. 150). On the basis of a close examination of the psychoanalytic literature, Beloff identified the following broad range of anal personality traits: obstinacy, orderliness, cleanliness, punctuality, thrift, craze for collecting, tendency to postpone, sadism in personal relationships, scrupulousness, pedantry, feelings of superiority, irritability, wish to dominate, and desire for autonomy. To assess these traits, Beloff constructed a questionnaire to measure overt behavior and attitudes related to anality. Analyses of the responses of 35 men and 40 women identified 28 items that defined an internally consistent scale, with a mean rt of .71 and a rt range of .53 to .93.

To test the validity of his scale, Beloff administered it to a new sample of 120 subjects. The 28 scale items were also presented to four friends of each subject, who were requested to report how they thought the subject would respond. Separate centroid factor analyses of self-ratings and peer ratings each yielded one general factor, with high loadings for 22 and 21 items, respectively. A significant correlation of .48 was also found between the peer ratings and self-ratings. The items with the highest loadings on the general factor were: feelings of superiority, wish to dominate, sadism, irritability, scrupulousness, and obstinacy. In contrast, thrift, cleanliness, and craze for collecting contributed relatively little to the total variance.

Beloff's scale seems to reflect an authoritarian attitude which involves an inclination to manipulate people and, to a lesser extent, strong interest in the possession or collection of objects. Lazare, Klerman, and Armor (1966) obtained results similar to those reported by Beloff. They also identified a general factor, defined by items related to orderliness (load: .74), strong superego (load: .62), and obstinacy and perseverance (load: .54). As in the Beloff study, thrift and cleanliness were not related as closely to the anal syndrome as originally assumed.

Kline (1967, 1968, 1969) has persistently focused on the problem of validity, which remains a major concern in studies of the anal personality. He constructed a 30-item scale (Ai 3), which he subjected to careful item analysis and checked for acquiescence and social desirability. The construct validity of this scale was then investigated in three studies. In the first study, responses to the Ai 3, Cattell's 16 PF Test, and Eysenck's EPI were factor-analyzed with varimax rotation. The Ai 3 loaded (.52) on only one factor, which was labeled "superego" by Kline. Other scales loading this factor were: Cattell's G (superego) .65; C (ego strength) .47; Q-3 (self-control) .54; and Q-4 (id pressure) –.28; and Eysenck's EPI, .69. Kline interpreted these results as providing confirmation of the anal personality, which he interpreted as resulting from the operation of defense mechanisms against anal sexuality. He further assumed that these defense mechanisms were mediated by the superego and executed by the ego.

In Kline's second validation study, the Ai 3 was factored (varimax rotation) along with the anality scales of Beloff (1957) and Hazari (1957). The Ai 3 loaded on the second extracted factor, which was labeled "obsessive traits," but not on the first factor, labeled "general emotionality and instability." In the third validation study, the Ai 3 and Grygier's DPI (1961) were factored (varimax rotation); anality loaded exclusively on a superego dimension (.62). Kline also obtained judgments about his experimental subjects from other persons, demonstrating the concurrent validity of the anality scale with this external criterion. Based on its correspondence with other anality scales, Kline concluded that his Ai 3 scale was a valid measure of anality.

The most important empirical contributions to research on the anal syndrome have now been reviewed. While other investigators have also reported evidence of an anal personality, for example, Finney (1963), Hazari (1957), Pichot and Perse (1967), and Sandler and Hazari (1960), the details of these studies are beyond the scope of the present paper. For our purpose, it is sufficient to assert Kline's (1972) conclusion: "There is firm evidence for the anal character" (p. 29). It should also be noted in passing that this conclusion contrasts with the lack of evidence for oral and other psychosexual syndromes (Winnubst, 1975).

ANALITY AND TIME ATTITUDE

Jones (1918) was among the first to draw attention to the symbolic meaning of time, and to examine the relationship between anality and time attitude. He contended that attitude toward time reflects personal values. Some people are remarkably sensitive to time, seeking to control their own time, not tolerating any interference with their own behavioral timetables, and typically demanding a large portion of other people's time. When frustrated in their temporal schemes, these individuals display reactions that range from irritability to fierce aggressiveness. Jones believed that such attitudes toward time were closely connected to obsessive-compulsive neurosis.

Abraham (1921) observed that an obsession with money is often deflected into an interest in time, and that many neurotics are constantly worried about time problems. Only time spent alone or working is considered by them to be well spent. The propensity for saving time is mainly exhibited in attempting to accomplish two or more tasks simultaneously. Work delays or interruptions cause extreme irritation; inactivity and relaxation are much disliked. As is often the case with money, compulsive patients save time on a small scale, but may on occasion waste it on a grand scale.

Summing up, according to psychoanalytic theory, the relationship between time attitudes, anxiety, and anality is expressed in the following traits:

- Inability to relax
- Possessiveness with respect to one's own time
- The idea that only time spent alone or at work is worthwhile
- Tendency to save time on a small scale, while wasting it on a larger scale
- Constantly feeling the lack of time
- Strong need to budget and control time
- Submissiveness to social norms about time, accompanied by internal rebellion against these same norms
- Irritation and aggression resulting from delay or interruption of work

In the psychoanalytic literature, there are numerous comments about time-related anxiety in compulsive neurosis and obsessive-compulsive behavior. Jones (1918) observed anal-erotic preoccupations and Von Harnik (1924) reported extensive time-related case history material in compulsive neurosis. It should be noted, however, that compulsive neurosis is more pathological, and more strongly associated with anxiety, than the more general theme of anal personality. In discussing the causes of compulsive neuroses, Bonaparte (1940) contends that unduly strict toilet training and the premature introduction of time awareness in childhood are important factors. Her description of compulsive neurotics clearly shows the underlying anal personality:

> *They have a horror of clocks, but at the same time they labor under a compulsion to take note of the most minute details concerning the hours, minutes and seconds. The flight of time is especially horrifying to them; they would gladly forget or deny its reality if they could but do so. (p. 442)*

In view of the above, Kline's (1972) failure to find a difference between anal and obsessive-compulsive traits in his factor analytic research should come as no surprise. Gorman and Katz (1971) contend that this is also likely to be true for the temporal aspects of anality and obsessive-compulsive neurosis. In essence, the relationship between time, anxiety, and obsessive style seems to be expressed in the following traits:

- Constant feeling that time is passing too quickly
- Experience time as being wasted
- Chronic feeling of lack of time
- Compulsive preoccupation with minutes and seconds
- Anxiety about clocks
- Disturbance in concentration

- Feelings of depression
- Great fear of death

An investigation by Pettit (1969) explicitly tested the hypothesized relationship between the anal personality and a specific attitude toward time. On the basis of Freud's anality theory, as extended to time attitude by Abraham (1921), Ferenczi (1914), and Jones (1918), Pettit assumes that people with an anal personality structure desire their experiences to be orderly, neatly organized, and clearly defined. Accordingly, they dislike diffuse, inarticulate expressions, continuously attempt to impose structure and exert control, and dislike spontaneous events and surprises.

Pettit hypothesized that the anal personality was positively related to a worried, meticulous, and obstinate attitude towards time, and that the relationship between anality and spontaneity was negative. To test this hypothesis he used the following four scales: the Grygier (1956) Anality and Spontaneity Scales, his own Time Scale, and the Composite Anality Scale (Schlesinger, 1963). As predicted, the two anality scales were highly correlated (.57). The Time Scale was also positively and significantly correlated with both the Composite Anality Scale ($r = .64$) and the Grygier Anality Scale ($r = .51$), and correlated negatively ($r = -.32$) with the Grygier Spontaneity Scale. Pettit interpreted these results as supporting his hypothesis, but he recognized that a strong objection might be raised with respect to the social desirability of his scales. Another possible interpretation is that the relation between anality and time attitude may be mediated by cultural factors, rather than resulting from reaction formation to early anal impulses. Pettit concludes that both factors play a role, and that longitudinal and experimental investigations are needed to settle these questions.

Gorman and Katz (1971) leveled three major criticisms against Pettit's study. First, they point out that anal character traits and the corresponding time attitudes are dominant Western cultural values, and that social desirability might be a crucial factor in mediating the relationship between anality and time attitude. Second, they note that Calabresi and Cohen (1968) identified at least four orthogonal time attitude factors: time anxiety, time submissiveness, time possessiveness, and time flexibility. The question, then, is which of these factors, or combination of factors, is related to anality. Finally, they ask whether the relationship between time and anality can be understood in terms of more general theoretical constructs such as rigidity, ego strength or obsessive-compulsive mechanisms. In this context, they cite Kline's (1969) findings of an association between anal characteristics and compulsive-neurotic traits.

Taking these criticisms into account, Gorman and Katz (1971) attempted to replicate Pettit's study. The following questionnaires were administered to 110 university students (58 females, 54 males): the Time Attitude Scale (Calabresi & Cohen, 1968); Pettit's Time Scale; the Composite Anality Scale (also used by Pettit); the Marlowe-Crowne Social Desirability Scale; and the Gough-Sanford Rigidity Scale. Correlations among the scales were computed and a prinicipal components factor analysis was performed. Except for social desirability, the scales all loaded on a single factor, which was labeled "obsessive-compulsive mode." A strong relation was also found between anality and several forms of time attitude, which concurred with Pettit's results. The investigators concluded that anality was a component of a more general concept of rigidity, and that social desirability appeared to have no effect on the results.

The findings for the Time Submissiveness subscale were especially interesting, yielding significant correlations with Pettit's Time Scale (.48), the Composite Anality Scale (.41), and the Rigidity Scale (.52). These findings led Gorman and Katz to theorize that the relation between anality and time attitude was primarily the result of a reaction formation against the anal expulsive stage, in which the desire to expel and manipulate feces is transformed into the opposite type of socially conforming behavior. This conclusion was supported by the absence of any relation between the Time Possessiveness subscale, which measures the retentive wish to save time, and the anal-retentive personality traits measured by the Composite Anality Scale.

TIME ANXIETY AND A/B TYPOLOGY

In 1975, I completed a 5-year study of time variables, reporting the findings in a book entitled *The Western Time Syndrome*. Four important molar time variables were described in this publication: time perspective, delay of gratification, time anality, and time competence. A new instrument, "The Western Time Attitude Scale" (WTAS) was also introduced (Winnubst, 1975). At about the same time, Appels drew my attention to a possible connection between my work on time and anality, and Type A behavior, which is associated with a higher prevalence of coronary disease for both men and women.

Friedman and Rosenman (1974) first described the Type A behavior pattern in 1959 as comprising a hurried, competitive, impatient lifestyle with the following overt characteristics: intense striving for achievement, competitiveness, time urgency, hyperalertness, overcommitment to work, and excessive hostility. In a recent paper, Jenkins (1978) reviewed the results of 8 prospective studies and 16 cross-sectional and retrospective studies, in which a positive relationship was found between the Type A behavior pattern and coronary heart disease.

Many of the Type A characteristics enumerated by Jenkins, Zyzanski, and Rosenman (1978) were strikingly similar to our findings for the anal-obsessive time attitude. Our time-anxious subjects experienced time as flowing too fast and as very threatening to them. They saw time as a tyrant and constantly felt extremely guilty over wasted time. According to Jenkins et al. (1978), Type A persons are:

- Strongly irritated when interrupted; frequently verbalize this irritation
- Hold two or more jobs simultaneously for a period of more than four years
- Never late for appointments
- Highly conservative with regard to time; often carry work materials and engage in work activities while waiting for others
- Impatient with people who work slowly; tend to hurry slow speakers

The accepted label for these behaviors is "time urgency." Time-urgent individuals are strongly goal directed and often view others as potential threats to their available time. These people are highly anxious about the flow of time, and seem to suffer increasingly from a chronic lack of time, which is indeed a scarce commodity for them. Since Jenkins' items did not tap this anxiety tendency, we decided to investigate the relationship between the "time urgency" of the A/B typology and the "time anxiety" of the Western Time Syndrome.

The Western Time Attitude Scale (WTAS), which was constructed from several existing scales (Winnubst, 1975), has 11 subscales that are anchored in four theoretical concepts: time persepective, delay of gratification, time anality, and time competence. From a factor analysis of the 11 WTAS subscales, two time-anality scales emerged: Time Anxiety and Time Submissiveness. The *Time Anxiety* (time obsession) subscale measures the degree to which time is experienced as passing too quickly. Persons with high scores on this scale typically feel they don't have enough time, and often feel panicky because of lack of time. They are pressed and hurried people. For them, a shortage of time is a continuing threat. The following are examples of items from the Time Anxiety scale:

- I get almost panicky when I don't have enough time
- I seem to be more pressed for time than most people
- It bothers me to think how fast time goes

The *Time Submissiveness* (punctuality) subscale measures an obsessive concern with being on time. Persons with high scores are very punctual. They worry about clocks and agendas. They are ruled by time. For example:

- I would be lost without a watch
- I would rather come early and wait, than be late for an appointment
- I like to have a definite schedule and stick to it

The relation of the two WTAS time dimensions with other time variables are reported in Figure 1. Within this network of relationships that define the Western Time Syndrome, time anxiety is associated with punctuality, the tendency to plan ahead and to postpone gratification, and with being occupied with thoughts about both positive and negative aspects of the past. Persons with time anxiety dwell more in the future and the past, than in the here and now. They are deeply worried about a lack of time in which to fulfill all of their plans and dreams. In essence, these highly motivated individuals have neurotic attitudes towards time.

The relation between the A/B typology and the Western Time Syndrome was examined in a cooperative research project with Nass and Verhagen, in which the empirical relationships between Type A behavior and time anxiety became clearer (Nass, Verhagen, & Winnubst, 1979). In a matched-control study, two groups of Dutch males, with a mean age of 46 years, were compared on the following personality variables: A/B typology, depression, rigidity, Western Time Attitude Scale, and achievement motivation. One group consisted of 58 myocardial infarction patients, whose infarct occurred less than

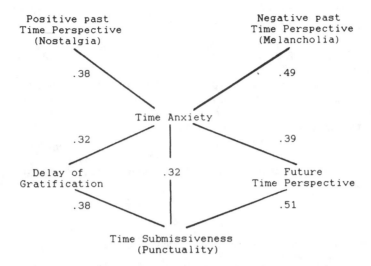

Figure 1 Network of relationships between the WTAS Time Anxiety and Time Submissiveness Subscales and other factors associated with the Western Time Syndrome (Winnubst, 1975). All correlations are significant at *p* < .005. Used with permission.

one year previous to the study. The control group consisted of 58 healthy males with no history of infarction. Differences between groups were assessed by means of discriminant-analysis (Wilks) to determine their respective influence on the dependent variables.

The results of this study are reported in Table 1, in which it may be seen that the depression and the Type A measures were the best indicators of differences between the coronary patients and controls. For our purpose, it was important to demonstrate the value of the Time Anxiety scale as a discriminating measure with relevance to cardiovascular disease. Another interesting finding was the correlation between the Jenkins A/B scale and the WTAS Time Anxiety scale:

Table 1 Differences between male patients with myocardial infarction and a control group of healthy males with no history of infarction

Personality scale	F
Depression	15.04**
JAS (A/B scale)	11.09**
Type A/B interview	8.54**
Fear of failure (Positive)	7.51**
Time anxiety	6.40*
Rigidity	4.73*

*p < .05.
**p < .01.

The correlations between these measures were .53 and .54, respectively, for the heart patients and the control group (both $p < .01$).

Specific attitudes toward time and a particular way of handling time appear to be critical dimensions of coronary-prone behavior. Friedman, Rosenman, and Jenkins, the pioneers of Type A coronary prone behavior research, emphasized the importance of time urgency in the etiology of cardiovascular disease. This writer's contribution resides in demonstrating that Type A time urgency is highly correlated with time anxiety, and that this theme is rooted within psychoanalytic theory, especially in the concepts of anal character and obsessive-compulsive neurosis. There appears to be a strong, but neglected, connection between the Type A coronary prone behavior syndrome of Friedman and Rosenman and the psychoanalytic theory of anal-compulsive behavior.

REFERENCES

Abraham, K. (1965). Contribution to the theory of the anal character. In K. Abraham (Ed.), *Selected papers*. London: Hogarth Press.

Barnes, C. A. (1952). A statistical study of the Freudian theory of levels of psychosexual development. *Genetic Psychology Monographs, 45*, 109–174.

Beloff, H. (1957). The structure and origin of the anal character. *Genetic Psychology Monographs, 55*, 141–172.

Bonaparte, M. (1940). Time and the unconscious. *International Journal of Psychoanalysis, 21*, 427–468.

Calabresi, R., & Cohen, J. (1968). Personality and time attitudes. *Journal of Abnormal Psychology, 78*, 431–440.

Ferenczi, S. (1970). Zur Ontogenie des Geldinteresses. In S. Ferenczi (Ed.), *Schriften zur Psychoanalyse*. I. (pp. 198–205). Frankfurt am Main: S. Fischer Verlag.

Finney, J. C. (1963). Maternal influences on anal or compulsive character in children. *Journal of Genetic Psychology, 103*, 351–367.

Freud, S. (1905). *Drei Abhandlungen zur Sexualtheorie*. Gesammelte Werke, Band V. London: Imago Publishing Company, (1942).

Freud, S. (1908). *Charakter und Analerotik*. Gesammelte Werke, Band VII. London: Imago Publishing Company, (1941).

Freud, S. (1913). *Die Disposition zur Zwangsneurose*. Gesammelte Werke, Band VIII. London: Imago Publishing Company, (1943).

Friedman, M., & Rosenman, R. H. (1974). *Type A behavior and your heart*. Greenwich, Connecticut: Fawcett.

Gorman, B., & Katz, B. (1971). Temporal orientation and anality. *Proceedings of the Annual Convention of the American Psychological Association*, 367–368.

Gottheil, E. (1965). An empirical analysis of orality and anality. *Journal of Nervous and Mental Disease, 141*, 308–317.

Grygier, P. (1956). The personality of student nurses: A pilot study using the DPI. *International Journal of Social Psychiatry, 2*, 105–112.

Grygier, T. G. (1961). *The dynamic personality inventory*. London: N.F.E.R.

Hazari, A. (1957). *An investigation of obsessive-compulsive character traits and symptoms in adult neurotics*. London: University of London.

Heimann, P. (1962). Notes on the anal stage. *International Journal of Psychoanalysis, 43*, 406–414.

Jenkins, C. D. (1978). Behavioral risk factors in coronary artery disease. *Annual Review of Medicine, 29*, 543–562.

Jenkins, C. D., Zyzanski, S. J., & Rosenman, R. H. (1978). Coronary-prone behavior: One pattern or several? *Psychosomatic Medicine, 40*, 24–43.

Jones, E. (1918). Anal-erotic character traits. In E. Jones (Ed.), *Papers on psychoanalysis*. London: Bailliere, Tindall & Cox.

Kline, P. (1967). *An investigation into the Freudian concept of the anal character*. Manchester: University of Manchester.

Kline, P. (1968). Obsessional traits, obsessional symptoms and anal eroticism. *British Journal of Medical Psychology, 41,* 299–305.

Kline, P. (1969). The anal character: A cross-cultural study in Ghana. *British Journal of Social and Clinical Psychology, 8,* 201–210.

Kline, P. (1972). *Fact and fantasy in Freudian theory.* London: Methuen.

Lazare, A., Klerman, G. L., & Armor, D. J. (1966). Oral, obsessive and hysterical personality patterns: An investigation of psychoanalytic concepts by means of factor analysis. *Archives of General Psychiatry, 14,* 624–630.

Menninger, W. C. (1943). Characterologic and symptomatic expressions related to the anal phase of psychosexual development. *Psychoanalytic Quarterly, 12,* 161–193.

Nass, C., Verhagen, F., & Winnubst, J. A. M. (1979). A/B typologie, de Protestantse Ethiek en het Westers Tijdssyndroom. Een empirische studie. *Gedrag, Tijdschrift voor Psychologie, 7,* 41–57.

Pettit, T. F. (1969). Anality and time. *Journal of Consulting and Clinical Psychology, 33,* 170–174.

Pichot, P., & Perse, J. (1967). *Analyse factorielle et structure de la personalité.* Lund: University of Lund.

Sadger, R. (1910). Analerotik und Analcharakter. *Die Heilkunde.*

Sandler, J., & Hazari A. (1960). The obsessional: On the psychological classification of obsessional character traits and symptoms. *British Journal of Medical Psychology, 33,* 113–121.

Schlesinger, V. J. (1963). *Anal personality traits and occupational choice—a study of accountants, chemical engineers and educational psychologists.* Unpublished doctoral dissertation, University of Michigan.

Von Harnik, J. (1924). Die triebhaft-affektiven Momente im Zeitgefühl. *Internationale Zeitschrift für Psychoanalyse, 10,* 33–35.

Winnubst, J. A. (1975). *The Western time syndrome: Concept integration and preliminary scale construct validation from a survey of molar time variables in psychology.* Amsterdam: Swets & Zeitlinger.

6

The Seven Kinds of Denial

Shlomo Breznitz
University of Haifa

Denial as a defense mechanism is viewed as a process through which people attempt to protect themselves from painful or frightening information related to external reality. In contrast to repression and other intrapsychic mechanisms, denial deals with problems emanating from the outside. More specifically, we are pursuing the various kinds and processes of denial and the ways they evolve in relation to anticipatory stress, namely, a situation in which there is some threatening information concerning an impending danger to a person.

As was noted in Breznitz (1981a), anticipatory stress occurs in a situation in which, as the danger comes closer, the involved person attempts to deal with it by a variety of changing mechanisms. These mechanisms may reflect a denial process if the person attempts to avoid the information or its emotional implications or tries to minimize stress by indulging in wishful thinking. Denial may also be involved even when the person develops stereotypic responses and no longer attends to stimuli around him or otherwise tries to protect himself by ready-made responses.

In the case of avoidance, this involves denial of the urgency or immediacy of a situation and the related need to take some kind of action. In the case of wishful thinking, it is the implication of impending danger or harm that is denied by an individual who attempts to focus on positive aspects of the situation. Finally, denial of fear is obviously related to our question; we would like to posit, however, that stereotypic behavior also reflects a kind of denial, in this case, denial of the information conveyed by the stimulus.

This chapter attempts to explicate a relatively simple model of denial-like behaviors. This model can serve as a framework toward a taxonomy of the various kinds of denial, as well as an analytic framework toward a closer understanding of the various components of this potent and prevalent response to stress. More specifically, *we postulate seven kinds of denial, each related to a different stage in the processing of the threatening information.* These kinds of denial represent attempts by the individuals to protect themselves from the impending danger by resorting to different strategies. By indulging in different ways to bias their perception of the world in which they live in a way more appropriate for themselves, people can keep in line with the pleasure principle.

In order to facilitate the intuitive analysis that will be presented, the model resorts to some metaquestions that the threatened person presumably attempts to answer. These metaquestions, in spite of their immediate appeal in terms of verisimilitude to an actually ongoing process of appraisal, should not, however, be seen as representing the actual way that the process of primary and secondary appraisals operate (Lazarus, 1966). The status of the metaquestions in the model will be further discussed at a later point in this analysis; at this juncture their main contribution lies in facilitating the taxonomy of the various kinds of denial. In no way do we argue that these questions actually represent the cognitive process going on consciously or unconsciously while a person is confronted with an objective threat. The model is presented in Figure 1.

Let us attempt a brief analysis. We start by assuming that a person is confronted by a situation in which he or she is objectively helpless. This implies that there is no way that the person can engage in instrumental action that will reduce the probability or the intensity of the danger. Next we assume that the threatening information is sufficiently clear and strong to be above the necessary threshold for its perception and registration. By postulating such obviously threatening information, we make sure that we deal with a stimulus definition of stress, irrespective of the particular response that a person will make. On the left side of the figure we have the metaquestions. On the right side of the figure we have the seven kinds of denial. Next to each kind of denial there is a letter which indicates its position in the sequential analysis of the process.

Let us assume an ideal hypothetical subject is confronted with obviously threatening information and is unable to actively cope. Let us now follow the processing sequence through its entirety. The first metaquestion is: Is there information? He may answer yes or no. Since we assume there is information, the answer in the absence of denial should be yes. The next metaquestion, then, is: Is it threatening? In view of our assumption, the answer should be yes. The next metaquestion is: Is it threatening to me personally? If the answer to that is yes, the next one is: How urgent is that threat to myself; is it threatening now? If yes, then the issue of coping comes up, and the next metaquestion is: Is there anything I can do about it? Can I cope? Assuming objective helplessness, the answer to that should be no. Such an answer in case of an imminent danger should give rise to emotional reactions, to anxiety, fear, or other unpleasant kinds of arousal. The next question, then, is: Am I anxious? The answer should be yes. What is the source of my anxiety? The correct answer in this intellectual exercise is that the source of the anxiety is indeed the threatening information. Thus the system is run through once without any denial taking place whatsoever.

Let us assume that our hypothetical subject is unable to face anxiety without resorting to some kind of denial. The first question that poses itself is, therefore, "Where should I start?" Our model assumes that *people attempt to engage in the least reality distortion necessary at any given point.* It is for this reason that we postulate that *the seven kinds of denial are indeed stages in the same process.*

If the obviously threatening information was brief or temporary only, there might have been actually no motivation to engage in denial at all. The problem, however, is that the threat is actually coming closer in time, and in addition,

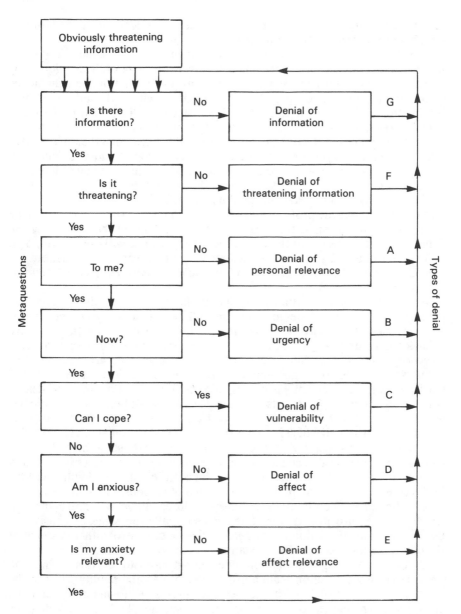

Figure 1 Denial-like behaviors assuming objective helplessness. From International Universities Press, 1981.

new incoming cues may signify its intensity, probability, as well as its imminence. Our model suggests that the first attempt to deny starts with the metaquestion concerning personal relevance. Thus, a person will perceive the information as threatening but may attempt to deny its personal relevance. By responding with "No" to this specific metaquestion, he engages in the first kind of denial, labelled *"denial of personal relevance."* It is denoted by the letter A, signifying its primacy in the entire sequence.

Denial of personal relevance is very well known and very frequent. It is often that a person will face a danger and yet perceive it as entirely devoid of any personal threat to himself. By maintaining this posture, he or she may indeed enjoy the advantages of denial, at least for a while. If the threatening information will not just disappear, and new signals indicate that it is actually coming closer, it will become increasingly difficult for a person to maintain the belief that it does not concern him personally. Once that belief starts to weaken, the next question concerning urgency becomes more salient than before. He or she may now become concerned with time: how much time went by, how much time is left, what can be done to use time, and so forth. If the denial tendency is still operative, and the person in our illustration is unable to face reality without the protective veil of distortion, he or she may now bias the information processing at the next stage, namely, denying the urgency of the danger. Thus the answer to the first three metaquestions will now be yes: Yes, there is information; yes, it is threatening; yes, it is threatening to me; but no, not yet, not now. Thus the second kind of denial is *"denial of urgency,"* and it is denoted by the letter B.

As the information continues to come in, however, even this solution may turn out to be impossible to maintain. While the urgency of the danger becomes more and more obvious, the next question dealing with protective behavior gains importance. It now poses the next option for denial, namely, *"denial of vulnerability."* Since our illustration assumes a situation of objective helplessness, a person who maintains that he or she can cope with the situation, is in fact denying his or her vulnerability. This third kind of denial, denoted by the letter C, reflects the specific situation of helplessness. In cases where there is a certain amount of objective control over the danger, there is another kind of denial which is diametrically opposed to denial of vulnerability. It is *"denial of responsibility."* By denying the ability to do something about the danger a person may abdicate his or her responsibility for what lies in store and for not taking any action. Thus type C denial is either "denial of vulnerability" in the case of objective helplessness or "denial of responsibility" in the case of objective control. In both instances, however, the cognitive mechanism through which the pleasure principle is served is essentially the same. It consists of psychological manipulation of the perceived level of control either one way or the other, contrary to its objective states.

If the threatening information does not terminate at this point, the psychological construction maintained by denial of vulnerability will also be short-lived; sooner or later it will become impossible to maintain, and the answer to the metaquestion will change from yes to no. No, I cannot cope. This automatically leads to anxiety.

The next stage during which the denial tendency can still intervene and reduce the anxiety is specifically tied to the perception of one's own emotions. By denying the affect itself, the person may, at least for a while, gain some psychological comfort. Thus, the fourth kind of denial is *"denial of affect,"* denoted by the letter D.

Once affect cannot be denied any longer, it may still be explained away. Trying to account for perceived emotionality by resorting to explanations and attributions unrelated to the objective facts, some psychological advantage can still be gained. There are many indications, for example, those from analysis of intrapsychic processes as well as reactions to external stressors, that people may for some time maintain the illusion that their fears, worries, and anxieties relate to something other than the primary threat in front of them. This fifth kind of denial, *"denial of affect relevance,"* is denoted by the letter E.

Once this defense breaks down there are no new metaquestions that may serve as the focus for the next stage of denial. There is no other possibility but to try to distort the answer to the preceding questions, those that were not tampered with yet.

The next possibility of denying threatening information and its implications to a person focuses on distorting the nature of the information itself. By using a filtering device, sifting information in a biased fashion, those aspects of the stimulus situation that are particularly threatening can be minimized, reduced, or even avoided altogether. In this case, we reach the stage of *"denial of threatening information,"* denoted by the letter F. This step in the denial sequence illustrates the need to invest greater amounts of energy in distorting objective reality. It is not just a function of the various evaluative processes taking place in the mind of the perceiver, but rather a brutal attempt to interfere with the kind of information that enters the processor in the first place. Needless to say, much psychological literature and experimentation in relation to the influence of motivation on perception deals specifically with this kind of denial. The best example, of course, is the whole advent of "new look" in perception, and particularly the issue of perceptual defense (see Allport, 1955; Bevan, 1964; Goldiamond, 1958; Lazarus & McCleary, 1951; Postman, 1953).

If the threatening aspects of the impending danger gradually spread to more and more content areas, the filter itself may become insufficient. Often, in this situation, there is no room for additional denial. It was attempted; it may have achieved its purpose for a while, and it ultimately failed. Only in very extreme cases is there yet another option available. By not taking chances with any information coming from the external world altogether, the need for a filter becomes superfluous. This, however, implies denial of information in its totality. Only in the rare extreme case of a psychotic withdrawal will such a pattern develop fully. In a more or less restricted form, however, it may become operative in extreme situational stresses as well. The stereotypic response of perseveration of the subjects in the experiments discussed in Breznitz (1981a) illustrate the point. By denying the informational value of the stimulus, they made sure that it will not be allowed passage through their already shaking and much weakened protective filters. Any such passage may induce additional anxiety, and thus by resorting to perseveration there was no need to attend to the stimulus at all. This last stage of denial, *"denial of information,"* is denoted by the letter G.

ASSUMPTIONS AND CONSTRAINTS

Needless to say, the sequential analysis presented in Figure 1 is based entirely on the assumption of an ongoing continuous objective input of threatening information. It indicates that at any point *the need to switch to a higher level category of denial is due to the fact that objective reality makes it impossible to maintain the previous level of adjustment.* This can be viewed on at least two levels: On the one hand, in the situation of anticipatory stress there are growing cues of imminence of the danger. Thus, even if there is no change in the actual content of the information, the very fact that the materialization of the threat is getting closer may suffice to upgrade the system of denial-like tendencies. On the other hand, even if there are no new cues whatsoever, not even cues of imminence, the very fact that the information is still there, still available, makes it more potent and reliable. It is therefore maintained that only when dealing with sufficiently prolonged threats can we witness processes that have been postulated in our model (Breznitz, 1981b).

It follows that even in situations of objective helplessness, if for some reason the danger goes away or the danger materializes quickly, before there is sufficient time to move through the various stages of denial-like behavior, before there is indeed sufficient time to exhaust one's options for coping and adaptation, denial can indeed serve an important psychological function.

The model does not claim that each person has to go through the entire sequence in that order. Indeed, it might very well happen that the implications of threatening information are so overwhelming that a person will immediately move into very advanced stages of denial. Thus, for instance, fainting or entering the state of emotional shock, so frequently reported in situations of major personal disaster, is a case in point. Fainting or emotional shock are both states in which there is denial of information altogether. It is also possible for a person to deny at level B before ever experiencing level A, or start directly with level D before experiencing any of the preceding ones. It is however our argument that *in no case will a person move backwards, that is to a less advanced stage of denial. The process may start at any level depending on one's predisposition and the intensity of the threat. Once started, however, it can only go in one direction, namely, forward.* It can only proceed towards more advanced stages of denial, never to the less advanced stages. Essentially, we claim that *the seven kinds of denial form a Guttman scale.* As such they imply *directionality* and *intensity,* without at the same time implying actual experiential passage through the entire sequence.

It must also be explicitly stated that denial begins only after the program has been run through in its entirety at least once. Therefore, we postulate that it is anxiety and other unpleasant affects that motivate the tendency to deny in the first place. Thus, at some initial stage, a certain amount of anxiety must be evoked by the threat in order to instigate the denial. We suspect that any other analysis will inadvertently lead to the logical problems of the Homonculus that we want to avoid at all costs. Denial in our analysis is therefore a mechanism that is evoked by appraisal of information that leads to certain psychological discomfort that a person wants to reduce. It is therefore essentially an escape from psychological pain rather than its total avoidance. Stated differently, denial protects us from additional discomfort rather than its initial onset.

Another assumption that is obviously untrue in any real-life situation and that, therefore, is maintained for heuristic purposes only, is the yes/no nature of the answers to the metaquestions. It is clearly the case that the answers to all of these metaquestions are ones of degree, and a more advanced development of the basic model postulated here must take this into consideration.

Increasingly, the issue of *minimization of stress* stands up as a potent way of reducing psychological impact (Lazarus, 1981). Minimization, however, indicates that the threatening properties of the situation are perceived as such, but in a milder form. Any dichotomy allowing only a yes/no analysis of the situation will do injustice to these important continuous phenomena. For analytic purposes, however, and specifically for taxonomic purposes, we think that the simple dichotomies used here may be more appropriate at this stage of our sophistication. At the same time, however, we have actually taken into account the continuous nature of these variables in our analysis of transitions from one stage to another. It was argued that if at any point due to additional information coming in, a particular answer, a particular construct cannot be maintained, there comes a point in time when the system has to be upgraded to the next stage of denial. But this, by its very nature, is an *additive, continuous process*, namely, that the inadequacy of the previous construct has to pass a certain *threshold* before a new stage is initiated.

To sum up then, we postulate seven kinds of denial of stress: denial of personal relevance, denial of urgency, denial of vulnerability or responsibility, denial of affect, denial of affect relevance, denial of threatening information, and finally denial of information. We claim that the order from A through G reflects the amount of reality distortion involved. Any kind of denial, even the most minimal one, must of course distort certain aspects of objective reality as perceived by the individual. *The more advanced the kind of denial is in terms of the sequence postulated by our model, the greater the amount of distortion involved.* In the absence of any change in the objective features of the situation, denial can move only in one way, namely, to more advanced stages.

DYNAMICS OF TRANSITION

There are two possible ways in which the present model can view the transition from one kind of denial to the next one:

1. The transition is entirely due to new information which makes the present answer to the last metaquestion inadequate and raises the salience of the next metaquestion. Assuming an ongoing tendency to deny, when the next question is raised, the biased answer is provided as an attempt to further postpone the full realization of the threat.

2. Because of new information the system runs again through the entire sequence leading to anxiety, and it is anxiety as such that leads to the next attempt to deny on a different, more advanced level of the process.

The difference between the two conceptualizations of dynamics of transition lies in the role of anxiety and in the issue of an ongoing general tendency for denial. If the first description is the adequate one, there is no need to expect any periods of anxiety intervening between the various transition points from one kind of denial to another. On the other hand, the second description of the process postulates that it is anxiety, and anxiety only, which maintains the denial tendency as operative, and thus one would expect that between any two different kinds of denial, that is at any transition point, there will be an experience of anxiety, however brief.

Furthermore, it is consistent with the underlying assumption of our model to postulate that following a serious experience of anxiety there will be an upgrading of the stage of denial used. This is based on the notion of effective learning from experience, namely, that failure of protection against anxiety will lead to a change in the defensive strategy employed. This need not of course be a single trial learning, and a few episodes of anxiety may be necessary.

MEANS AND CONSEQUENCES

Our taxonomy describing the seven kinds of denial of stress makes it now possible to analyze the various psychological devices that have to be employed in order to achieve a particular kind of denial. Let us try a preliminary analysis of the psychological processes that can be conducive to each of the seven types.

Denial of Personal Relevance

In order for people to view a particular threat as unrelated to them personally, they must psychologically maximize the perceived differences between themselves and other individuals involved in the situation. Such maximization of personal differences may lead to a variety of consequences, many of them quite negative ones. Thus, for instance, the maximization of perceived uniqueness of an individual can make it very difficult to maintain good social bonds when they are most needed. It may also lead to a situation where an individual will find him- or herself unable to model the behavior of others when such modeling could provide a good way to reduce personal anxiety and increase a sense of safety. It ought to be mentioned in this context that as Schachter (1959) and others have often demonstrated, it is during periods of anxiety and stress that we need to affiliate most, particularly with people who are in the same situation. By taking the temporary advantages of denying personal relevance of a threat the individual may sacrifice the ability to interact well with peers, and particularly with those who are in the same danger. At the same time, however, it must be mentioned that this first type of denial is often the basis of courageous acts under duress. By feeling unthreatened and naively exceptional, soldiers or civilians will often endanger their own lives and protect others without concern or anxiety that might otherwise inhibit their action. The same psychological device, however, that can sometimes lead to courageous action may lead to neglect in many areas, including one's health. The story of medicine, and particularly of preventive medicine, illustrates the potency of this kind of denial. While fully aware of the dangers of certain behaviors or the dangers of certain inactions to others, even an intelligent person may often plead the case of uniqueness, and refrain from taking the right course of action. The psychological advantages, at least the immediate psychological advantages of such denial of personal relevance are quite obvious. So, unfortunately, is their long-term cost.

Denial of Urgency

Here the psychological process must utilize ways to subjectively slow down time. This can be achieved by a variety of means, such as attempts to more differentiate the time left into a greater number of smaller units. In this way, a person can perceive the situation as less urgent than before.

Denial of Vulnerability

In this case, what is called for is a certain amount of maximization of perceived personal strengths. By maximizing one's image of strength, the illusion can be created of greater control over the events. There is yet another way to achieve denial of vulnerability, namely, by stressing the important role of experience. Since it can be taken for granted that major disasters including terrible suffering, wounds, and of course, death, were either relatively rare or even absent in a person's history, stressing the importance of experience leads to the belief that whatever was true before is the best prediction of what will happen in the immediate future. This of course augments the sense of control and produces denial of vulnerability. It should be stressed, however, that these attempts lead automatically to the neglect of some unique, possibly important features of the present threat. It is only if the present situation is seen as similar to other previously experienced situations that experience as such becomes a meaningful guide for the future. Thus, there is a psychological need to neglect the specific unique features of the present threat and to concentrate on its common denominators with other previously experienced situations. The cost of all this is quite obvious. By sensing the unjustified control over the situation a person may neglect to take necessary protective action while it is still possible, or if he cannot deal with it alone, by asking for the much needed help from other people or organizations.

In the case of a threat which does not leave the person objectively helpless, Type C denial relates to the opposite of vulnerability, namely, denial of responsibility. In such a situation, what has to be done in order to bring such denial about is to minimize the sense of control over the situation. The person must perceive him- or herself as more helpless than he or she really is. The individual prefers to view the situation as one that is totally out of personal control, tending to maximize the perceived similarity between this situation to other situations in the past where it turned out that one's control was rather limited. It is also necessary for them to concentrate on those features of the information that support the notion of helplessness. Our concern here is with the subjective sense of helplessness, not necessarily based on objective facts, but rather on subjective needs. Once again, this kind of denial can be quite costly because it precludes action. It disarms the motive for action and leaves the person passively awaiting his fate in some kind of fatalistic mood.

Denial of Affect

In order for a person to achieve even a limited sense of neutrality in the face of emotional arousal, it is necessary to invent procedures that will reduce the emotional impact of the threatening situation. There are many ways to do this, such as increased automatization of behavior, development of certain routines that are always followed, stereotypic behavior, and engaging in anything that will distract one's mind from what is in store. Such continuous "neurotic preoccupation" may indeed deflate the emotional impact of the impending danger at least to some extent. Another, altogether different way to deal with the psycho-physiological feedback emanating from the emotional reaction is to explain it away by resorting to nonemotional causes. Thus, for instance, a person may perceive himself as being very tired, attributing the symptoms to fatigue, illness, and other similar causes. He or she may even attempt to intellectualize the situation and account for the arousal by a sense of great curiosity, excitement in the positive sense, and in fact interest in whatever is happening.

Once more, however, the cost can be quite great. After all, emotions are one of the most reliable triggers of escape and avoidance, and if blunted or reduced or accounted for by irrelevancies, there is always a danger that they will fail in fulfilling this very basic function.

Denial of Affective Relevance

Once the emotion itself cannot be explained away by other means, or denied its status, it is still possible to explain it in terms of other causes. Anxiety, yes, the person thinks, but, not from the threat. Fear, yes, but not related to the impending danger. People may engage in diverting their attention to secondary issues and thus try to de-emphasize the anxiety-provoking nature of the stressor. For instance, they may use projection, such as claiming that they are terribly worried about somebody else. Or, alternatively, about something else. Or about somebody being unduly influenced by their anxiety and therefore being anxious not to show their emotions, and so forth. People have an incredible capability to concentrate on secondary issues and focus all their attention and emotion on them in order to deflect their apprehension and anxiety from its main focus.

Denial of Threatening Information

Psychological theory and experimentation spent a great deal of effort in trying to understand the mechanisms that underlie selective inattention and selective perception, subception, perceptual defense, and other related phenomena. While it is not within the scope of this chapter to analyze the complex issues involved, suffice it to mention that information processing is perceived as constituting various levels of analysis and control, whereby one level can influence whatever is happening on the next, and thus reduce the chances of awareness of certain significant stimuli. At the same time, however, it is quite clear that in order to eliminate dangerous information that is threatening to the ego, the person must on some level of interpretation and analysis be aware of the content of all information available, including that to be rejected. It is this partial processing and partial understanding, this partial awareness, that makes the process of filtering possible. Otherwise there would be a transition to the next level of denial, Type G, which has no problem with selection, since it consists of denial of all information. Type G thus solves the problem of filtering by overgeneralization. It is the least sophisticated of all kinds of denial, probably very much akin to what Freud called the primitive stimulus barrier put between the external environment and the person's psyche.

Whereas denial of threatening information implies the need for continuous on-line monitoring of all information, where very sensitive probes test at all times whether a particular item of information is neutral, partially threatening, or very threatening, the last kind of denial, that of all information, is totally indiscriminate. The cost of that, however, is tremendous. One becomes entirely at the mercy of the internal world without the much needed corrective features coming from the outside. The psychotic person is obviously a most dramatic illustration of what happens when reality as such is denied in its totality.

One of the most important criteria for cost-effectiveness of any psychological mechanism is its sensitivity to changes in the situation. Thus, any device, whatever its psychological benefits, that does not allow for its own correction subject to changes in the actual situation in which the person operates, is bound to be disastrous in the long run. Looking at the various stages of denial, we find that if there are changes for the better in the situation, irrespective of the causes for such a change, the person may find out that the need for distorting the reality is reduced and eventually reduce his or her protection and revert back to a normal appraisal of information coming from external sources.

Once resorting to Type G, however, there is very little room for self-correction. If information from the external world is rejected indiscriminately, there is no way for a person to discover that much of the information is benign and unthreatening, if indeed such is the case. He may go on and protect himself even when the need for it no longer exists. Thus, one of the tragic aspects of psychotic defense is its lack of responsiveness to changes in one's life. It is, in fact, shielded from any reality testing whatsoever.

Refutability of the Model

One of the strengths of the proposed model is that it is relatively easy to refute. In order to further enhance this property, the model deliberately attempts to state very strong propositions, the truth value of which can be ascertained quite easily. Thus, for instance, instead of just enumerating the seven kinds of denial, there is a direct claim concerning their differential intensity, the explication of the process underlying their respective formation, as well as their sequentiality.

The following may illustrate the strength and relatively easy refutability of our model. On the basis of the analysis proposed here, two kinds of denial cannot happen at the same time, at least not concerning the same aspects of the information. After all, according to our reasoning, the person who is using denial must be at a certain stage of the process, and he cannot be in more than one point at the same time as the sequence was described in Figure 1. The only exception to this general rule concerns differentiation of the threatening information. While within a particular segment of information concerned, the process must operate on one specifiable level, and one level only. It is possible to differentiate the information into more specific categories, not all of which have to be treated in exactly the same way. Thus, for instance, a person may relate to one particular feature of the information by denying its threatening implications, and at the same time defend against the implications of vulnerability from another cue or another item related to the same threat but belonging to another aspect of the informational input.

It ought to be relatively easy to study whether a person's behavior is in this sense monolithic, that is, whether it exhibits features of defense belonging only to a single level of processing, or whether the behavior indeed shows denials of different kinds at the same time. If such is the case, this will clearly refute one of the underlying principles proposed here.

A closer look at the model indicates that each kind of denial acts, in a sense, as a short circuit, and keeps the process from advancing to more advanced stages. By denying at a certain point the implications of the metaquestions involved, the analytic process exits into a circuit which starts from the very beginning. Figure 1 illustrates this very clearly. In this way, the person avoids the need to face the next metaquestion and the ones following it as well. So it is not clear whether the only way to describe denial behaviors within the context of our model is to view them as attempts to avoid the rise of anxiety, or whether they fulfill another function, namely, that of protecting the individual from confrontation with subsequent metaquestions.

What is the status of these metaquestions? On the one hand, they can be viewed as analytic tools attempting to explicate the kinds of information processing taking place in the various stages of the sequence, and at the same time, they can be seen as explicating what is sometimes called the process of appraisal. Lazarus (1966) made an important contribution in viewing primary appraisal and secondary appraisal as the basic features of psychological stress. While primary appraisal denotes the way a person interprets particular information as threatening to himself, secondary appraisal constitutes the cognitive processes that underlie the choice of a particular coping strategy. The metaquestions proposed here indeed deal with those aspects of the situation, but particularly with the question of coping. The threatening aspect of the situation is taken for granted by postulating that the information is a priori obviously threatening. By utilizing a stimulus definition of stress, whatever processing occurs from that point on relates to the implications of that information and to possible actions that one may take as a consequence of understanding those implications.

Another way to view the metaquestions is to consider the possibility that they indeed depict some of the features of what is essentially sequential information processing. At any given time, at any given point in the sequence, another aspect of the information becomes the focus of the analysis. The metaquestions describe the content areas of this sequential focusing.

Once again, the model is deliberately very explicit about the content areas involved, as well as their finite number. Any study that will refute the sequence proposed here or illustrate the existence of a different kind of denial, one which does not appear among the seven listed here, will clearly refute the model in its stringent sense. It will also illustrate the need to pose a new metaquestion and perhaps add a new transition point in the sequential focusing proposed here.

While the model is easily refutable in its strict sense, it may very well survive experimentation by accommodating new information and weakening some of the propositions and assumptions developed here. It is our contention that by starting with a very strong model the research in this complicated and rather neglected area of study will profit even if the model as such will sooner or later be changed beyond recognition.

Individual Differences

One obvious shortcoming of the proposed model lies in its total neglect of individual differences. It is concerned only with the central tendency that may be attributable to all individuals facing threatening information. Needless to say, experience teaches that sooner or later a more sophisticated and more differentiated approach will be needed.

Thus, for instance, there are some obvious personality characteristics which are highly relevant to the process proposed here. Among the most obvious ones is the question of ego strength and one's vulnerability to anxiety. Individual differences in these characteristics and in a person's ability to manage his own anxiety will clearly monitor the intensity and frequency with which the process of denial will be activated.

Another clear personality variable relates to the distinction between repressors and sensitizers. It is a basic tendency of individuals to confront threatening situations by either trying to learn as much as possible about them, being at all times cued to new information and receptive to it, or on the contrary, by putting barriers between themselves and the information, and protecting themselves from some of its implications. The seven kinds of denial described here all illustrate the operation of the tendency to repress and to protect against external threats. We will thus postulate that a major advance concerning this area will obviously necessitate the study of individual differences along some of these dimensions.

Another obvious characteristic very much under the control of individual differences relates to the issue of ambiguity and tolerance of ambiguity. The present model suggests that it is when a person cannot maintain a particular construct concerning a specific metaquestion that is in the focus of the information processing sequence, it becomes necessary to change the previous answer and move to the next metaquestion. This is obviously a statement about threshold. It indicates that only when there is inconsistency beyond a tolerable level between a person's answer to a metaquestion, and information coming from external sources, is there a need to change the present situation. Individual differences in tolerance of ambiguity will therefore influence, to a great extent, the likelihood of transition from one state to another. Persons rating high on intolerance of ambiguity will need to abandon the present level of coping sooner than those who can manage an ambiguous situation with greater ease. An interesting prediction would be that intolerance of ambiguity will be associated in the long run with more advanced stages of denial.

There is one obvious difference between individuals that relates to their tendency to engage in denial-like coping in the first place. While it was already briefly mentioned in conjunction with the repression-sensitization dimension, there might be other components to the same dilemma. Not everyone copes with threatening information by always resorting to denial. There are many other kinds of coping mechanisms, and they may all be preferred to denial in various stages of the anticipation situation. It is an open question whether a person who is engaged in, let us say, Type B denial (urgency denial), moves to a

different, more advanced stage of denial, or exits into entirely different modes
of coping if the need to abandon it becomes obvious. The present model
indicates that if there is a tendency to deny, then the next stage would be denial
of vulnerability or denial of responsibility, respectively. In the absence of such
an ongoing tendency to engage in denial as a coping mechanism, the individual
may indeed exit our system and move to different modes of coping altogether.
If at any time, however, he returns to the denial tendency, he will once again
have to follow the sequential process as indicated here.

It is difficult to predict what the situational determinants are that lead to
either denial or other kinds of coping strategies. One parameter of the
threatening situation, however, suggests itself already at this point of our
knowledge. It appears to be a safe assumption that when the intensity of the
threat is very high, the tendency towards denial may be intensified as well.
Threats that clearly indicate a very potent danger to a person usually tend to
evoke particularly strong denial-like tendencies. We would also suggest that
the higher the intensity of the threat, the more advanced the stage of denial
that will be reached, either during an ongoing process, or already in its initial
stage. This is tantamount to claiming that if the initial impact of the
threatening information is very potent, the process described here moves very
rapidly into that particular stage where it produces certain positive hedonistic
results. The more potent the initial threat, the more advanced the first
satisfying stage of denial would be.

When the threatening information is ambiguous in its own right, it allows a
greater amount of disconfirmation at any stage of the information processing.
Thus, a person may take advantage of inherent ambiguity and use it to
maintain a given construct before having to move to a new one. As already
stated by Lazarus (1981), ambiguity can be an important asset in any stressful
situation because it allows a greater amount of cognitive manipulation of the
information. We will therefore predict that ambiguous situations will keep the
denial process at a lower stage of development than less ambiguous ones.

Denial in Patients with a History
of Heart Attack: An Illustration

In order to bring the discussion, which until now was perhaps too abstract,
closer to real life situations, we will concentrate on patients who have
experienced a heart attack. The experience of a heart attack is a very dramatic
psychological stress, which poses a grave danger to the person involved. The
chances of using denial-like tendencies in coping with this situation are,
therefore, quite high, and this might allow us to look for the variety of denials
as postulated in the present model.

Type A

In the study of a coronary-care unit, Hackett, Cassem, and Wishnie (1968),
found that while 11 out of their 50 subjects witnessed a fatal cardiac arrest
during their stay in the unit, none identified with the victim. This clearly
demonstrates the operation of denial of personal relevance. It is particularly
dramatic to witness in the case where the objective personal relevance is quite
obvious. It might very well be that there is a need on the part of some of those

patients to maximize the perceived difference between themselves and other patients in similar circumstances, in order to ensure themselves that theirs is not a grave condition.

Type B

There are vast amounts of data on the tendency of many individuals, including individuals who have experienced either a heart attack itself or something which made its probability and relevance quite high, to delay in calling for help in case of a personal emergency. It seems that many patients could have profited from help much sooner than they actually did, and some of them actually could have saved their lives if they would have consulted a physician or a hospital earlier than they did, were it not for their wish to procrastinate and to delay as much as possible. This is a classical situation of denial of urgency: "Yes, I might sense certain pains in the chest, and yes, they may be dangerous or serious, but there is plenty of time. Let me wait for a while and see what happens. Let me postpone and see how it develops; there is no need to act immediately."

This denial of urgency can also be seen in the prevalent postponement of change in behavior. Thus, for instance, although many people are sophisticated enough to understand the danger of smoking, being overweight, having high blood pressure, lacking exercise and a proper diet, to mention only the major risk factors, there is a clear tendency to refrain from taking immediate action in relation to one's behavior. It is not a rare exception to see a person who intellectually understands the threatening aspects of the neglect of his personal health, and yet does not act on it. Here we have a clear demonstration of Type B kind of denial, namely, denial of urgency. This denial of urgency takes advantage of the fact that none of the risk factors produces clear indications of growing imminent threat. On the contrary, one of the greatest problems with preventive medicine is that considering risk factors such as those mentioned in this context the danger lies in their long-term cumulative impact, rather than in any immediate clearly visible consequence. It is therefore relatively easy for the interested individual to utilize denial of urgency in order to reduce the anxiety which might be related to personal neglect and its potentially threatening outcomes.

Type C

As is always the case in this kind of denial, we ought to distinguish between two distinct situations. In the instance of objective helplessness, Type C denial relates to denial of vulnerability. In case of objective control over the situation, however, we will deal with denial of responsibility. Let us illustrate them one by one.

Denial of Vulnerability It is often the case that patients who experience one heart attack and survive tend to exaggerate the belief in the control over the situation, beyond that justified by objective data. Thus, they often tend to think that by following the physician's prescriptions they do not only protect themselves from future similar experiences, but that their physical condition actually becomes better than that of other people, even if they never experienced a heart attack in the first place. The motivational advantage of denial of vulnerability in this situation is quite obvious, and one should be hesitant to tamper with it. A patient who trusts that he will gain total control over his personal destiny by engaging in exercise, watching his weight, being very careful in his diet, and stopping smoking, will gladly follow the often difficult regimen prescribed by medicine. And yet, denial it is, and as such it can pose a very dangerous trap. The truth of the matter is that those risk factors which are under the control of the individual patient do not account for all of the variance in heart attacks, and thus situations arise in which even those who followed all the prescriptions exactly may experience another heart attack for reasons unrelated to those risk factors. Witnessing such an episode in someone else, or, experiencing it may cause a grave psychological breakdown and depression. The thinking is "if it could have happened after all these precautions, after all these difficult changes in one's life, then anything can happen, and there is not much use in following the physician's prescriptions."

Denial of Responsibility This, the other side of the coin, follows almost naturally from what was said above. By abdicating one's responsibility over fate, even though this may indicate a sense of fatalistic passivity, the patient is no longer responsible for what happens. Furthermore, in our own studies (Nitzan, 1977), we have found to our great amazement that contrary to what we expected, many patients view the advent of a heart attack as being totally outside their sphere of control. More frequently than control subjects who did not experience a heart attack, patients claim that what happens to them has nothing to do with their way of conducting their lives. On the contrary, they frequently state that heart attacks are due to luck, fate, and other such uncontrollable factors. While such a belief clearly undermines the ability of the patient to comfort himself concerning his prospects for the future, it at the same time reduces any feeling of guilt concerning the past.

Type D

In a study of patients who had just experienced a heart attack, it was found that while most of them admitted thoughts of death, few admitted experiencing fear during that time (Hackett et al., 1968). This indicates that some of them must have used the denial of anxiety as a coping device.

Type E

One of the main reasons for this dangerous delay in asking for medical help is the ability of the patient to explain away his own symptoms. While they are often quite obvious, and the person is very familiar with them, he or she may attribute them to other causes and thus reduce their anxiety which might be due to the implication of experiencing heart problems. Often a patient will attribute his symptoms to such causes as fatigue, or some sort of indisposition. He might even engage in vigorous exercise to make his symptoms credible, or alternatively, to convince himself that if he could climb so many stairs so quickly then it obviously cannot be a heart attack which he is going through but something much less threatening.

Type F

Out of the variety of different possible ways in which a patient who experiences a heart attack will resort to biased filtering of relevant information, I wish to concentrate on a single example which is of particular interest. It indicates a situation in which there is a paradoxical influence of protective behavior on the defense mechanisms employed.

Consider the case of an individual who engages in a variety of activities, or refrains from a variety of activities in which he was involved before his heart attack, all with the intention of reducing the danger of another similar experience. *These protective measures, however, have the important property of serving as constant reminders of what happened and what can in principle happen again.* Thus, for instance, a person who starts his early morning activities by engaging in exercise, something which he did not do before his heart attack, creates a constant reminder of his problem in the form of this very protective behavior. If the individual wants to deny the fact that something very important has changed his normal way of life, and that he was, so to speak, marked by an important reminder of his vulnerability, he might very well try to refrain from confrontation with such reminders. One of the consequences of such protection from cues implying his vulnerable condition will be that protective behavior as such will be reduced.

The above may very well be one of the reasons why people often backslide even if they are well aware of the benefits of a particular change in their behavior (Janis, 1981). Protective behavior will be safer from inducing such potential backsliding if it does not dominate one's attention. In other words, only if it does not serve as a reminder can it be maintained safely. The reminding property of a particular behavior depends primarily on whether it is a part of a routine, or if it is a specific change due to the heart attack which the person experienced. If it is a part of a routine, then the patient may not be reminded of his precarious condition and may profit from it without at the same time having to defend against its implications. There are obviously quite significant practical conclusions to be drawn from the above analysis, but this is out of the scope of the present paper.

Type G

Denial of all information is such a drastic way of coping, that it is fortunately quite rare. There is, however, one clinical syndrome following a heart attack that might be related to this sort of denial. It is quite often mentioned in the medical literature that after the initial recovery from the heart attack a deep depression often sets in. Such depression during the convalescence might indeed indicate the operation of denial in this extreme form. During the depression phase itself, patients often minimize their interaction with their environment, and attend mostly to their internal states rather than to external stimulation. In a sense, one may claim that depression always implies a certain amount of Type G denial, namely, denial of information coming from one's immediate environment.

In conclusion, it may be stated that a serious threat such as the one posed by a heart condition often leads to denial-like behaviors of a great variety. The model presented here argues that there are essentially seven kinds of denial, all of which find expression in this particular condition. Needless to say, this much neglected area of study requires a great deal of additional research. It is hoped that the model proposed here may serve an important catalytic function in that direction.

REFERENCES

Allport, F. (1955). *Theories of perception and the concept of structure.* New York: John Wiley.

Bevan, W. (1964). Subliminal stimulation: A pervasive problem for psychology. *Psychological Bulletin, 61,* 81–91.

Breznitz, S. (1981a). Anticipatory stress and denial. In S. Breznitz (Ed.), *The denial of stress.* New York: International Universities Press.

Breznitz, S. (1981b). Methodological considerations in the study of denial. In S. Breznitz (Ed.), *The denial of stress.* New York: International Universities Press.

Goldiamond, I. (1958). Indicators of perception: I. Subliminal perception, subception, unconscious perception: An analysis in terms of psychophysical indicator methodology. *Psychological Bulletin, 55,* 373–411.

Hackett, T. P., Cassem, N. H., & Wishnie, H. A. (1968). The coronary-care unit. *The New England Journal of Medicine, 279,* 1365–1370.

Janis, I. L. (1981). Stress inoculation as a means for preventing pathogenic denial. In S. Breznitz (Ed.), *The denial of stress.* New York: International Universities Press.

Lazarus, R. S. (1966). *Psychological stress and the coping process.* New York: McGraw-Hill.

Lazarus, R. S. (1981). The costs and benefits of denial. In S. Breznitz (Ed.), *The denial of stress.* New York: International Universities Press.

Lazarus, R. S., & McCleary, R. A. (1951). Autonomic discrimination without awareness: A study of subception. *Psychological Review, 58,* 113–122.

Nitzan, N. (1977). *Anger, calming down, and personality characteristics of heart disease patients.* Unpublished Master's thesis, University of Haifa.

Postman, L. (1953). On the problem of perceptual defense. *Psychological Review, 60,* 298–306.

Schachter, S. (1959). *The psychology of affiliation.* Stanford: Stanford University Press.

II

PSYCHOPHYSIOLOGY OF STRESS AND ANXIETY

II

7

Psychosocial Stressors and Their Psychophysiological Implications in Rats

Jan Snel
University of Amsterdam

Stress research in animals uses procedures that make generalizations to man difficult. There is a general tendency, for example, to use acute intensive stimuli of a more or less unnatural nature for the animal. Relatively few studies make use of prospective longitudinal research designs, and traditionally, only a few dependent variables are measured concurrently. In an effort to circumvent some of these limitations, the effects on several biochemical, and pathological variables of a long-term low-level competition for food were investigated in this study. These effects were measured longitudinally in groups of male Wistar rats.

METHOD

The experimental design was based on the studies of Henry and Stephens (1977) and Alexander (1974) and previous work in the laboratory of Psychophysiology of the University of Amsterdam. One week after arrival in the lab, 35 3-week old rats were housed individually for 13 weeks to keep them preexperimentally "stress naive" and to induce socially inadequate behavior.

In the seventh week of this period, the experimental group (group 1; $n = 10$) and a control group (group 2; $n = 10$) were respectively operated on, to implant either a tuned circuit or a dummy. The tuned circuits made it possible to detect automatically selected behavioral categories and to record them on a computer. The rats with dummy circuits did not need to compete for food but served as controls for the experimental rats. Another 10 animals (group 3), remained undisturbed for comparison with the operated noncompeting rats of group 2.

The aim of the implantation was to objectively measure and reliably rank the animals. The rank order of animals serves to evaluate the effect of stressors (Christian, 1975; Lloyd, 1975). If a stable rank order exists, this could reflect rapid habituation to the situation and a diminishing urge to compete, invalidating competition for food as a long-term stressor. Since stable dominant-subordinate relationships among animals imply a differentiated physiological response pattern, it was necessary to avoid a stable social order in

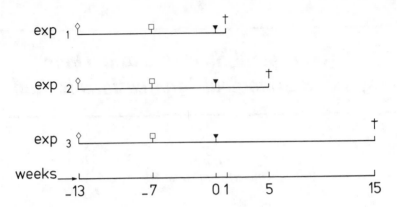

◇ start of isolation period
□ implantation of tuned circuit
▼ start of competition period
† end of experiment

Figure 1 Experimental design.

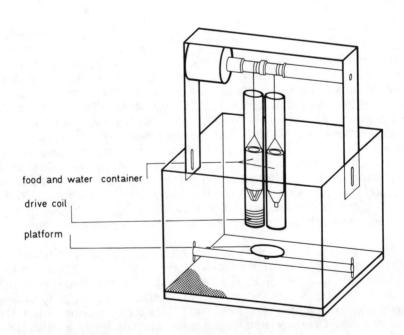

food and water container
drive coil
platform

Figure 2 Experimental situation to compete for food.

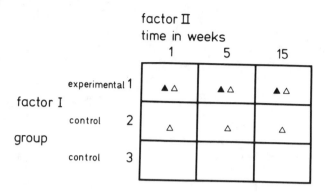

Figure 3 The experimental design depicted as a 3 × 3 factorial design.

the experimental groups. After the social isolation period the rats were placed together, in groups of 10, in the experimental situation on a 23-hour food deprivation schedule. In experiment 1, they stayed for 1 week; in experiment 2 for 5 weeks, and in experiment 3 for 15 weeks. Observation of spontaneous aggressive encounters and the electronic recordings of the rats' behavior during feeding time revealed that continuous social disorders existed in the experimental groups during the whole length of the experiments. The experimental design (Fig. 1) concerned a 3 by 3 factorial design. The hypotheses was tested in two ways:

1. Cross-sectionally, it was tested to determine whether or not effects of the psychosocial stimulus could be found, that is competition (factor 1, or group-factor).

2. Longitudinally, the sequential course of effects was assessed to evaluate differences in effects during a certain time period (factor II or time-factor).

RESULTS

Final body weights and differences between initial and final weights are reported in Table 1. Compared to their controls, rats competing for food for 15 weeks (exp. 3), had significantly lower final body weights, which might reflect a strong active coping with the food deprivation. The results of the analysis of variance indicated that the group factor had a significant main effect on body weight and relative organ weights.

On a univariate level, competing animals showed significantly increased adrenal weight, which might illustrate an increased function to release large amounts of corticosterone (Goldberg & Welch, 1972; Henry, Ely, Watson, & Stephens, 1975; Tharp & Buck, 1974; Welch & Welch, 1969). Competing animals also showed the lightest liver weights, possibly reflecting a depletion of liver glycogen and a functional breakdown and lower thymus weights. These findings suggest an exhaustion of the immunity system (Mountcastle, 1974).

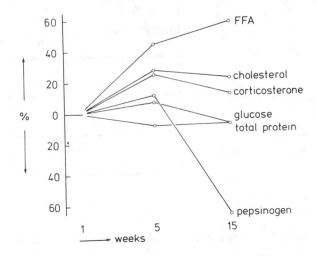

Figure 4 Percentage of change in means of biochemical data for the 5 and 15 weeks experiments, compared to those of the experiment lasting 1 week.

While these results confirmed our hypotheses, the data on the biochemical measures, reported in Table 3, did not support them, since no significant results were found.

A further analysis was made on the protein fractions. Unbound protein fractions play an important role in the stressor-induced increase in lymphocytes. Mettrop's study (1972) of the relationship of stressors and contact dermatitis strongly suggested an involvement of the lymphocyte mediated immunity system. Amkraut, Solomon, and Kraemer (1971) state as an accepted fact that protein changes in inflammatory conditions are in general a decrease of the albumin concentrations and an increase of the globulin fractions.

Although the MANOVA on the globulin fractions showed nonsignificant results, the significant lower albumin levels ($p = .02$) in the food competing groups illustrate the impact of this long-term low level psychosocial stressor.

Gastric erosions in the corpus and antrum of the stomach, rated on a 5-point scale by two independent judges (interjudge reliability .80; Brandjes, 1977) did not differentiate between experimental and control groups, although there is a trend, indicating that competing rats experience somewhat more stress than their controls.

Summarizing the results of the comparison of the rats competing for food with their controls leads to the conclusion that an activation of supposed physiological substrata for responses to stressors could not be sustained. Another aspect of the experimental design was to evaluate the effects of competition for food longitudinally. Tables 2, 3 and 4 reveal a striking time effect. Since the group factor (competing vs. noncompeting) was of minor significance, a comparison was made among the three food competing groups in the three experiments.

Table 1 Final body weights and difference with initial body weights at W_0

Group	1			2			3		
Experiment	m	s	D	m	s	D	m	s	D
1	330.3	31.8	-43.2	323.9	25.7	-50.1	339.7	35.0	-33.6
2	258.9[a]	45.9	-60.4	254.0	21.8	-65.6	258.9	22.0	-60.3
3	321.6	36.7	-68.8	359.5	28.1	17.5	362.3	32.4	1.0

[a] $n = 8$; other groups $n = 10$.

97

Table 2 Two-way MANOVA of body weight and *relative* organ weights

Factor	I: group			II: time			I & II: interaction		
Dependent variables	df	F	p	df	F	p	df	F	p
Multivariate	16/144	1.825	.03		41.326	*	32/267	1.682	.02
Body weight	2/79	1.999	.14		65.641		4/79	1.791	.14
Adrenals	2/79	3.287	.04		76.156		4/79	.341	.85
Thymus	2/79	5.367	.007		24.869		4/79	3.943	.006
Spleen	2/79	2.407	.10		31.474		4/79	2.105	.09
Heart	2/79	.333	.72		9.148		4/79	.456	.77
Kidneys	2/79	.747	.48		83.233		4/79	.717	.58
Testes	2/79	.478	.62		32.600		4/79	2.892	.03
Liver	2/79	3.118	.05		111.614		4/79	1.498	.21

*All F-values $p < .001$.

Table 3 Two-way MANOVA of biochemical variables for group factor I at 3 levels and time factor II at levels 1, 5 and 15 weeks without protein fractions

Factor	I: group			II: time		I & II: interaction	
Dependent variables	df	F	p	F	p	F	p
Multivariate	12/148	.759	.69	29.968	<.001	1.868	.01
Corticosterone	2/79	.694	.50	3.728	.03	3.753	.008
Cholesterol	2/79	.945	.39	15.080	<.001	2.533	.05
Free fatty acids	2/79	1.300	.28	25.532	<.001	1.576	.19
Glucose	2/79	.731	.48	19.029	<.001	.345	.85
Total protein	2/79	.197	.82	31.263	<.001	1.392	.24
Pepsinogen	2/79	.652	.52	68.258	<.001	2.127	.09

Table 4 Means and SDs of albumin, globulin fractions and albumin/globulin ratios in the groups of experiment 2 and 3

Experiment	2						3					
Group	1 (8)		2 (9)		3 (9)		1 (10)		2 (10)		3 (10)	
Fraction	m	s	m	s	m	s	m	s	m	s	m	s
Albumin	4801	294	5228	621	5020	256	4496	327	4540	315	4818	220
γ	986	436	1021	454	1329	356	1172	297	949	323	646	75
α_1	1395	441	1321	273	1222	302	1794	185	1938	330	2112	210
α_2	751	112	648	182	651	107	666	95	721	163	739	75
β_1	2048	178	1834	179	1790	223	1871	162	1893	225	1773	111
β_2							1450	169	1330	209	1304	149
alb/glob							650	78	674	96	736	62

Table 5   Gastric erosions rated on a 5-point scale

Group	1		2		3		All groups	
Experiment	m	s	m	s	m	s	m	s
2	3.0	.87	3.1	.83	2.5	1.02	2.86	.91
3	4.0	.00	3.8	.60	3.7	.64	3.83	.56
Total 2 + 3	3.56	.58	3.45	.72	3.1	.85		

Quite strikingly, the hypotheses were supported until the fifth week; however, after that time the levels of relative organ weights and biochemical measures showed an opposite picture. This raises the question of whether, in our experimental design, the long-term low level competition for food, induced by a 23-hour deprivation schedule, was adequate to sustain a continuous activation of an underlying physiological response mechanism, or did it induce active (and successful) coping with regard to the applied deprivation schedule?

CONCLUSIONS

In this study, a systematic longitudinal comparison of Wistar rats competing for food that bases conclusions on the significant results for the group factor, the forced competition for food deprivation schedule did not result in distinct response patterns. Or to phrase it otherwise, competing rats did not differ on a number of biochemical, physiological, and pathological variables from noncompeting animals.

A further tentative conclusion is that considering the levels of the dependent variables, the rats from all groups (both competing and control groups) were exposed to some form of intensive stressor stimulation, which in spite of our attempts was probably elicited by some inconspicuous aspects of the food deprivation and could have masked the effects of the competition. Yet the differences found (mainly weight of essential internal organs) do suggest that the experimental animals had more severe long-term after effects. This may justify the further use of competition for food as a long-term, low-level psychosocial stressor in future research.

Concerning the time factor (1, 5 or 15 weeks of exposure to the stressor) a statistically significant main effect was found for all absolute and relative organ weights and some of the biochemical variables. A more detailed investigation of these results indicated to some extent the existence of habituation to the aversive stressor (Snel, 1979).

This first attempt to study longitudinally long-term effects of a psychosocial stressor is sufficiently promising to continue research in this area.

REFERENCES

Alexander, N. (1974). Psychosocial hypertension in members of a Wistar rat colony. *Proceedings of the Society for Experimental Biology and Medicine, 146,* 163–169.
Amkraut, A. A., Solomon, G. F., & Kraemer, H. C. (1971). Stress, early experience and adjuvant induced arthritis in the rat. *Psychosomatic Medicine, 33,* 203–214.

Brandjes, M. (1977). *Onderzoek naar de relatie tussen dominantie-hiërarchie en enige biochemische, fysiologische en pathologische variabelen bij de rat.* Doktoraal werkstuk, University of Amsterdam, The Netherlands.

Christian, J. J. (1975). Hormonal control of population growth. In B. E. Eleftheriou, & R. L. Sprott (Eds.), *Hormonal correlates of behavior: A lifespan view* (Vol. 1). New York: Plenum.

Goldberg, A. M., & Welch, B. L. (1972). Adaptation of the adrenal medulla: Sustained increase in choline acetyltransferase by psychosocial stimulation. *Science, 178,* 319–320.

Henry, J. P., Ely, D. L., Watson, F. M. C., & Stephens, P. M. (1975). Ethological methods as applied to the measurement of emotion. In L. Levi (Ed.), *Emotions: Their parameters and measurement.* New York: Raven Press.

Henry, J. P., & Stephens, P. M. (1977). *Stress, health, and the social environment: A sociobiological approach to medicine.* Berlin: Springer.

Lloyd, J. A. (1975). Social behavior and hormones. In B. E. Eleftheriou, & R. L. Sprott (Eds.), *Hormonal correlates of behavior: A lifespan view* (Vol. 1). New York: Plenum.

Mettrop, P. J. G. (1972). *Stress and experimental contact dermatitis.* Unpublished doctoral dissertation, University of Amsterdam, The Netherlands.

Mountcastle, V. B. (1974). *Medical physiology* (2 vols.). St. Louis: Mosby.

Snel, J. (1979). *Morphological, biochemical and pathological effects of a long-term, forced food competition in male Wistar rats.* Unpublished doctoral dissertation, University of Amsterdam, The Netherlands.

Tharp, G. D., & Buck, R. J. (1974). Adrenal adaptation to chronic exercise. *Journal of Applied Physiology, 37,* 720–722.

Welch, B. L., & Welch, A. S. (1969). Sustained effects of brief daily stress (fighting) upon brain and catecholamines and adrenal, spleen, and heart weights of mice. *Proceedings National Academy of Science USA, 64,* 100–107.

8

Threat, Anxiety, and Sensory Deprivation

Tytus Sosnowski and Jan Strelau
University of Warsaw

The concepts of optimal activation (Hebb, 1965; 1966) and optimal stimulation (Leuba, 1965) provide a framework for describing and classifying situations differing in character on the basis of a common, nonspecific property—their stimulating capacity.* The possibility also arises of analyzing changes in different behavioral variables in terms of this dimension of stimulation, but the concepts of optimal activation and optimal stimulation are difficult to define in operational terms.

In experimental psychology, the concept of optimal stimulation seems to be more useful than optimal activation because it assumes the possibility of direct manipulation of situational variables. Still, the effects of such manipulation are not always easy to predict, for we do not know how to compare the actual level of stimulation with the optimal level for a given individual.

Another factor which complicates the prediction of the effect of stimulus intensity variations on behavior is the wide range of individual differences in the need for stimulation. Recently this issue has gained considerable attention, which has resulted in the development of a number of questionnaires for measuring individual differences in the strength and mode of responding to stimulus intensity variations, for example, the Sensation Seeking Scale (Zuckerman, 1975), Temperament Inventory (Stelau, 1972), and Stimulus Screening Scale (Mehrabian, 1977).

Trait anxiety seems to be an individual difference variable that may influence behavior in highly and moderately stimulating situations. This trait is usually defined as directly related to individual differences in responding to certain types of highly stimulating situations, namely, threat situations. Yet, there are also data indicating that trait anxiety may influence behavior in situations that are extremely low in stimulating capacity, namely, sensory deprivation situations. For example, Zuckerman (1975) assumes that: "The sensation-seeking trait seems to be a more important factor in volunteering to

The studies reported in this chapter were part of a more extensive research program. This research was supported by the Space Research Center of the Polish Academy of Sciences (Project MR-I-29).

*Although the two conceptions differ in many respects, it seems justified to view them as referring, at least to a large extent, to the same regulative mechanism. One important distinction is generally made: The concept of optimal stimulation focuses on changes in stimulus intensity, while the concept of optimal arousal is concerned with the effects of such changes on the central nervous system.

enter this situation (i.e., sensory deprivation), but as the curiosity factor is reduced (usually in the first two hours) anxiety increases and measures of trait anxiety, not sensation seeking, become the best predictors of reaction to the experiment" (p. 27).

The studies reported in this chapter had two basic goals. The first was to assess and compare certain variables which characterize the functioning of individuals in two experimental situations that represent the extremes in level of stimulation: threat and sensory deprivation. The second goal was to compare the functioning of persons high and low in trait anxiety in these situations. Two psychophysiological variables, heart rate and level of skin resistance, and one self-report variable, the level of state anxiety determined by a questionnaire method, were selected as the measures of functioning.

METHODS

Anxiety was measured by means of the Polish version of the State-Trait Anxiety Inventory (STAI) developed by Spielberger, Gorsuch, and Lushene (1970) and adapted to Polish conditions. The STAI is a self-report questionnaire with two 20-item scales that measure anxiety proneness as a relatively stable personality trait and state anxiety as a transitory emotional reaction, consisting of consciously perceived feelings of apprehension, nervousness and tension, and activation or arousal of the autonomic nervous system.

Heart rate was measured by three electrocardiographs: a 3-channel Multicard E-30 apparatus for determining the initial level of heartbeat, a 3-channel Multicard E-30, and a 1-channel Simplicard apparatus for measurements in the deprivation chamber (cell). In all cases, bipolar-extremity outputs were applied. In addition, a manual measurement of pulse rate was taken in the decompression cell. The final measurement was taken by the medical doctor in charge of the cell.

Skin resistance was determined by means of "JANMAZ" psycho-galvanometers. The electrodes were attached to the fingertips of the index and the middle fingers of the right hand. The magnitude of skin resistance was indicated on the dial of the apparatus, gradated in kiloohms.

Experimental Procedure

The two experimental conditions were designed to induce threat and sensory deprivation. In the threat condition, the subjects were seated in a decompression cell (DCC) in which the pressure was reduced to approximate the physical conditions at an altitude of 5000 meters. The procedure was adapted from the standard periodical testing of pilots in order to examine their capability for flying at high altitudes. Before the DCC session, the subjects were instructed by the staff in the use of the alarm system and breathing masks, in case of sudden indisposition. The subjects stayed in the DCC for about 50 minutes. During the first 10 min, they ascended up to 5000 m, where they remained for 30 min. Next, they descended to the starting level.

The properties of the arranged experimental situation, which were most significant according to the goals of the study, were the following:

1. Physical and psychological discomfort associated with oxygen deficiency at the altitude of 5000 m.

2. Physical threat resulting from the possibility of experiencing uncomfortable feelings or sudden indisposition (loss of consciousness).

3. Social threat associated with the possibility of failing to meet the requirements of the experimental situation, with the anticipation of receiving negative evaluations from peers and the staff.

4. Novelty of the situation; there were no pilots among the subjects who could be familiar with such tests.

At least two of the factors listed above may be considered as threatening, and the situation as a whole was highly stimulating.

Testing in the DCC was performed on two or three subjects at the same time; security regulations did not allow individual examinations in the DCC. During confinement in the DCC, three variables were measured: state anxiety, heart rate, and skin resistance. State anxiety was measured twice: after the subjects entered the cell, that is, right before the door was closed, but before ascending was started; and after the descending was accomplished and the door was opened, but before leaving the cell. A questionnaire was handed to subjects, with instructions to describe their feelings at the time right before ascending and immediately after descending.

Heart rate was measured at the same time or, more precisely, right after the first and right before the second anxiety test. These measurements were taken manually by a medical doctor in charge of the decompression cell.

Skin resistance was measured at nine different times but at the same time for each subject. The stages of the experiment in which skin resistance was measured were (1) right before closing the door of the cell; (2) after closing the door, when ascending had been started; (3) at the altitude of 2500 m; (4) at the altitude of 5000 m; (5) after 10 min; (6) after 20 min; (7) after 30 min of staying at the altitude of 5000 m (the seventh measurement was taken at the moment when descending began); (8) at the altitude of 2500 m; and (9) after the descending was completed and the door was opened.

In the condition of *sensory deprivation,* each subject was tested individually, in two cells of the same type as described above. The subjects were seated inside the cells in airplane seats lined with blankets, in a semireclining position. A flannel hood over the subject's head and goggles with dark lenses provided isolation from light stimuli. Isolation from sound was attained by the use of a helmet with earphones, through which white noise was transmitted from a tape recorder during the entire session. Since the tapes had to be changed every 90 min, there were short breaks in the emission of noise.

In order to reduce possible movements or shifts in position, the subject's arms and bodies were fastened to the chairs. They were also requested not to make large movements, with the explanation that these might damage the electrodes of the measuring device. The experimenter could make observations through an illuminator in the wall of the cell, right behind the subjects. There was no communication with the subjects during the session, except for the final moment when the experimenter announced the end of testing.

Before entering the deprivation cell (DPC), subjects gave their watches to the experimenter. No precise information was given on the time limits of the session: Subjects were simply told that it would last quite long. Nevertheless, since the subjects participating in the study had an opportunity to communicate with each other outside of the testing hours, they became familiar with the time and the procedures of the experiment.

The conditions described above did not guarantee total sensory deprivation. The subjects could still receive thermal stimuli, due to variations in the temperature of the surroundings, tactile and kinesthetic stimuli, and probably also some vibrations resulting from the experimenters' movements in the vicinity of the cell. The conditions, however, were minimally stimulating, particularly in comparison to the DCC conditions.

The same variables were measured during the DPC session as in the DCC condition, that is, state anxiety, heart rate, and skin resistance. State anxiety was measured right before the beginning and right after the end of the deprivation period. Heart rate and skin resistance were measured by means of an electrocardiograph and a psychogalvanometer. A total of 14 measures of these variables were taken. The times of testing were (1) at the very beginning of the session; (2) after 15 min; (3) after 30 min; (4) after 45 min; (5) after 60 min; (6) after 120 min; (7) after 180 min; (8) after 240 min; (9) after 300 min; (10) after 315 min; (11) after 330 min; (12) after 345 min; (13) after 360 min of deprivation; and (14) after announcing the end of the session.

Examinations of each individual case lasted for two consecutive days and involved a number of additional measurements besides those reported in this study. During the first day of testing, various medical examinations were carried out to evaluate the capability for participating in the DCC sessions. Heart rate at rest and EEG measurements were also taken. During the second day, examinations in the DPC were accomplished. Questionnaires were also administered, including the STAI State and Trait Anxiety Scales. Additionally, before and after the session, in both the DCC and the DPC, the subjects completed tasks measuring their intellectual and psychomotor efficiency.

Subjects

Conscripts and cadets participated in the studies; there were no flight personnel among subjects. The sample also included soldiers selected by their superiors with regard to the experimenters' suggestions. About 60 subjects participated in the studies; however, some of them did not, for various reasons, take part in the entire cycle of testings, for example, lack of medical permission for participating in DCC sessions, apparatus failure, absence at some stage of the experiment. Complete data were available for 37 subjects; the results have been further processed only for these subjects.

RESULTS FOR THE ANXIETY MEASURES

In all, six measurements of anxiety were taken: measures of trait and state anxiety in the nonexperimental conditions, and four measures of state anxiety in the experimental situations, that is, at the beginning and the end of the DCC and the DPC sessions.

Table 1 shows the correlations found among the anxiety measures. What attracts attention is the fact that the state anxiety indexes obtained in the

Table 1 Correlations between measures of trait and state anxiety

Measures	Initial level Trait	Initial level State	State-DCC Before	State-DCC After	State-DPC Before
State (initial)	0.71				
State (before DCC)	0.55	0.76			
State (after DCC)	0.68	0.73	0.65		
State (before DPC)	0.67	0.70	0.58	0.65	
State (after DPC)	0.68	0.79	0.70	0.71	0.68

experimental conditions were more highly correlated with the initial level of state anxiety than with the level of trait anxiety.

The mean anxiety measures for the entire sample are presented in Table 2. As can be seen, four of the five state anxiety means were quite similar, whereas, the mean for the state anxiety measure taken before the DCC sessions was markedly and significantly higher, as determined by t tests. These findings indicate that the subjects experienced more anxiety while they were waiting for the beginning of the DCC session than in the other conditions in which a measurement of this variable was taken.

The mean state anxiety scores for subjects within the sample who were high or low in trait anxiety are also presented in Table 2. Subjects whose STAI trait anxiety scores were above the median for this scale were assigned to the high anxiety (HA) group; those with scores below the median were assigned to the low anxiety (LA) group. Consistent with our expectations, the HA group attained significantly higher mean state anxiety scores than the LA group on all four occasions on which these measures were taken. As for the total sample, the highest means for both groups were obtained for the measurement taken before the DCC session.

RESULTS FOR THE SKIN RESISTANCE AND HEART RATE MEASURES

Figure 1 shows the changes in skin resistance during the DCC sessions for the entire sample and for the HA and LA groups. Although we measured resistance (in kiloohms), it is more convenient to use the concept of skin conductance in reporting and interpreting the results. Therefore, on the vertical axis in Figure 1, the lowest values of resistance correspond to the

Table 2 Mean anxiety scores for the total sample and for the HA and LA groups

Groups	Initial level Trait	Initial level State	State-DCC Before	State-DCC After	State-DPC Before	State-DPC After
Total ($N = 37$)	35.92	32.51	35.05	31.50	32.85	32.81
HA ($N = 19$)		37.00	39.71	34.00	37.42	36.43
LA ($N = 18$)		27.21	30.47	27.56	27.22	28.63

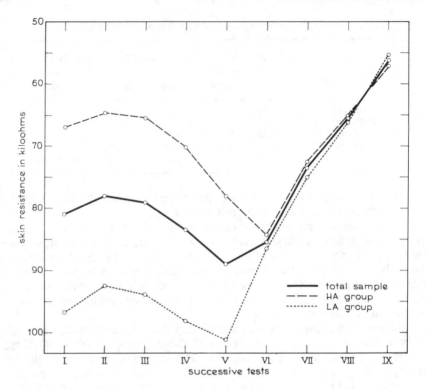

Figure 1 Mean skin resistance in the DCC for the total sample and for the HA and the LA groups.

highest values of conductance. As the graph shows, the highest level of skin conductance was found in the final stage, while the lowest level appeared in the middle stage of the DCC session. When the entire sample was considered, significant differences were found ($p = .05$) between index V (lowest conductance) and the following points: I, II, III, VII, VIII, and IX.

Figure 1 also reveals the differences in the curves for the HA and LA groups. For the first five measurements, higher conductance was noted in the HA group. Then, the divergency disappeared and both curves were almost identical. Statistical analysis yielded significant differences between the HA and the LA group for measures I through IV; the difference in test V approached significance. Although the correlations between trait anxiety and skin resistance were relatively small, the highest correlation coefficients (for the entire sample) were found for indexes I through IV ($r = -.23$), but these correlations were nonsignificant ($p < .05$). Still, the constancy of the coefficients computed for the first four indexes is notable.

The mean heart rate measures taken in the DCC, reported in Table 3 for the HA and LA groups, did not reveal any significant differences, either between the rate before ascending and after descending, or between these rates and the initial level of heartbeat. Also, no significant differences were found between the HA and the LA groups in any of the three measures. There were, however,

Table 3 Indexes of heart rate in the DCC for the total sample and for the HA and the LA groups

Groups	Initial level	Before DCC	After DCC
Total (N = 37)	79.9	77.8	76.0
HA (N = 19)	79.4	76.8	78.4
LA (N = 18)	80.4	78.9	73.5

some differences in the dynamics of the changes in heart rate between the two groups. A significant (p < .05) decline in heart rate occurred in the LA group after the DCC session, both in comparison to the rate before the session and to the initial rate. In contrast, a weak tendency in the opposite direction was noted for the HA group, that is, an acceleration of heart rate occurred after the session, but these differences were insignificant.

Results for the skin resistance measures taken in the DPC are presented in Figure 2. The curve for the total sample is U-shaped; the highest levels of conductance were found at the first and the final measurements. The mean for index IV (lowest conductance) differs significantly from the means for indexes I, II, VIII, XI, XII, XIII and XIV (p < .05). It also seems worthwhile to note the

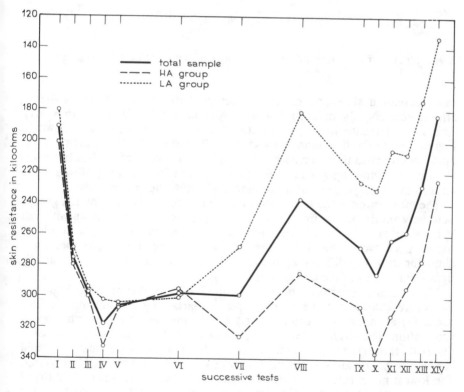

Figure 2 Mean skin resistance in the DPC for the total sample and for the HA and the LA groups.

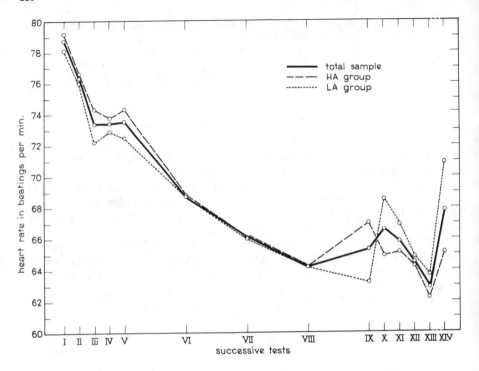

Figure 3 Mean heart rate in the DPC for the total sample and for the HA and the LA groups.

rapid increase in skin conductance between the XIII and XIV measures, that is, after announcing the end of the session, was statistically significant ($p < .01$). This rapid increase in skin conductance was more marked than shown in Figure 2, since the time lapse between the XIII and the XIV measurement was much shorter than the intervals between other consecutive tests. This lapse was less than a minute long, that is, the time required for switching off the white noise, announcing the end of the session, and taking the measurement.

The mean value of the skin conductance measure for the HA and LA groups were very similar in the first stage of the experiment, but beginning with test VII, taken at the end of the third hour of deprivation, higher levels of conductance were found for the LA group, and this trend persisted. Unfortunately, the differences between the two groups were not statistically significant for any of the measures ($p > .05$).

Mean rates of heartbeat, obtained in the DPC, are illustrated in Figure 3. The curve charted for the total sample is marked by a systematic decline, beginning at index I and ending at index VIII, the end of the fourth hour of deprivation. The tendency was perturbed in the last two hours of the session (index IX through XIII). In addition, as for the skin resistance indexes, a rapid increase in heart rate was recorded between the XIII and the XIV measures. The lowest mean rates of heartbeat (index VIII and IX) significantly differed from the rates obtained in the tests from I through VI ($p < .05$). Also, the difference between indexes XIII and XIV was significant ($p < .05$). Mean heart rates for the HA and the LA groups were similar to the means for the total sample, and did not differ significantly in any test.

DIFFERENCES BETWEEN EXPERIMENTAL CONDITIONS IN SKIN RESISTANCE AND HEART RATE

The mean value of skin resistance obtained in the DCC differed markedly from those recorded in the DPC, that is, the former were much higher. When the total sample was considered, statistical analysis indicated that the highest mean skin resistance in the DCC (index V) was significantly lower ($p < .02$) than the lowest mean resistance obtained in the DPC (index XIV). In other words, the mean value of skin conductance in the DCC did not drop down, for any measure, to the level of the highest mean obtained in the DPC.

Considerable differences between the DCC and the DPC conditions were also observed in the heart rate measures. The rates obtained in the DCC were close to the initial level of heart rate, whereas those recorded in the DPC were considerably lower than the three DCC measures.

DISCUSSION

The levels of skin conductance and heart rate obtained in the DCC were considerably higher than the same measures found in the DPC condition. Also, the level of state anxiety before the DCC session was higher than in the DPC; however, this difference was not significant. In general, the findings lead to the conclusion that the DCC experimental situation was more stressful and stimulating than the DPC condition.

The level of state anxiety was relatively constant, except in the situation of waiting for the beginning of the DCC session. However, large and highly significant differences in state anxiety between the HA and the LA groups were noted. These differences suggested that if the STAI State Anxiety scale measures state anxiety evoked by situational factors, then the mere fact of participating in the experiment was the most important factor of this kind. In all the stages of the experiment, subjects with higher trait anxiety exhibited more state anxiety than those with lower trait anxiety, independently of the type of experimental condition.

The differences in state anxiety for the HA and LA groups is even more remarkable when one considers that the sample was in fact split at the median. Such results are consistent with the views of many researchers (e.g., Shedletsky, & Endler, 1974; Spielberger, 1977) that most tests for measuring trait anxiety assess individual differences in the readiness to respond with state anxiety in situations involving social and evaluation threat. Thus, large differences in state anxiety between HA and LA groups would be expected in a rather difficult psychological examination.

The observed changes in heart rate under the conditions of sensory deprivation may be explained, to a large extent, by workload, defined as the effort which has to be spent to meet the requirements of a task (compare Roscoe, 1978). In the sensory deprivation condition, the effort expended was minimal, which resulted in a systematic decline in heart rate. The elevation in heart rate in the final stage of the experiment, particularly between tests XIII and XIV, which corresponds to a simultaneous increase in skin conductance, seems to reflect emotional arousal associated with the announcement of the end of the session.

In the DCC, no differences were found between the first and second heart rate measurements, probably due to the fact that these measurements were taken, for technical reasons, right before and immediately after the end of the session when the door was opened, and not during the session itself. Previous reports indicate that subjects exhibit various compensating reactions to oxygen deficiency at the altitude of 5000 m., including changes (acceleration) in heart rate (compare Błoszczyński, 1977). Thus, heart rate was not measured in the most interesting stage of the experiment.

The skin resistance curve for the DCC condition clearly negates the assumption that the level of emotional arousal, as measured by this indicator, increases in proportion to the altitude, which is related to the degree of physical and psychological discomfort and the extent of objective physical threat. Indeed, this curve reveals an opposite trend. Certainly, the influence of the physical environment cannot be excluded totally since the lowered pressure could directly influence perspiration, that is, reduce it. In this case, the skin resistance curve would be determined by environmental factors having nothing to do with the level of emotional arousal. Yet, it seems worthwhile to consider an alternative hypothesis, since the resistance curve resembles the U-shaped anticipation charts known in the literature (compare Epstein, 1972). This similarity suggests that if the skin resistance curve reflects changes in the level of emotional arousal, this arousal was evoked by the anticipated end of the session, and that it was due to social rather than physical factors. The anticipation of being evaluated immediately after the examination could be such a factor. Such interpretative hypotheses are supported by empirical data obtained in factor analysis of questionnaire scores that indicate physical threat determines state anxiety most strongly when an individual must face the threat all alone; whereas the threat is perceived as a social one in the presence of others (compare Ekehammar, Magnusson, & Ricklander, 1974; Endler, Hunt, & Rosenstein, 1962). Unfortunately, such interpretations of the findings of the present study cannot be verified because introspective data concerning the content of the experienced emotions is lacking.

The skin conductance curve during DPC sessions was also U-shaped, but in this case an interpretation is much easier to provide. The initial elevation of the curve, followed by a rapid decline, is probably related to the novelty of the experimental situation, which declines with the passage of time. The further gradual rise in the curve may reflect psychological discomfort, which grew as the period of deprivation increased. In the final stage of the experiment, the elevation presumably reflected the anticipated end of the session, which was confirmed by announcing the end of the session. The above conclusions are generally consistent with those drawn by Zuckerman (1975), based on his studies of sensory deprivation that were previously described.

No significant differences in heart rate were found between the HA and LA groups in either of the two experimental situations, or in initial heart rate.

Some divergent tendencies of changes in heart rate from the first to the second measurement were observed in the DCC, that is, a decline for the LA group and a slight increase in the HA group. This finding is difficult to interpret because we could not identify the specific time of the changes in heart rate measurement, having no continuous control over the measurement of this variable. Assuming that the second measurement was taken at the stage of relaxation after the session, one could conclude that demobilization (relaxation) develops faster in low trait anxiety subjects.

Trait anxiety was related to interesting differences in the dynamics of change in skin resistance in the DCC and the DPC condition. During the first stage of the DCC session, the HA group had higher skin conductance than the LA group, but this difference disappeared in the second stage of testing. The results provide evidence that high trait anxiety in the initial stage of the emergency situation was associated with higher levels of emotional arousal, but the low correlations between the two variables indicated that this relation was neither strong, nor clear. In the second stage of the experiment, no differences in skin conductance were found between the HA and the LA group, which is interesting in that the highest level of conductance was noted for both groups in the final measurements. Thus, two different mechanisms appeared to regulate the changes in skin conductance in the first and second stages of the experiment.

The results for the DPC condition also indicate differences in skin conductance between the HA and the LA groups. These differences were not significant, however, in spite of their consistent appearance in tests VII through XIV. The differences appeared after three hours of deprivation and subsisted until the end of the experiment. According to Zuckerman (1975), after a few hours of sensory deprivation high trait anxiety subjects should exhibit higher levels of state anxiety and arousal in comparison to LA subjects because the ambiguity of the situation has a greater impact on HA subjects in leading them to anticipate unusual and possibly dangerous effects. Our results, however, are contrary to this view: The LA subjects attained higher indexes of emotional arousal (lower skin resistance) in the second stage of the experiment than the HA subjects. Perhaps this was due to the fact that contrary to the studies conducted by Zuckerman and his colleagues the subjects who were about to participate in our study could contact other subjects who already participated in the examinations, and could thus gain much information about the experimental conditions that could considerably reduce the ambiguity factor (Zuckerman, Albright, Marks, & Miller, 1962). But this explanation would also require the HA subjects to engage in information-seeking before the experiment in order to account for their lower conductance during the DPC condition.

The results of our studies indicate that an individual difference variable, such as trait anxiety as measured by means of the STAI (Spielberger et al., 1970), may be differentially related to the functioning of individuals in physically and psychologically threatening and sensory deprivation situations. But the results obtained in this study should be considered with cognition, they require further empirical verification.

REFERENCES

Błoszczynski, R. (1977). *Psychologia Lotnicza, (Aviation Psychology)*, Warszawa: Wydawnictwo MON.

Ekehammar, B., Magnusson, D., & Ricklander, L. (1974). An interactionist approach to the study of anxiety. *Scandinavian Journal of Psychology, 15,* 4–14.

Endler, N. S., Hunt, J. M., & Rosenstein, A. J. (1962). An S-R inventory of anxiousness. *Psychological Monographs, 76,* (17, Whole No. 536).

Epstein, S. (1972). The nature of anxiety with emphasis upon its relationship to expectancy. In C. D. Spielberger (Ed.), *Anxiety: Current trends in theory and research* (Vol. 2), New York: Academic Press.

Hebb, D. O. (1965). Drives and CNS: Conceptual nervous system. In H. Fowler (Ed.), *Curiosity and exploratory behavior.* New York: Macmillan.

Hebb, D. O. (1966). *A textbook of psychology.* London: W. B. Saunders.

Leuba, C. (1965). Toward some integration of learning theory: The concept of optimal stimulation. In H. Fowler (Ed.), *Curiosity and exploratory behavior.* New York: Macmillan.

Mehrabian, A. (1977). A questionnaire measure of individual differences in stimulus screening and associated differences in arousability. *Environmental Psychology and Nonverbal Behavior, 2,* 89–103.

Roscoe, A. H. (1978). Stress and workload in pilots. *Aviation, Space and Environmental Medicine, 4,* 630–636.

Shedletsky, R., & Endler, N. S. (1974). Anxiety: The State-Trait Model and interactional model. *Journal of Personality, 42,* 511–527.

Spielberger, C. D. (1977). State-Trait Anxiety and interactional psychology. In D. Magnusson, & N. S. Endler (Eds.), *Personality at the crossroads: Current issues in interactional psychology.* Hillsdale, New Jersey: Lawrence Erlbaum & Associates.

Spielberger, C. D., Gorsuch, R. L., & Lushene, R. E. (1970). *Manual for the State-Trait Anxiety Inventory.* Palo Alto, California: Consulting Psychologists Press.

Strelau, J. (1972). A diagnosis of temperament by nonexperimental techniques. *Polish Psychological Bulletin, 3,* 97–105.

Zuckerman, M. (June 1975). Sensation seeking and anxiety, traits and states, as determinants of behavior in novel situations. Paper presented at the NATO conference of Dimensions of Anxiety and Stress, Oslo.

Zuckerman, M., Albright, R. J., Marks, C. S., & Miller, G. L. (1962). Stress and hallucinatory effects of perceptual isolation and confinement. *Psychological Monographs, 76,* (30, Whole No. 549).

9

Motor Skill Learning as a Paradigm for Heart Rate Feedback Therapy

K. Janssen
University of Tilburg

Biofeedback is becoming a major mode of treatment for several stress-related disorders. In recent years a score of publications have appeared that accumulate evidence in this respect (Blanchard, & Epstein, 1978; Olton, & Noonberb, 1980). Yet little is known about most clinical applications of biofeedback, however promising and useful they appear to be, either in terms of specific effectiveness or the conditions under which the method is most successfully applied. Well-designed and controlled investigations are needed in order to establish the specificity of the effects of biofeedback as well as the optimal conditions for applications of this method.

Given the prevailing need for evidence with reference to direct clinical applications, the quest for a theoretical framework for biofeedback learning might seem only secondary and academic. Indeed, for many researchers and clinicians working in the field of biofeedback, the question of how acquisition of self-control over a physiological function can be explained has fallen into the background. They seem to have forgotten that biofeedback research originated from a controversy regarding Skinner's (1938) dogmatic stand on the mutual exclusiveness of the operant and classical conditioning paradigms. Mowrer (1938) should, in fact, be acknowledged as the heroic predecessor of the contemporary biofeedback researcher, for he was the first to challenge Skinner's dogma, thereby initiating new avenues of inquiry.

Does the practitioner need theoretical explanatory models with regard to the clinical application of biofeedback? The point I want to make here is that although the development of theoretical models may seem to be of purely academic importance, such endeavors have strong implications for clinical practice. A theoretical model backed by empirical evidence would provide needed guidelines for identifying the critical factors in biofeedback treatment, while suggesting ways and means of optimizing clinical applications of biofeedback.

Miller's (1969) experiments on the operant conditioning of heart rate illustrate this point very clearly. In collaboration with DiCara, he carried out a series of experiments in which he tried to rule out neuromuscular mediation as

I am indebted to Dr. W. de Moor for criticizing a previous draft and inspiring me for the last draft.

a possible explanation for the operant conditioning of heart rate. The early experimental data obtained on curarized rats did, indeed, seem to support the conclusion that such learning did not necessarily involve somatic mediation. Subsequent research, however, either did not establish true operant conditioning of autonomic functions or achieved only very limited effects (Hahn, 1974; Roberts, 1977; Van Kalmthout, 1979), and this was even true of replication experiments in Miller's own laboratory (Dworkin, 1973; Dworkin, & Miller, 1977).

Since 1970, a 7% change in heart rate was the strongest effect that has been obtained by operant conditioning in curarized rats (Gliner, Horvath, & Wolfe, 1975). In addition, evidence has accumulated that curare blocks peripheral motor activity, while central motor activity remains unaltered by it. Since central motor activity is intrinsically coupled with autonomic activity, we need sophisticated studies to single out operant conditioning as the core of the process in visceral learning. As far as humans are concerned, we can conservatively state that voluntary control over heart rate can readily be learned, but that the learning of an effective, clinically significant control of heart rate is probably impossible without the aid of some kind of mediation. It is now questionable whether operant conditioning plays an essential role in this learning process.

Biofeedback research is an example of how clinical practice can profit from fundamental research. If operant conditioning is not at the core of the process by which voluntary control is obtained in biofeedback, then reinforcement contingencies need not be our first concern in the clinical application of this method. And if in some way mediation seems critical to establishing voluntary control over an autonomic function, we could use this in clinical practice to adjust the format of the training procedure and thus optimize the effect.

Obrist, Howard, Lawler, Galosy, Meyers, & Gaebelein (1974) state: "One can argue that the issue of mediation should be put in a different perspective in that one should also exploit, not just control or ignore the relationship between cardiovascular and somatic activity" (p. 153). Obrist and his colleagues (Obrist, 1976; Obrist, Galosy, Lawler, Gaebelein, Howard, & Shanks, 1975) convincingly demonstrated that cardiac activity indeed is strongly related to EMG, breathing and overall activity. Such evidence provides a good rationale for using, for example, breathing instructions, progressive relaxation, or frontalis EMG feedback, as effective approaches to biofeedback treatment of autonomic functions such as heart rate or blood pressure.

Besides the lack of support for operant conditioning as an explanatory model for biofeedback training, the operant paradigm also fails to specify the mechanism by which the change in a physiological function is brought about in biofeedback training. This descriptive theory is concerned only with the contingency and/or the contiguity between response and reinforcer, and the consequent change in behavior. The reinforcer is seen to bring about this change only because of its drive-reducing properties. But, as Thorndike (1933) noted many years ago, reinforcers as response-contingent stimuli inevitably have a certain information value, since they provide the subject with information about the effects of his preceding response. This idea has already been worked out systematically in the psychology of motor skill leaning where response feedback in this sense is referred to as "knowledge of results." In Bartlett's (1948) words, it is not just practice, but "it is practice the results of which are known, that makes perfect."

Engel (1972) suggested that the acquisition of voluntary control over a cardiovascular function can best be understood as analogous to a motor skill learning process (e.g., Bilodeau, & Bilodeau, 1969; Fleischman, 1966). Lang (1974), Brener (1974), and Schwartz, Young, & Volger (1976), have followed this line of thought, and Lang (1974) very explicitly states that "the acquisition of voluntary control over a viscus is a skill ... it requires an organized sequence of activities, movements, and symbolic information, such as those required to play darts or hit a tennis ball accurately." This point of view is related to one of the basic conceptions in the psychology of information processing, in which an essential role is assigned to feedback. A rule of thumb is that a variable cannot be controlled unless the controller (the subject) is provided with information pertaining to that variable (Ashby, 1963).

BRENER'S MODEL

Three skill models have been proposed in recent years for biofeedback learning (Brener, 1975; Lang, 1975; Schwartz, 1975), and a comprehensive review of these models is offered by Williamson and Blanchard (1979). I will describe Brener's in some detail, since it pays attention to the nature of the learning process, which is a neglected aspect of biofeedback in the operant conditioning literature on this topic. Moreover, several hypotheses derived from this model can be tested empirically.

Basically Brener's model is an extension of a hypothesis formulated by James (cited in Brener, 1977), stating that the performance of a response leads to afferent information that is fed back into the central nervous system and stored there in the form of a "response image" (RI). In fact this RI is a memory of feedback stimuli of a previous response, fixing the nature of the response in the RI, so that new performances of the response can be compared with it. Consequently, feedback of a response is a necessary condition of the generation of the RI, and, subsequently, for the development of voluntary control over the response.

There are several ways in which response feedback can loop back towards the RI. In this brief outline, it suffices to mention only two of them, which help to clarify Brener's model, that is, internal sensory feedback (proprioception and interoception; Sherrington, cited in Brener, 1975) and external sensory feedback ("while writing I see my hand make movements, and I see the effects on the paper"). True voluntary control over a physiological function can be said to exist only when that particular function can be influenced by the subject without the aid of external sensory feedback from it. Nevertheless, external sensory feedback plays an essential role in the acquisition of such voluntary control, in that it allows the subject to simultaneously tune in the external and internal sensory feedback. Eventually however, the internal sensory feedback will be sufficient to allow the RI to make the comparison between response goal and performed response. This process of mutual tuning in internal and external sensory feedback is comparable to the calibration of a temperature scale on a thermometer with the aid of external physical anchor points. Brener uses the term calibration to label this process.

For those physiological functions where the performance of the response is naturally accompanied by external sensory feedback, people somehow in their development engender a calibration of the inherent internal sensory feedback. Since this is the case for most responses involving the striate muscular system, most people are able to acquire voluntary control over those responses, that is, become able in the course of their development to perform them without any need of external sensory feedback.

In conditions of pathology wherein this internal sensory feedback is impaired the only way for a person to perform the particular responses is to regress to the corresponding external sensory feedback. Brener (1977) illustrates this for tabes dorsalis, a syphillitic condition in which the patient has no proprioception of the legs, but which generally allows the patient to follow instructions to stand and walk, provided he can continuously watch the position and the movement of his legs. In some way, the external sensory feedback serves as a prosthesis, but if this feedback is not available, the patient would be handicapped completely. Recently Van Wieringen (1980) has described how other conditions of the striate muscular system and their treatment by EMG feedback can be understood by the same model.

For autonomic functions, the performance of a response will generally not be accompanied by external sensory feedback; hence, calibration of such responses will not be possible. This implies for such functions that voluntary control cannot emerge spontaneously by nature. Development of voluntary control of autonomic responses can only come about when external sensory feedback is explicitly provided, and this is precisely what is done in biofeedback therapy.

Evidence for Brener's Model

A basic construct in Brener's (1974) model is the calibration of internal sensory feedback, which implies that a person must acquire an ability to discriminate the internal consequences of a response in order to develop voluntary control of that response. Although Brener carefully avoids the use of cognitive-mentalistic terminology, his discriminability formulation sounds very similar to the so-called "awareness" conception of biofeedback. The most extreme version of this view holds that the ability of an individual to discriminate between different levels of an internal physiological function or response (e.g., low heart rate vs. high heart rate), is both a necessary and sufficient condition to obtain control over that function.

One way to operationalize the ability to discriminate the consequences of body functions has been the Autonomic Perception Questionnaire (APQ) designed by Mandler, Mandler, & Uviller (1958). In responding to this questionnaire, the subject is asked to what extent he is aware of specific autonomic reactions in certain situations.

Results reported by Bergman (1972) and Bergman, & Johnson (1971) show that the relationship between acquisition of voluntary control over heart rate and APQ scores was extra difficult to interpret or virtually absent. The same holds for the results obtained by Blanchard, Young, & McLeod (1972) and by

McFarland (1975). Blankstein (1975) compared the ability to control heart rate with APQ subscores reflecting a general awareness of autonomic activity and specific awareness of heart functioning. While specific awareness did show a positive correlation with ability to control heart rate, general awareness failed to show any relationship. Although evidence based on the APQ has provided little support for Brener's model, such evidence can never be very convincing because this questionnaire is easily invalidated by biasing factors, for example, subjective reports of being strongly aware of a certain autonomic reaction can be easily contaminated by anxiety about a dysfunction in the viscus which is involved in the reaction. Thus we can even question whether this instrument offers a valid operationalization of "autonomic awareness." Whitehead, Drescher, Heiman, & Blackwell (1977) investigated the validity of the APQ against a direct measure of ability to discriminate own heart beat. APQ scores did not correlate with perceptual sensitivity of heart beat, and even those items pertaining directly to the awareness of heart beat were not significantly correlated with actual sensitivity. Consequently, even Blankstein's suggestion of the need for a more specific relationship between APQ subscores and the ability to control an autonomic function might not hold.

Investigations in which direct measures of discrimination ability are used would provide a better test for Brener's model. In one such investigation on discrimination of muscle activity, Sime, De Good, & Noble (1976) find positive correlations with EMG feedback learning of m frontalis. In the field of heart rate (HR) McFarland & Campbell (1975) provide evidence supporting the hypothesis that awareness of HR as measured by a discrimination task is predictive for performance in a subsequent biofeedback training of HR increment. Results by Clemens & McDonald (1976) confirm this finding. They also show that the ability to increase HR and the ability to lower HR are positively related to different aspects of the discrimination. A series of experiments by Whitehead et al. (1977), however, shows that when heart beat perception is assessed by the more sophisticated method of signal detection theory, no relation can be found between heart beat perception and voluntary HR control or HR learning.

Another source of evidence for the calibration hypothesis may be found in the influence on HR learning of disruption of the temporal contiguity between internal and external feedback stimuli, as was briefly reported by Williamson & Blanchard (1979). They compared the HR speeding and slowing performances of four groups of subjects receiving analogue HR feedback that was either immediate, or delayed by 1.4 sec, 5 sec, or 14 sec. The results of this study show that the degree of temporal disruption correlates with the ability of HR control, both for speeding and slowing. It was also found that the group receiving immediate feedback consistently improved self-control of HR speeding and slowing. This evidence is in support of the calibration hypothesis.

In summary, the body of evidence thus far backing Brener's construct of calibration is very shallow and discordant. Fair tests of the model have to wait until valid procedures to measure "awareness" and ability to discriminate in autonomic functions have been developed. The most powerful test of the calibration hypothesis would be to demonstrate that improvements in discrimination occur concurrent with progress in performance (i.e. control with the aid of a feedback signal) and precede progress in self-control (without a signal) of HR. Validation of this prediction would require the use of statistical methods based on time series analysis, for example, cross correlation function as described by Box and Jenkins (1976).

In Brener's model a second basic construct is the response image (RI). Brener leans heavily on the authority of that great American psychologist James to justify his use of this construct. Nevertheless, it is evident that we need much more empirical evidence of its existence. It is necessary for instance, to assess the exact way in which storage of images takes place, and how the comparison between response goal and response in performance is made by the RI. Without a backing by neurophysiological data, this very construct would remain highly speculative.

In general, to assume a straight analogy between motor skill learning and visceral learning may prove to be an oversimplification. One basic assumption in motor skill learning is that there exists a positive one-to-one relationship between neural efferent output towards the motor system and its activity. Visceral organs, on the other hand, are innervated by both the sympathetic and the parasympathetic nervous system. Consequently, the relationship between neural efferent output to a visceral organ and its activity level need not necessarily be positive, nor one-to-one (Schwartz et al., 1976).

IMPLICATIONS FOR CLINICAL PRACTICE: A THREE-STAGE MODEL OF BIOFEEDBACK THERAPY

Brener's view, if backed up by empirical evidence, has promise for successful clinical applications of biofeedback. Once calibration has been accomplished then the voluntary nature of the response can be maintained in the absence of exteroceptive feedback, granted that adequate interoceptive feedback is present. This model thus leads to the expectation that patients can transfer in-session learning to everyday life situations. Brener's viewpoint can also be of help in the search for specific factors involved in the process of biofeedback therapy, and thus provide guidelines for its optimization.

Nevertheless, before discussing specific factors in biofeedback therapy, we must first deal with nonspecific factors, more specifically placebo components. Placebo is defined here according to Peek (1977) as a component in a treatment that has an effect on the phenomena under study (e.g., anxiety, psychosomatic complaints) and is not explained in terms of the theoretical framework used to explain the phenomena in question (e.g. learning theory). In most biofeedback studies in which a placebo feedback condition was included in the design, a considerable placebo response did indeed occur. In the Budzynski, Stoyva, Adler, & Mullaney (1973) study on the application of EMG feedback for muscle tension headache, decreases in EMG level and in subjective pain score occur in both the feedback group and the placebo feedback group. But the decrements for the placebo group are considerably smaller (25 and 15% respectively) than for the true feedback group (60 and 90% respectively). The decrements in subjective pain score and EMG scores for the placebo group equal those of the waiting list control group. Besides a placebo factor, other nonspecific factors might have played a role in this study such as habituation and reactivity. Moreover, for the feedback group the decrements in EMG level and in headache score are interdependent (r = +.90), whereas for the placebo group they are actually independent (r = -.05).

A good deal of specificity can be assumed to exist in other applications of EMG feedback for complaints in the striate muscle system, such as sphincter training and revalidation training for spasms and hemplegias (Blanchard & Epstein, 1978). In other applications of biofeedback, such as HR feedback for anxiety, placebo effects can be demonstrated even to a greater extent than in the field of EMG feedback, but here also specific effects may add significantly to a placebo effect when a true HR feedback group is compared with a false feedback group (Gatchel, Hatch, Mainard, Turns, & Taughton-Blackwood, 1979).

Stern, Miller, Ewy, & Grant (1980) propose that it is the patient's subjective perception of acquiring control over the occurrence of symptoms that largely constitutes the placebo effect in biofeedback therapy. In their study, individuals experiencing stressful life events were offered a false feedback of their pulse rate, informing half of the subjects of an increase in ability to control pulse rate, and the other half of an equally distributed ability. Subjects in the *"increase"* condition reported a significant reduction in several symptoms (headache, racing heart, shortness of breath, sweaty hands, chest pains). Even more striking was the finding that this effect was maintained at a three-week follow-up session. Stern et al. (1980) conclude that it is the perceived control over a desirable outcome that leads to the reduction in symptom report. This is in line with several laboratory studies (Geer, Davison, & Gatchel, 1970) that have demonstrated that perceived control over aversive outcomes leads subjects to report lower degrees of physical distress, as compared to subjects without perceived control.

Biofeedback as an active coping skill for the subject could serve the function of increasing the subject's sense of controlability of the situation he is engaged in, and hence decrease his anxiety. Seligman's (1975) theory on learned helplessness offers an adequate framework for these effects. Hence, it becomes questionable whether, as Peek's definition of placebo suggests, we can still regard the sense of controlability as a placebo effect, since a theoretical framework to describe the phenomenon adequately is indeed available. In passing, it should be stated that it is proper in this context to distinguish between placebo effects and cognitive effects. Perceived control should rather be conceived of as a cognitive effect. Part of this cognitive effect may also be present under placebo conditions, much the same as physiological effects may partly be engendered under placebo conditions.

However, in their study Stern et al. (1980) do make an implicit use of the subjects' (psychology students) conviction that voluntary control of autonomic functions can be acquired and can thus influence symptom occurrence. The suggestion of these authors that biofeedback treatment be used as a method to reduce the perception of symptom distress by individuals exposed to cumulative stressful experiences, does in fact parasitize other studies aimed at demonstrating the specific effects of the method. Even Wickramasekera (1980) recently acknowledged that "therapists who routinely use active ingredients in their therapy, get stronger placebo effects than those who routinely use inert ingredients." This emphasizes the need to search for active ingredients in order to trace relevant factors with reference to placebo effects.

Starting from the skill-learning conception to delineate specific factors in human biofeedback training, I eventually arrive at a working model, consisting of three elements (stages) in the process of biofeedback therapy:

1. First the subject has to develop an ability to discriminate "internal states." This can be conceived of as a cognitive-physiological learning process, and the manner in which it takes place can well be understood by Brener's model: The external feedback loop serves as a check to validate and calibrate the internal sensoric feedback.

2. The subject can thereupon frame hypotheses about methods by which to bring about desirable changes in the target response. These could be hypotheses pertaining to the cognitive domain: For example, does certain imagery or do certain types of visualization lead to a desirable change in the physiological function under concern? Or these can be hypotheses relating to a somatic strategy: Does a certain breathing pattern, or a change in body posture lead to the desired change? The validity and usefulness of any hypothesis can be assessed during this stage of therapy by means of the external feedback signal. In a later stage, when calibration of intero- and proprioception has been sufficiently developed, the internal feedback can gradually take over the role of the external feedback signal in testing the validity of the hypotheses.

3. Once calibration of internal perception has been completed, and the subject has been able to find one or several hypotheses that proved to be effective in the training situation, the subject has the opportunity to try out these hypotheses in real life situations. If implementation of a hypothesis in daily life situations subsequently leads to a reduction in symptomatology, the validity of the hypothesis would be reinforced. With this, a first step is achieved towards transfer of effect of training. From here onwards autonomy of the patient can be expected to develop. And that of course, has to be the final aim of any therapeutic effort.

The formulation by the subject of hypotheses in order to obtain desirable changes, certainly also occurs in other therapies based on self-control. It could very well be hypotheses handed over and explicitly formulated by the therapist, for example, in the form of relaxation instructions as in progressive relaxation (Bernstein, & Borkovec, 1973; Jacobson, 1938), or it could be hypotheses developed by the subject himself as happens in autogenic training (Schultz, & Luthe, 1969). In these verbal relaxation methods, however, the subject has no way to directly validate the usefulness of a hypothesis. This may sometimes result in frustration for the trainee. In autogenic training the number of therapy dropouts may largely be determined because in the absence both of explicit instructions (progressive relaxation) and of any direct possibility of validating any hypothesis (biofeedback), the period for many subjects to develop any effective hypothesis is too long to bridge.

CONCLUSION

Biofeedback therapy can profit highly from fundamental research. The choice between operant conditioning and skill learning as the core of the process in biofeedback therapy might have consequences for the optimal display of the feedback signal to the subject. Skill-learning theory for instance, would predict that with greater amounts of information, learning will be more rapid and extensive. This would lead to a preference for analogue feedback systems, where the subject is continuously being informed about the activity level in the response concerned.

Brener's skill-learning model assisted us to arrive at the description of biofeedback therapy as a three-stage process. This does not preclude, however, that operant conditioning factors may be of influence in this model also. Skill learning and operant conditioning need not be mutually exclusive, since both paradigms may just focus on different aspects of the same process. As Shapiro and Surwit (1976) state, "Rather feedback seems to be necessary for a subtle response to be learned, while reinforcement affects performance. It appears as though those working in the area of feedback and information have concentrated most of their attention on habit *development,* while those interested in reinforcement and motivation have concerned themselves mainly with habit *maintenance.*"

In our model for biofeedback therapy, the first stage (discrimination learning) can be considered as a skill-learning situation. This also holds for the second stage when the subject is to develop hypotheses by which to influence the activity level of the response concerned. Here the information value of the signal plays a significant role. In the third stage these hypotheses have to be implemented in the life situation of the patient. This can be conceived of as bringing a newly acquired operant (relaxation hypothesis) under appropriate stimulus control. Reduction in symptom occurrence or distress then provides contingencies (e.g., reduction of pain) reinforcing the implementation of the hypothesis.

REFERENCES

Ashby, W. R. (1963). *An introduction to cybernetics.* New York: Wiley.

Bartlett, F. C. (1948). The measurement of human skill. *Occupational psychology, 22,* 83–91.

Bergman, J. S. (1971). Sources of information which affect training and raising of heart rate. *Psychophysiology, 9,* 30–39.

Bergman, J. S., & Johnson, H. J. (1971). The effects of instructional set and autonomic perception on cardiac control. *Psychophysiology, 8,* 180–190.

Bernstein, D. A., & Borkovec, T. D. (1973). *Progressive relaxation training.* Champaign: Research Press.

Bilodeau, E. A., & Bilodeau, I. McD. (Eds.) (1969). *Principles of skill acquisition.* New York: Academic Press.

Blanchard, E. B., & Epstein, L. H. (1978). *A biofeedback primer.* Reading, Massachusetts: Addison-Wesley.

Blanchard, E. B., Young, L. D., & McLeod, P. (1972). Awareness of heart activity and control of heart rate. *Psychophysiology, 9,* 63–68.

Blankstein, K. R. (1975). Note on relation of autonomic perception to voluntary control of heart rate. *Perceptual & Motor Skills, 40,* 533–534.

Box, G. E., & Jenkins, G. M. (1976). *Time series analysis.* San Francisco: Holden-Day.

Brener, J. (1974). A general model of voluntary control applied to the phenomena of learned cardiovascular change. In P. A. Obrist, A. H. Black, J. Brener, & L. V. DiCara. *Cardiovascular psychophysiology,* Chicago: Aldine.

Brener, J. (1975). Learned control of cardiovascular processes: Feedback mechanisms and therapeutic applications. In K. S. Calhoun, H. E. Adam, & K. M. Mitchel (Eds.), *Innovative treatment methods in psychopathology,* New York: Wiley.

Brener, J. (1977). Sensory and perceptual determinants of voluntary visceral control. In G. E. Schwartz, & J. Beatty (Eds.), *Biofeedback: Theory and research*, New York: Academic Press.

Budzynski, T. H., Stoyva, J. A., Adler, C. S., & Mullaney, D. J. (1973). EMG biofeedback and tension headache: A controlled outcome study. *Psychosomatic Medicine, 35*, 484–496.

Clemens, W. J., & McDonald, D. F. (1976). Relationship between heart beat discrimination and heart rate control. *Psychophysiology, 13*, 176.

Dworkin, B. R. (1973). *An effort to replicate visceral learning in curarized rats.* Unpublished doctoral dissertation, The Rockefeller University.

Dworkin, B. R., & Miller, N. E. (1977). Visceral learning in the curarized rat. In G. E. Schwartz & J. Beatty (Eds.), *Biofeedback: Theory and research*, (pp. 221–242). New York: Academic Press.

Engel, B. T. (1972). Operant conditioning of cardiac function: A status report. *Psychophysiology, 9*, 161–177.

Fleishman, E. A. (1966). Human abilities and the acquisition of skill. In E. A. Bilodeau (Ed.), *Acquisition of skill*, New York: Academic Press.

Gatchel, R. J., Hatch, J. P., Mainard, A., Turns, R., & Taunton-Blackwood, A. (1979). Comparison of HR biofeedback, false biofeedback, and SD in reducing speech anxiety: Short- and long-term effectiveness. *Journal of Consulting & Clinical Psychology, 47*, 620–622.

Geer, J. H., Davison, G. C., & Gatchel, R. J. (1970). Reduction of stress in humans through nonveridical perceived control of aversive stimulation. *Journal Personality Social Psychology, 16*, 731–738.

Gliner, J. A., Horvath, S. M., & Wolfe, R. R. (1975). Operant conditioning of heart rate in curarized rats: Hemodynamic changes. *American Journal of Physiology, 228*, 870–874.

Hahn, W. W. (1974). The learning of autonomic responses in curarized animals. In P. A. Obrist et al. (Eds.), *Cardiovascular psychophysiology: Current issues in response mechanisms, biofeedback and methodology*, (pp. 295–311). Chicago: Aldine-Atherton.

Jacobson, E. (1938). *Progressive relaxation.* Chicago: University of Chicago Press.

Kalmthout, M. van (1979). *Operante konditionering van autonome aktiviteit.* Unpublished doctoral dissertation, Nijmegen University.

Lang, P. J. (1974). Learned control of human heart rate in a computer directed environment. In P. A. Obrist, A. H. Black, J. Brener, & L. V. Dicara (Eds.), *Cardiovascular psychophysiology*, Chicago: Aldine.

Lang, P. J. (1975). Acquisiton of heart rate control: Method, theory, and clinical implications. In D. C. Fowles (Ed.), *Clinical applications of psychophysiology*, New York: Columbia University Press.

Mandler, G. J. M., Mandler, J. M., & Uviller, E. T. (1958). Autonomic feedback: The perception of autonomic activity. *Journal of Abnormal Social Psychology, 58*, 367–373.

McFarland, R. A. (1975). Heart rate and heart rate control. *Psychophysiology, 12*, 402–405.

McFarland, R. A., & Campbell, C. (1975). Precise heart rate control and heart rate perception. *Perceptual & Motor Skills, 41*, 730.

Miller, N. E. (1969). Learning of visceral and glandular responses. *Science, 163*, 434–445.

Mowrer, O. H. (1938). Preparatory set (expectancy): A determinant in motivation and learning. *Psychological Review, 45*, 62–91.

Obrist, P. A. (1976). The cardiovascular-behavioral interaction as it appears today. *Psychophysiology, 13*, 95–107.

Obrist, P. A., Galosy, R. A., Lawler, J. E., Gaebelein, C. H., Howard, J. L., & Shanks, E. M. (1975). Operant conditioning of heart rate somatic correlates. *Psychophysiology, 12*, 445–455.

Obrist, P. A., Howard, J. L., Lawler, J. E., Galosy, R. A., Meyers, K. A., & Gaebelein, C. J. (1974). The cardiac-somatic interaction. In P. A. Obrist, A. H. Black, J. Brener, L. V. DiCara (Eds.), *Cardiovascular psychophysiology*, Chicago: Aldine.

Olton, D. S., & Noonberg, A. R. (1980). *Biofeedback, clinical applications in behavioral medicine.* Englewood Cliffs, New Jersey: Prentice Hall.

Peek, C. J. (1977). A critical look at the theory of placebo. *Biofeedback and Self-regulation, 2*, 327–335.

Roberts, L. E. (1977). Operant conditioning of autonomic responses: On perspective on the curare experiments. In G. E. Schwartz & D. Shapiro (Eds.), *Consciousness and self-regulation*, (Vol. 2) New York: Plenum Press.

Schultz, J. H., & Luthe, W. (1969). *Autogenic Methods.* New York: Grune & Stratton.

Schwartz, G. E. (1975). Biofeedback, self-regulation, and the patterning of physiological processes. *American Scientist, 63*, 314–324.

Schwartz, G. E., Young, L., & Volger, J. (1976). Heart rate regulation as skill learning: Strength-endurance versus cardiac reaction time. *Psychophysiology, 13*, 472–478.

Seligman, M. E. P. (1975). *Helplessness.* San Francisco: Freeman.

Shapiro. D., & Surwit, R. S. (1976). Learned control of physiological function and disease. In H. Leitenberg (Ed.), *Handbook of behavior modification and behavior therapy,* Englewood Cliffs, New Jersey: Prentice Hall.

Sime, W. E., De Good, D. E., & Noble, B. J. (1976). Awareness of frontalis muscle tension before and after EMG biofeedback relaxation training. *Psychophysiology, 13,* 164.

Skinner, B. F. (1938). *The behavior of organisms.* New York: Appleton-Century.

Stern, G. S., Miller, C. R., Ewy, H. W., & Grant, P. S. (1980). Perceived control: Bogus pulse rate feedback and reported symptom reduction for individuals with accumulated stressful life events. *Biofeedback & Self-Regulation, 5,* 37–49.

Thorndike, E. L. (1933). An experimental study of rewards. Columbia University, Teacher's College, Publication Number 580. In Annett 1969, *Feedback and human behavior,* Baltimore: Penguin Books.

Wickramasekera, I. (1980). A conditioned response model of the placebo effect: Predictions from the model. *Biofeedback & Self-Regulation, 5,* 5–18.

Wieringen, P. van (1980). *Klinische toepassing van EMG feedback: Een overzicht.* Preprint. Amsterdam: Vrije Universiteit.

Williamson, D. A., & Blanchard, E. B. (1979). Heart rate and blood pressure biofeedback II. *Biofeedback & Self-Regulation, 4,* 35–50.

Whitehead, W. E., Drescher, V. M., Heiman, P., & Blackwell, B. (1977). Relation of heart rate control to heartbeat perception. *Biofeedback & Self-Regulation, 2,* 371–392.

10

Hyperventilation, Anxiety, and Coping with Stress

P. B. Defares
University of Amsterdam

P. Grossman
Agricultural University and Foundation for Stress Research, Wageningen

In health psychology the concept of stress has conspicuously come to the fore, because of its relevance as a causal agent for disease, behavioral malfunctioning, and mental deficiencies (Stone, Cohen, & Adler, 1979). It is generally recognized, however, that the coping ability of the individual is among the best preventive resources to preserve mental tranquility and an optimal health state (Coelho, Hamburg, & Adams, 1974; Meichenbaum, 1977; Rodin, 1980).

Lazarus' stress model emphasizes the mediating cognitive process of appraisal, which is "a perception distinguishing the potentially harmful from the potentially beneficial or irrelevant" (Lazarus, Averill, & Opton, 1974). According to Lazarus, the process of appraisal is the outcome of the interaction of antecedent situational or ecological cues and dispositional personality traits, beliefs, and cognitive styles. Other stress researchers agree that the coping capability of an individual is directly linked to appraisal, which plays a decisive intermediary role in determining whether stress will emerge or equilibrium will be preserved (Lumsden, 1975; Rodin, 1980). In this context it seems exceedingly important to scrutinize those conditions that may severely hamper the capacity of the subject to cope with external stressors.

Feelings of anxiety, apprehension, and unrest caused by heightened arousal levels may indeed cripple the coping ability of the stress victim. The psychophysiological functioning of the individual is a crucial aspect of the elicited stress response. Though the alarm or emergency reaction to a powerful stressor includes a variety of physiological changes, which are partially mediated by the activity of the adrenal glands, our focus will be on respiratory responses. In a recent paper (Janis, Defares, & Grossman, 1983), we stated: "In response to oncoming danger or anticipations of imminent threat, most everyone will begin breathing hard. This, in effect, changes the rate and depth of respiration in the direction of hyperventilation, which is characterized by respiratory activity in excess of immediate metabolic requirements (p. 7)."

Hyperventilation bears strong repercussions for the adequacy of cognitive functioning, as has been shown in empirical studies (Hardonk & Beumer, 1979; Weimann, 1968; Wyke, 1963).

Negative appraisals of a stressor result in anxiety reactions and enhance feelings of subjective incompetence (Sarason, 1975; Spielberger, 1972). If hyperventilation is indeed a concomitant of anxiety under certain conditions, the foregoing considerations suggest that a state of temporary hyperventilation would further augment the likelihood of inadequate coping.

Before examining the relationship between anxiety and hyperventilation in greater depth, the psychophysiology of respiration will be briefly reviewed, with special reference to hyperventilatory breathing.

THE PSYCHOPHYSIOLOGY OF HYPERVENTILATION

Respiratory, cardiovascular, and metabolic activities function in the healthy organism in an integrated and interdependent fashion in order to achieve optimal homeostasis. Hence, respiratory parameters are highly correlated with measures of general metabolic activity and cardiovascular events (Grossman & Defares, 1983; Sheperd & Vanhoutte, 1979). Frequency of respiration, for example, is positively correlated with both heart rate and oxygen consumption. In the fight-flight emergency response, as discussed by Selye and Benson, the body's resources are rapidly mobilized, requiring specific respiratory alterations to meet increased metabolic activities (Benson, 1975; Selye, 1979). Recent research has demonstrated that elevated respiratory rate and volume, achieved by a predominantly thoracic mode of breathing, is most characteristic of the anticipation of stress (Ancoli & Kamiya, 1979; Dudley, 1969; Suess, Alexander, Smith, Sweeney, & Marion, 1980). Moreover, in experimental situations in which stress reactions are elicited by confrontation with imminent danger, hyperventilatory breathing has repeatedly been reported. Such breathing involves a decrease in end-tidal carbon dioxide level, which accurately reflects both alveolar and arterial carbon dioxide pressures (Dudley, 1969; Suess et al., 1980).

In normal breathing, a certain amount of carbon dioxide is eliminated by means of gas exchange. In order to preserve homeostasis and adequate acidity levels, the carbon dioxide tension in the arterial blood should be relatively stable and should remain within fixed boundaries. In hyperventilation, carbon dioxide tension in the blood decreases, and simultaneously, the pH (acidity level), is altered, which results in the blood becoming more alkaline. This shift in pH has immediate consequences which are reflected in altered EEG patterns, and in reflex-activity of the sympathetic nervous system.

At the neuronal level, hyperventilation appears to produce a biphasic response to the reduction of arterial CO_2 tension (Lum, 1981). First, with the initial drop in CO_2 pressure, there is immediate migration of the CO_2 out of the neurons, an increase in intracellular pH, and increased neuronal activity and electrical discharge in associated nerve fibers. A more pronounced decline in CO_2 tension may result in alterations in neuronal metabolism, in which the lactic acid that is produced further alters pH, and neuronal activity may greatly diminish. Ultimately a state of tetany may ensue, partly mediated by the instability of nerve membranes.

Wyke (1963) reports evidence from several investigations that respiration-induced changes in carbon dioxide tension alter the activity of the hypothalamus and the reticular activating system. Reduced arterial CO_2 seems to depress reticulocortical activation, resulting in decreased awareness of the environment, deceleration and enhanced synchrony of brain waves, and defective cortical excitability. It has been established that a reduction in CO_2 level produces immediate cerebral vasoconstriction and inhibits release of oxygen from hemoglobin molecules. This apparently results in a state of cerebral hypoxia, and synchronous high-voltage, slow-wave EEG activity appears (Lum, 1981; Wyke, 1963). A highly condensed model of the physiological effects of hyperventilation is given in Figure 1.

A brief state of hyperventilation appears to be a normal response to stressful situations (Dudley, Holmes, Martin, & Ripley, 1964; Suess et al., 1980), but some individuals suffer from chronic, frequent, and prolonged attacks of hyperventilation, or sustained low levels of arterial carbon dioxide pressure, that is, hyperventilation syndrome. These conditions may result from prolonged exposure to stress or habitually faulty breathing patterns. Patients typically present a wide range of complaints that can vary considerably from person to person.

Perhaps the most universal symptoms of hyperventilation are psychological in nature. Patients appear anxious and often report feeling tense, jittery, confused, or disturbed. Phobic and depressive responses are also frequently noted. The somatic complaints often fall into the categories of cardiovascular, cerebrovascular, neurological, gastrointestinal, and muscular problems. These include heart palpitations, irregular heartbeat, tingling sensations in different body parts, dizziness and faintness, excessive gas, stomach or intestinal cramps, trembling, and muscular pain. Unless the subject is examined while hyperventilating, no underlying physiological basis for the symptoms can be found. For this reason, incorrect labels are attached to the person's problem, for example, hypochondriasis, hysteria, psychasthenia, or some physical misdiagnosis. Patients suffering from chronic hyperventilation syndrome are

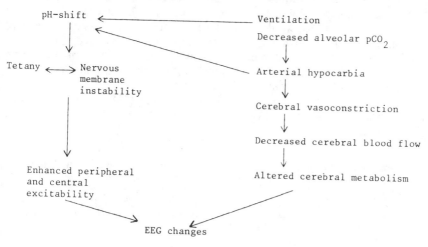

Figure 1 The physiological effects of hyperventilation.

usually labeled as hyperventilators or hyperventilation-prone individuals (Hardonk & Beumer, 1979; Weimann, 1968).

HYPERVENTILATION AND ANXIETY REACTIONS

In this section, we will elaborate on the relationship between anxiety responses and hyperventilatory breathing. Spielberger (1972) describes anxiety reactions emerging subsequent to a negative appraisal of a stressor in terms of feelings of apprehension mediated by an activation of the autonomic nervous system that may ultimately lead to highly overlearned responses to threatening stimuli. In further elaborating upon coping responses, Spielberger (1972) contends that adequate coping can be severely hampered by feelings of intense anxiety and panic due to anxious *expectation.*

Hamilton's information processing model of neurotic anxiety is generally consistent with this view. Hamilton contends that neurotic anxiety is due to "excessive and or threatening information." In explicitly referring to anticipatory responses he further states: "This information resides in cognitive data which encode in schemata an individual's expectancies and anticipation of pain, rejection, isolation and personal incompetence."

There are strong indications that hyperventilation plays an important role in the anticipation of stress, which have been substantiated in studies of anticipated physical harm, and in mental test situations (Dudley et al., 1964; Holmes, McCaul, & Solomon, 1978; Garssen, 1980; Motta, Fagiani, Dolcetti, Bellone, & Borello, 1971). The effect of the anticipation of stress on hyperventilation may be more substantial *when imminent danger of a severe threat is involved,* such as anticipation of electric shock in the laboratory (Suess et al., 1980). In real life, the following examples seem relevant: sudden announcement of the imminent death of a spouse, alarms signaling hazardous events such as life threatening earthquakes or hurricanes, and anticipation of a dangerous operation with high mortality rates (Janis et al., 1983).

Anticipation of examinations may also induce symptoms of hyperventilation, especially when the outcome is of high personal relevance to the subject and failure would have strong social repercussions, such as expulsion or severe punishment. Garssen (1980), for instance, found that normal persons, that is, subjects who did not suffer from breathing disturbances or trait anxiety, showed significant drops of carbon dioxide *prior* to a test session of high relevance to the subjects.

The following quotation from Janis et al. (1983) describes our interpretation of the interaction between anxiety and the symptoms of hyperventilation:

> We conceptualize the build up and persistence of high fear in such instances as a positive feedback loop resulting from the person's awareness of his excited state due to hyperventilation. In many cases, a crucial component of the loop is the person's correct appraisal of his or her current state of deficient self-control for coping effectively with the danger situation. The person's self-derogatory appraisals not only augment the magnitude of perceived threat but also markedly lower self-confidence; these two adverse factors are well-known determinants of the level of fear. (p. 12)

Colla (1985) has postulated analogous feedback loops in an instructive schematic representation of the relationship between anxiety, hyperventilation, and autonomic neurological reactions (figure 2).

HYPERVENTILATION, TRAIT ANXIETY, AND COPING

Hyperventilation may play a decisive role in anticipatory stress responses as was suggested in the previous section. It is important to note, however, that so far we have referred to actual stressors, which evoke emotional, *state* anxiety reactions. We also postulate that *trait* anxiety (i.e. individual proneness to anxiety) may be related to generally elevated levels of physiological arousal and that hyperventilation syndrome may often be accompanied by unusually high trait anxiety. This latter hypothesis was indeed corroborated in a study with *severe* hyperventilators in which 35 of 46 subjects suffering from the hyperventilation syndrome (assessed by means of capnography) showed extremely high trait anxiety levels (Grossman, Swart, & Defares, 1985).

The implications of the foregoing analysis for coping can be explained by a three-dimensional coping model proposed by Lazarus et al. (1974), which is presented in Figure 3. Basically, this model provides a heuristic conceptual analysis of the factors that contribute to variability in coping behavior. In line with Lazarus' general stress model, two classes of potential determinants of coping variability are postulated: situational demands and personality dispositions (Lazarus et al., 1974). Lazarus' model stipulates different qualitative coping modes R_1 R_2–R_n. Though the model does not make explicit references to quantitative analysis, it permits quantification in the case of a single coping response.

Our analysis involves anticipation of stress, and further assumes an intricate relationship between anxiety and hyperventilation. Coping, in our view, refers to different degrees of subjectively perceived competence (coping ability); the Personal disposition (P) variable refers to hyperventilation proneness; and the

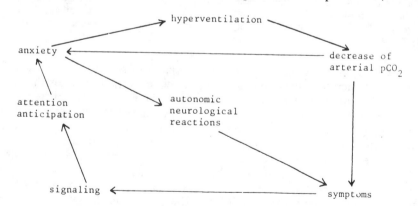

Figure 2 Vicious circle re: hyperventilation syndrome. From P. Colla, (1985). Hyperventilation a disease? In P. B. Defares and P. Grossman, eds., *Hyperventilation* (Dutch). Leiden: Stafleu.

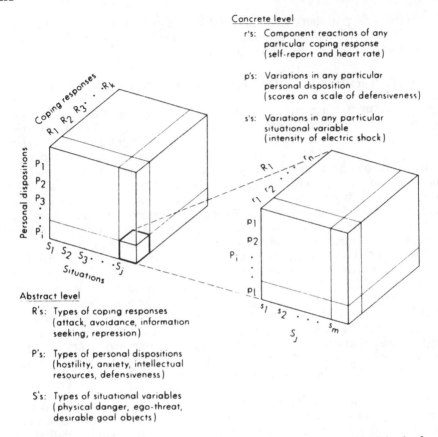

Figure 3 3-way sources of variance model on abstract (left) and concrete (right) levels of analysis. From R. S. Lazarus, J. R. Averill, and E. M. Opton, Jr. (1974). The psychology of coping: Issues of research and assessment. In G. V. Coelho, D. A. Hamburg, and J. E. Adams, eds., *Coping and adaptation* (p. 270). New York: Basic Books. Used with permission.

Situational (S) variable stands for different degrees of severity of a particular stressor in inducing anticipation stress. (Our model further assumes that the severity of a stressor does not exceed the tolerance of the most stable individuals in terms of homeostatic balance.) Focusing on the concrete level of the model, given that Rs represent different degrees of subjectively perceived coping ability, a low level of hyperventilation proneness associated with a relatively strong but still bearable stressor would not necessarily cause deterioration in (perceived) coping ability. Conversely, the same stressor might be disastrous for the high hyperventilation-prone subject, in whom very low levels of subjectively perceived competence would be induced.

The hypothetical sequence of events depicted in phenomenological terms is presented for high hyperventilation prone subjects in Figure 4. It should be noted that negative appraisal of the stressor, according to the flow diagram, is further enhanced in high trait-anxious individuals by self-attribution of responsibility for defective coping, and by negative evaluation of subjective competence. A crucial aspect of adaptation in the case of repetitious confrontations with the same stressor is the manner in which the person processes noxious information.

Successive cognitive coding analogous to Lazarus' primary and secondary appraisal and reappraisal ultimately sets the stage for either adequate or defective habituation. With severe hyperventilators who suffer from high trait anxiety, confrontations with similar hazardous events induces negative feedback loops, preventing habituations from taking place. Subsequently,

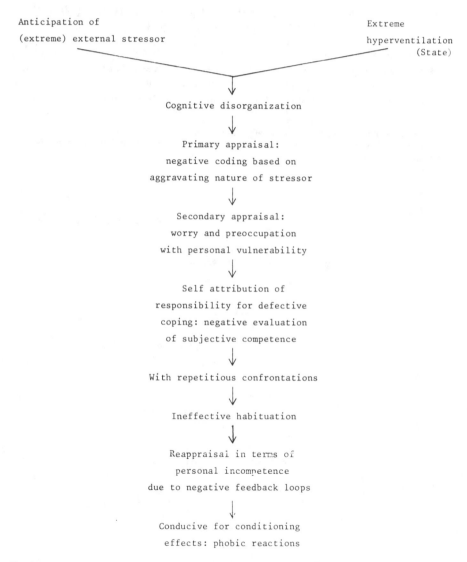

Anticipation of
(extreme) external stressor

Extreme
hyperventilation
(State)

Cognitive disorganization

Primary appraisal:
negative coding based on
aggravating nature of stressor

Secondary appraisal:
worry and preoccupation
with personal vulnerability

Self attribution of
responsibility for defective
coping: negative evaluation
of subjective competence

With repetitious confrontations

Ineffective habituation

Reappraisal in terms of
personal incompetence
due to negative feedback loops

Conducive for conditioning
effects: phobic reactions

Figure 4 Anticipation of extreme external stressor: Coping and habituation of high hyperventilation prone subjects (high trait anxiety).

phobic reactions may ensue, as conditioning mediated by a prolonged state of heightened arousal is likely to occur.

The hypothetical sequence of events in the interpretation of an extreme stressor for low trait-anxious subjects who are not hyperventilation prone is presented in Figure 5. People with low hyperventilation proneness have a much greater chance of gradually habituating to these events and reappraising their coping capability in terms of personal competence.

ENHANCEMENT OF COPING CAPABILITY BY MEANS OF BIOFEEDBACK INTERVENTION

The foregoing theoretical analysis suggests that a substantial proportion of subjects with high levels of trait anxiety may be dispositional hyperventilators.* Consequently, reducing hyperventilation could indirectly have a positive impact on anxiety proneness and the appraisal of future harm. Therapies

*In epidemiological terms, it is generally estimated that 6 to 10% of the population suffers from dispositional hyperventilation; many hyperventilators also show symptoms of phobic behavior (Weimann, 1968).

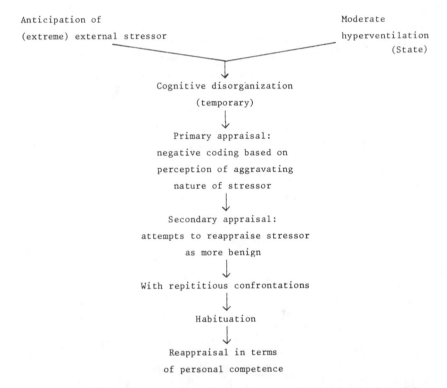

Figure 5 Anticipation of extreme external stressor: Coping and habituation of low hyperventilation prone subjects (low trait anxiety).

directed toward reestablishing homeostatic functioning by means of modifying breathing patterns toward abdominal, slower-, and larger-volume respiration have indeed been remarkably successful at quickly removing or reducing physical and psychological disturbances (Compernolle, Hoogduin, & Joele, 1979; Defares, & Grossman, 1980; Lum, 1981; Sprague, 1977). The goal of the present study was to modify the patterns of hyperventilators by means of a biofeedback procedure.

In this intervention study, we examined the respiratory and psychological effects of a breathing-based biofeedback treatment aimed at altering the ventilatory pattern of hyperventilators in a stable fashion. The general goals and procedures for the study are as follows:

- Objective: Learning of an appropriate breathing pattern by way of auditory steering.
- Respiratory Biofeedback Device: Auditory stimuli by way of ear-telephone (simulation of respiratory pattern) as a method of training the breathing pattern, followed by monitoring of breathing frequency to detect deviations from a pre-set pattern (Grossman et al., 1985).

We compared the effects of biofeedback therapy given to 25 hyperventilation syndrome patients with that of a control treatment applied to 21 hyperventilators. The therapy consisted of receiving instruction by the use of a portable respiratory biofeedback instrument which monitored respiration rate and emitted an auditory pattern, simulating a desired breathing pattern, when the criterion for the appropriate respiration rate has been exceeded. This study was carried out in cooperation with Grossman, De Swart, and Defares 1985; see also Defares, Grossman, & De Swart, 1983).

The subjects were referred to our laboratory by general practitioners and went through an extensive procedure in order to ascertain whether they were to be considered severe hyperventilators. Strict criteria were applied, using a standard provocation test and obtaining measurements of the following physiological variables: base-line end-tidal CO_2 level, CO_2 prior to the provocation test, CO_2 level *after* 5 minutes recovery, a ratio-score indicating the amount of CO_2 recovery, base-line breathing rate, and subjective somatic complaints.

Once accepted as hyperventilators, subjects completed several psychological tests, which were assumed to be linked to the symptoms of hyperventilation on the basis of theoretical considerations and the results of a pilot study. The following tests were administered: The Dutch version (Van der Ploeg, Defares, & Spielberger, 1980) of the State-Trait Anxiety Inventory (Spielberger, Gorsuch, & Lushene, 1970); a social anxiety scale developed by Willems, Tuender-de Haan and Defares, (1973); a modification of Eysenck's Maudsley Personality Inventory, developed by Wilde (1970), which consisted of three independent dimensions: neuroticism, neurosomatic instability, and extraversion; a self-esteem scale, derived from a widely used Dutch personality inventory (Luteijn, Starren, & Van Dijk, 1975); and a Dutch version of the Locus of Control scale developed by Rotter (Andriessen, 1972).

For most scales population norms were available, which permitted comparison of the subjects in this study with other populations. As with regard to the physiological measurements, the psychological inventories were administered before and after therapy. Within- and between-group comparisons were made in order to ascertain the effects of the feedback intervention.

The subjects in the therapy group came into the laboratory once a week, for eight weeks. During half-hour sessions, biofeedback devices were adjusted, questions about the therapy were answered, and subjects were instructed to practice using the device at home, three times a day, for 10 minutes each time. The control group subjects, who were also told they were receiving therapy, were exposed to the biofeedback device weekly, for the same number of sessions. However, no attempt was made to alter their normal breathing patterns and the feedback device merely reinforced their usual respiration pattern. At home, they were merely instructed to lie down twice a day for 20-minute sessions.

RESULTS

In presenting the results of this study, the therapy and control groups will be compared. It is important to note that the data for the repeated measures were collected one month following treatment. Two-tailed t tests for dependent samples yielded highly significant changes for the therapy group in trait anxiety, state anxiety and neurosomatic instability (see Table 1). The only significant difference obtained for the control group concerned locus of control, showing a shift in the direction of greater externality after the pseudo-treatment.

In order to assess the *net* therapy effect, *between*-group comparisons were carried out on discrepancy scores (difference between before and after

Table 1 Comparisons of therapy group (T, $n = 25$) and control group (C, $n = 21$) with respect to eight psychological variables

		Before therapy		After therapy		Paired t-test
		Means	S. Dev.	Means	S. Dev.	p
Self-esteem	T	23.2	5.8	25.8	6.1	n.s.
	C	20.2	6.7	18.5	8.0	n.s.
Trait anxiety	T	46.8	8.7	40.6	9.1	.002
	C	50.8	10.8	49.4	8.8	n.s.
State anxiety	T	48.2	12.7	39.4	9.4	.001
	C	50.2	11.7	47.3	9.5	n.s.
Neuroticism	T	78.3	23.9	73.0	24.1	n.s.
	C	83.1	22.5	87.8	18.6	n.s.
Neuro-somatic instability	T	30.6	5.3	27.3	7.7	.001
	C	31.8	5.6	31.2	5.2	n.s.
Extraversion	T	55.4	16.9	57.4	16.5	n.s.
	C	45.8	19.0	43.5	20.1	n.s.
Locus of control	T	12.1	4.6	13.0	6.0	n.s.
	C	12.2	5.4	10.0	4.6	.001
Social anxiety	T	47.0	15.8	46.2	14.1	n.s.
	C	52.6	19.1	50.7	20.8	n.s.

Table 2   Significant differences between therapy group and control group

Subjective complaints	F = 13.288	p = .001
HVPT pCO_2 – 5 min	8.133	.007
Recovery capnogram	6.408	.015
Base-line breathing frequency	8.749	.005
Trait anxiety	3.914	.05
State anxiety	4.519	.039
Neuroticism'	3.758	.021
Neuro-somatic instability	4.480	.04

Note. 1-way analysis of variance based on discrepancy scores.

measurements) of the therapy and control group. Applying one-way analyses of variance, 4 of the 6 physiological variables, and 4 of the 8 psychological variables indicated significant changes, corroborating the positive effect of the respiratory-based feedback treatment.*

In closing, we would like to dwell briefly upon a theme that seems directly relevant for anxiety theory. This pertains to the question of the role of psychological moderator variables in mediating changes in other psychological dimensions, once a fundamental somatically based restructuring of the personality has been engendered. Intercorrelations among the change scores, that is, discrepancy scores, offer interesting indications in this regard. Half of the variables are significantly related at the .05 level. However, trait anxiety, the most frequently correlated change score, was significantly related to change in *all* of the other psychological parameters, and was highly associated with changes in the measure of self-esteem, neuroticism, extraversion, and locus of control. Since improvement on trait anxiety was exhibited by 80% of the therapy group, its correlations with these other psychological change scores suggests that the biofeedback treatment induced improvements across a range of psychological dimensions among many subjects.

It should be noted that only covariance is considered in the correlations among the variables, but the results suggest that, inasmuch as other variables underwent a change, this may have been at least partially mediated by trait anxiety. In retrospect, it is our opinion that the results of our intervention study are in line w.ih Spielberger's theory, which predicts that trait anxiety will remain stable over time, unless a fundamental restructuring of the organism has taken place. If this is the case, it is not surprising to find that once trait anxiety does undergo a shift, the impact is indeed pervasive and mediates changes in other psychological dimensions.

CONCLUSIONS

In dealing with the effects of stress and anxiety on cognitive functioning, Lazarus' stress model was taken as a starting point in order to clarify the

---

*In passing, it should be emphasized that control-group subjects received a more adequate therapy in a later stage.

Table 3 Correlation between change-scores of the psychological variables (therapy group) $N = 25$

	Trait anxiety	State anxiety	Self-esteem	Neuroticism	Neurosomatic	Extraversion	Locus of control	Social anxiety
Trait anxiety		.37	.62	.54	.40	.52	.49	.39
State anxiety				.35	.29			
Self-esteem								.32
Neuroticism					.34	.66	.30	.43
Neurosomatic						.41	.40	
Extraversion							.31	.35
Locus of control								
Social anxiety								

p values of significant correlations range from 0.05 to 0.001. The values of empty cells were deleted, because of the low (nonsignificant) correlations.

relationship between hyperventilation and coping behavior. It was contended that anticipation stress plays a decisive role in eliciting anxiety responses, and concomitantly, hyperventilatory breathing.

Our research corroborated that severe hyperventilators indeed possess high trait anxiety, and that among high trait-anxious subjects, a substantial proportion may be dispositional hyperventilators. Furthermore, there are strong indications that severe hyperventilators with high trait anxiety are especially susceptible to defective coping behavior when confronted with imminent danger or the anticipation of hazardous events.

The positive results of a ventilatory-based biofeedback treatment in diminishing severe hyperventilation and concomitant trait anxiety has important implications for coping. It seems that restoring homeostasis and psychological tranquility by means of ventilatory techniques might greatly enhance the coping capability of the vulnerable individual. One should bear in mind, however, that neuroticism and other factors such as psychotraumatic life events often play a decisive role in the etiology of the hyperventilation syndrome. For these "sequelae" of the mind, other therapeutic procedures are needed, such as cognitive restructuring, desensitization and insight therapy.

REFERENCES

Ancoli, S., & Kamiya, J. (1979). Respiratory patterns during emotional expression. *Biofeedback and Self-Regulation, 4,* 242 (Abstract).

Andriessen, J. H. T. H. (1972). Interne of externe beheersing. *Nederlands Tijdschrift voor de Psychologie, 27,* 173–191.

Benson, H. (1975). *The relaxation response.* New York: Marrow.

Coelho, G. V., Hamburg, D. A., & Adams, J. E. (1974). *Coping and adaptation.* New York: Basic Books.

Colla, P. (1985). Hyperventilation, a disease? In P. B. Defares & P. Grossman (Eds.), *Hyperventilation* (Dutch). Leiden: Stafleu.

Compernolle, T., Hoogduin, K., & Joele, L. (1979). Diagnosis and treatment of the hyperventilation syndrome. *Psychosomatics, 20,* 612–625.

Defares, P. B., & Grossman, P. (1980). *The treatment of hyperventilation by steered audio-ventilation.* Abstracts Wold Congress Behaviour Therapy, Jerusalem.

Defares, P. B., Grossman, P., & Swart, J. C. G. de (1983). Test anxiety. In R. H. M. Schwarzer, H. M. van der Ploeg, & C. D. Spielberger (Eds.), *Advances in test anxiety research* (Vol. 2). Lisse: Swets & Zeitlinger.

Dudley, D. L. (1969). *Psychophysiology of respiration in health and disease.* New York: Appleton-Century-Crofts.

Dudley, D. L., Holmes, T. H., Martin, C. J., & Ripley, H. W. (1964). Changes in respiration associated with hypnotically induced emotion, pain, and exercise. *Psychosomatic Medicine, 26,* 46–53.

Garssen, B. (1980). Role of stress in the development of the hyperventilation syndrome. *Psychotherapy and Psychosomatics, 33,* 214–225.

Grossman, P., & Defares, P. B. (1983). To the heart of the matter. In C. D. Spielberger, I. G. Sarason, & P. B. Defares (Eds.), *Stress and anxiety* (Vol. 9). Washington: Hemisphere.

Grossman, P., Swart, J. C. G, de, & Defares, P. B. (1985). A controlled study of a breathing therapy for treatment of hyperventilation syndrome. *Journal of Psychosomatic Research, 29,* 49–58.

Hamilton, V. (1979). Information processing aspects of neurotic anxiety and schizophrenia. In V. Hamilton & D. M. Warburton (Eds.) *Human stress and cognition.* Chichester: Wiley, 1979.

Hardonk, H. J., & Beumer, H. M. (1979). Hyperventilation syndrome. In P. J. Vinken & G. W. Bruyn (Eds.), *Handbook of clinical neurology* (Vol. 38). Neurological manifestations of systemic diseases, Part 1. Amsterdam: North-Holland Publishing Company.

Holmes, D. S., McCaul, K. D., & Solomon, S. (1978). Control of respiration as a means of controlling responses to threat. *Journal of Personality and Social Psychology, 36,* 198–204.

Janis, I. L., Defares, P. B., & Grossman, P. (1983). Hypervigilant reactions to threat. In S. Selye (Ed.), *Selye's guide to stress research* (Vol. 3). New York: Van Nostrand Reinhold.

Lazarus, R. S., Averill, J. R., & Opton, E. M. (1974). The psychology of coping: Issues of research and assessment. In G. V. Coelho, D. A. Hamburg, & J. E. Adams (Eds.), *Coping and adaptation.* New York: Basic Books.

Lum, L. C. (1981). Hyperventilation and anxiety state. *Journal of the Royal Society of Medicine, 74,* 1–4.

Lumsden, D. P. (1975). Towards a systems model of stress: Feedback from an anthropological study of the impact of Ghana's Volta River project. In I. G. Sarason & C. D. Spielberger (Eds.), *Stress and Anxiety* (Vol. 2). Washington: Hemisphere.

Luteijn, F., Starren, J., & van Dijk, H. (1975). *Nederlandse Persoonlijkheids Vragenlijst.* Lisse: Swets & Zeitlinger.

Meichenbaum, D. (1977). *Cognitive behavior modification.* New York: Plenum Press.

Motta, P. E., Fagiani, M. B., Dolcetti, A., Bellone, E., & Borello, G. (1971). Modificazioni dei gas nel sangue nello stato ansioso di media gravitá. *Archivio per le Scienze Mediche, 128,* 111–119.

Ploeg, H. M. van der, Defares, P. B., & Spielberger, C. D. (1980). *Handleiding bij de Zelf-Beoordelings Vragenlijst, ZBV.* Een Nederlandstalige bewerking van de Spielberger State-Trait Anxiety Inventory STAI-DY. Lisse: Swets & Zeitlinger.

Rodin, J. (1980). Managing the stress of aging: The role of control and coping. In S. Levine & H. Ursin (Eds.), *Coping and health.* New York: Plenum Press.

Sarason, I. G. (1975). Anxiety and preoccupation. In I. G. Sarason & C. D. Spielberger (Eds.), *Stress and anxiety* (Vol. 2). Washington: Hemisphere.

Selye, H. (1979). *The stress of life.* New York: McGraw-Hill.

Sheperd, J. T., & Vanhoutte, P. M. (1979). *The human cardiovascular system.* New York: Raven.

Spielberger, C. D., Gorsuch, R. L., & Lushene, R. E. (1970). *Manual for the State-Trait Anxiety Inventory (STAI).* Palo Alto, CA: Consulting Psychologists Press.

Spielberger, C. D. (1972). Current trends in theory and research on anxiety. In C. D. Spielberger (Ed.), *Anxiety, current trends in theory and research* (Vol. 1). New York: Academic Press.

Sprague, D. B. (1977). *Effectiveness of respiration biofeedback and study skill training in alleviating test anxiety in college students.* Unpublished doctoral dissertation, University of Kentucky, 1977.

Stone, G. C., Cohen, F., & Adler, N. E. (1979). *Health psychology, a handbook: Theories, applications and challenges of a psychological approach to the health care system.* San Francisco: Jossey-Bass.

Suess, W. M., Alexander, A. B., Smith, D. D., Sweeney, H. W., & Marion, R. J. (1980). The effects of psychological stress on respiration: A preliminary study of anxiety and hyperventilation. *Psychophysiology, 17,* 535–540.

Weimann, G. (1968). *Das Hyperventilationssyndrom.* München: Urban and Schwarzenberg.

Wilde, G. J. S. (1970). *Neurotische labiliteit gemeten volgens de vragenlijstmethode.* 2e druk. Amsterdam: Van Rossen.

Willems, L. F. M., Tuender-de Haan, H. A., & Defares, P. B. (1973). Een schaal om sociale angst te meten. *Nederlands Tijdschrift voor de Psychologie, 28,* 415–422.

Wyke, B. (1963). *Brain function and metabolic disorders.* London: Butterworths.

III

STRESS AND ANXIETY IN CARDIOVASCULAR DISORDERS

11

Vital Exhaustion and Depression as Precursors of Myocardial Infarction

A. Appels
University of Limburg

Chronic diseases have a history in that they constitute the final stage of a development over a long period of time. In contrast to most infectious diseases, chronic diseases are characterized by prolonged exposure to a number of harmful factors. This implies that we have to study individuals on their way to myocardial infarctions. The stress factors that we study are parts of a biography. Each factor is embedded in a stage of the individual's development.

The road leading to the development of myocardial infarction is characterized by an abundant mobilization of energy. This surplus mobilization may be attributable to personality factors, such as the Type A behavior (Dembroski, 1978), or to typical conditions of an occupation or function (Russek, 1960), or to sociocultural configurations, such as those found in immigration, or as those occurring in times of profound changes in the economic situation of a country (Eyer, 1977; Marmot & Syme, 1976).

People who live a hyperenergetic life are more likely to encounter all kinds of pleasant as well as unpleasant experiences. So-called "A" types will experience more stressful life events than the more sedate-living "B" types (Falger, 1984; Suls, Gastorf, & Witenberg, 1979). What will happen when a Type A is confronted with a stressful situation? Glass (1977) developed a model that illustrates this process (and tested it more or less successfully in the psychological laboratory).

If we place this model in a somewhat wider context, it also helps us to gain insight into the individual's life prior to the infarction. When a Type A is confronted with a new stressful situation, he seems to react in accordance with the following pattern: First, he mobilizes extra energy in order to get the situation under control. This is a phase of hyperresponsiveness. If, however, the Type A is incapable of overcoming the new problems, a reversal in this behavior may occur in that the amount of activities decreases. This second phase is characterized by hyporesponsiveness and is often accompanied by symptoms of fatigue and helplessness/powerlessness. After some time the stressful period will be passed, and the individual will regain his usual level of activity. Figure 1 presents this model.

This way of life may continue for decades. Beneath the surface, two "scars" are formed. The first is a somatic one: the tightening of the coronary arteries as

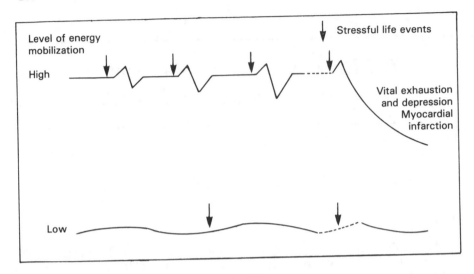

Figure 1 A simplified model of the pathogenesis of CHD.

a result of atherosclerotic plaque formation. The second "scar" consists in an acquired disposition to respond with feelings of helplessness and listlessness to new problematic situations.

Chronic diseases have a history. If we carefully follow an individual on his way to his myocardial infarction, we will find that prior to the occurrence of the disease he passes through a period of helplessness and listlessness, or, as we call it now, a state of vital exhaustion and depression. The basic hypothesis in our studies is that feelings of vital exhaustion and depression belong to the prodromes of myocardial infarction and sudden cardiac death. The coronary event does not hit the individual out of the blue (even if it will often be experienced as such) but follows after an accumulation of fatigue and depression.

Feelings of fatigue and general malaise have been reported as elements of the prodromata of myocardial infarction and sudden death by some epidemiologists. Alonzo found that 38% of 160 patients who had been hospitalized because of their first myocardial infarction had possessed feelings of "fatigue-weakness" in the month prior to the event. In his study 14% reported "emotional changes" and 16%, feelings of "general malaise" (Alonzo, 1975). Rissanen found that "unusual fatigue" was the most frequently mentioned prodrome of sudden death (32%), followed by discomfort in the chest (24%), dyspnea (15%), and changed angina pectoris (15%) (Rissanen, 1978). Kuller reports that in his study about the prodromata of sudden death, 56% had complained about "undue fatigue," 42% about dyspnea, 37% about chest pain, and 28% about difficulty in sleeping in the two weeks before their deaths (Kuller, 1979). From a psychological point of view the feelings of fatigue-weakness, general malaise, and difficulties in sleeping do not form discrete categories but seem to form a coherent pattern which tentatively might be labeled as a "syndrome of vital exhaustion and depression" or as a reflection of a status of "conservation-withdrawal." An attempt to measure and to analyze this syndrome by means of the construction of a questionnaire seems to be worthwhile both from a scientific and a practical point of view.

THE MAASTRICHT QUESTIONNAIRE

The first step towards the construction of such an instrument was made in the Imminent Myocardial Infarction Rotterdam (IMIR) study. The design and the results of this study were published elsewhere (Appels, 1979; Appels, Pool, Kazemier, & van der Does, 1979). Summarizing, it can be described as follows. A new questionnaire was developed for the purpose of measuring the envisaged syndrome. This questionnaire was submitted to 382 men who visited their family doctors because of complaints of possible cardiac origin. This group was monitored for 10 months. It appeared that those who suddenly died or suffered a myocardial infarction in this period or whose cardiac condition seriously deteriorated had a higher mean score when they first contacted their family doctors than those who did not develop a new heart disease in that period. This indicates that the item pool has some predictive validity. Since it was uncertain at the time what theoretical construct was actually measured by these items, the test was given the neutral name, "Maastricht Questionnaire," (MQ) (Fig. 2).

A second indication of the validity of the questionnaire was found in a study by Verhagen et al., who compared 58 infarction patients with 58 healthy persons (Verhagen, Nass, Appels, van Bastelar, & Winnubst, 1980) on several behavioral factors, including the Type A behavior pattern and the Maastricht Questionnaire. As Table 1 shows, the questionnaire discriminated significantly between the two groups. It discriminated even better than the structured interview for the assessment of the Type A behavior, probably because the syndrome of vital exhaustion and depression is closer in time to the occurrence of myocardial infarction than the Type A behavior.

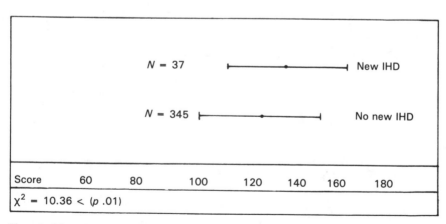

Figure 2 Maastricht questionnaire predictive validity (IMIR study) 10 months follow-up.

Table 1 Univariate F and discriminant analysis

	Univariate F	Discriminant function coefficient	Wilks' lambda
Maastricht questionnaire	15.04	.45	.88
Type A interview	11.09	.33	.83

58 patients and 58 healthy controls (Verhagen et al., 1980).

Subsequent to these studies, the Maastricht Questionnaire was revised. Some items were removed because they were of the same tenor as other items, which resulted in a high intercorrelation. Other items were added, mainly derived from clinical interviews.

This revised edition is currently subjected to a new prospective cross-validation. The subjects of this study are municipal employees of Rotterdam who voluntarily cooperate in a periodic medical examination. Simultaneously, the questionnaire is presented to all male patients under 66 who are admitted to the Annadal Hospital at Maastricht because of their first infarction (Fig. 3). These 57 patients were compared with 406 municipal employees whose medical history, according to the examination, showed no apoplexy, old myocardial infarction, or angina pectoris. The mean score of the coronary patients was 86 (standard deviation 21). The mean score of the reference group was 63 (standard deviation 15). This difference is larger than one standard deviation. Since the mean age of the reference group is higher than that of the patients' group, the difference cannot be accounted for by age.

In the description of the model it was said that in the course of the development towards myocardial infarction, two scars are formed: the atherosclerotic plaques, and an acquired disposition to respond with feelings of helplessness and listlessness to new problematic situations. Or, in other words, the syndrome of vital exhaustion and depression originates in earlier periods of fatigue and helplessness/hopelessness. We have tested this hypothesis by asking

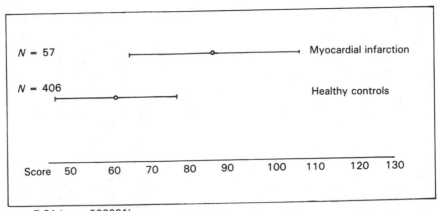

$t = 7.64$ $(p < .000001)$

Figure 3 Maastricht Questionnaire concurrent validity (Means and Standard Deviations).

28 patients and the reference group of 406 healthy controls whether they had ever been overstrained. This is a difficult question because it is so difficult to define what the term "overstrained" means. But this difficulty exists to an equal degree for both groups. Of the 28 patients, 18 replied "yes," and 10, "no." Of the controls, 106 answered "yes," and 300, "no." Here, too, a significant difference was found. The odd-even ratio equalled 5.09 ($p < .001$).

Summarizing, it can be said that two retrospective studies and one prospective study indicate that feelings of vital exhaustion and depression are often a typical feature of the period prior to the infarction.

A further specification of the syndrome can be given by a psychometric analysis of the questionnaire and by clinical interviews. Psychometric analyses of the MQ show that the questions have a high internal consistency (Cronbach's alpha is .91). At the same time some subelements can be recognized: (a) feelings of listlessness and tiredness (Do you often feel tired? Do you lately feel more listless than before?); (b) loss of vitality (Do you feel less capable of doing something useful now-a-days?); (c) helplessness and hopelessness (Have you experienced a feeling of hopelessness recently?); (d) depressive and hypochondriac feelings (Do you sometimes wish to be dead? Is your mind filled with the idea that you are ill?); (e) exhaustion (Do you sometimes have the feeling that your body is a battery which is losing its power?); (f) projections of feelings of insufficiency upon the outer world (Do you have the feeling that the younger people try to remove the older people?) and (g) sleep disturbances (Do you often wake up during the night?).

The following interview illustrates the syndrome. This clinical description also illustrates that the syndrome of vital exhaustion and depression is often a part of a developmental phase of an individual. Mr. V (59 years old) is a well-known actor. He is married and has three children not living in the parental home anymore. In World War II he was a district leader of the underground resistance organization. For 12 years he has suffered from hypertension. His manner of speaking has all the characteristics of the Type A behavior. Shortly before his infarction, he was engaged in the translation of a stage play. The commission for that piece of work had been given to him long before, but he did not start working on it until he had only three weeks left to finish it. "I could not start working until I was under pressure."

His friends had noticed that he had grown quieter during the last year. He began to retire from company. He had also disposed of his television ("The only thing you see on that screen is naked womenfolk"). He has all but stopped reading. He is too listless, too apathetic to read. "What I felt is what the poet J. Engelman called 'ironic laziness': doing nothing anymore because everything is just too relative, nothing is worth your while."

"I used to depend on crowds for my living. Now I avoid them. Once, the applause tickled my vanity. Now I just grin and think, where can I get a good glass of wine? I get more out of that. Why am I standing here anyway?"

He is inclined to go to bed early. "That is a form of withdrawing. Why stay up if the evening has nothing to offer for you?" It is against this background that the irritation arises.

One has been warned that nothing is valuable. By nature, I am a perfectionist. In the past I became overstrained twice because I made too high demands of myself and others. Now I can get furious if a clock does not run true. A clock should function properly. If it doesn't, it confirms to the world that it is of no value. To me, the cardiac infarction is a refuge. Society cannot call on me anymore. I now have a certificate in my pocket, my legalized excuse for not having to be active anymore. What I like best is to retire, take a sleeping pill on the pretence of having a headache. If there is nothing to stay awake for, there is not anything as wonderful as sleeping.

I do not long for death, either. My problems are not great enough for me to do so. I am in the grey area in between, no violent emotions anymore, no profound sadness. It is the domain of "l'ennuie" in the sense meant by Bernanos. What's the meaning of it all, the theatre company, the performances, the resistance during the War? Where is the sting, the enthusiasm? The heyday is past. All that is left for me to do is to become a decent old grandpa.

I am too rational to enter into new human relations. But it would be wonderful to fall in love once more. I feel as if I am in a small boat passing by the harbor. It is an age-bound depression. One has no experiences anymore that make life worthwhile. Sometimes I get terribly annoyed by my wife's patronizing remarks like: "Wouldn't it be wiser for you to take tonic instead of beer?"

I have no real grit anymore, either. Sometimes, when I have done some little job, like repairing a clock, I can lie deadbeat on the couch for an hour. I also checked four to five times if I had made no mistakes in doing something. When I went out I walked back as often as three times to check if the door was properly locked. That's a symptom of insecurity. One doesn't have oneself under control anymore. My wife said: "You've become so uncertain." (Personal communication)

DISCUSSION

Except for the data of the prospective IMIR study all other data that were presented above were obtained in retrospective studies. This raises the question whether or not these data have been biased by the nature of these studies. The dramatic experience of having a myocardial infarction works like a lighthouse that illuminates its surroundings. The coronary event influences the perception and the recall of feelings and emotions experienced in the months preceding the event. Feelings of depression caused by the myocardial infarction may color the perception of the past which may result in an overestimation or overreporting of the number of symptoms of vital exhaustion and depression experienced in the period before the infarction. To what extent have the retrospective data been influenced by this "lighthouse" effect?

Table 2 shows the distributions of five items which discriminated significantly between cases and controls in both the prospective cohort study (IMIR) and the case-control study, in which 57 patients were compared with 406 healthy controls. These distributions can be compared by looking at the odd-even ratios. (The formula of this ratio is ad/bc). Inspection of Table 2 shows that all odd-even ratios of the case-control study are somewhat higher than those found in the prospective study. Does this indicate that symptoms of vital exhaustion and depression are overreported by those who recently experienced a myocardial infarction? The differences are not large and can partly be explained by the differences in the control groups, the first being composed of people who visited their doctor with complaints of possible cardiac origin, the second one being formed by healthy persons who voluntarily participated in a screening program. Guided by a close inspection of Table 2 we do not believe that retrospective studies are strongly biased by the "lighthouse effect" as far as reporting of premonitory symptoms is concerned. The final proof, however, will be the comparison of the odd-even ratios using the same type of control group in the retrospective study as was used in the prospective study.

Table 2 Odd-even ratios of five items in prospective and retrospective studies

Item		Prospective study			Retrospective study	
		Symptom			Symptom	
		Reported	Not reported		Reported	Not reported
Do you have a feeling that little comes out of your hands lately?	Cases	19	18	Cases	17	39
	Controls	106	211	Controls	45	363
	OER = 2.10			OER = 3.52		
Do you have a feeling that you have come to a dead end?	Cases	12	25	Cases	16	41
	Controls	53	264	Controls	28	378
	OER = 2.39			OER = 5.27		
Do you have a feeling that nobody can help you with those problems deep down inside?	Cases	17	20	Cases	22	35
	Controls	82	235	Controls	76	330
	OER = 2.44			OER = 2.73		
Have you ever had a feeling lately like "I do not achieve enough, I could achieve more if only I were healthier, not so weak, not so limp?	Cases	22	15	Cases	21	36
	Controls	104	213	Controls	43	363
	OER = 3.00			OER = 4.92		
Do you feel less capable of doing something useful nowadays?	Cases	19	18	Cases	17	40
	Controls	98	219	Controls	50	356
	OER = 2.36			OER = 3.03		

A second difficult question is why this syndrome is related to coronary heart disease (CHD). Should these feelings primarily be understood as reflecting a psychic status which has resulted from a long exposure to stress or as symptoms of an increasing disfunction of the left ventricle, causing a low output, which results in feelings of tiredness?

This is probably not a good question. The syndrome forms a part of the total set of the prodromata of myocardial infarction and sudden death which consist mainly of angina pectoris, palpitations, and dyspnea. These elements influence each other in a cyclic way. It is unlikely that the presence of the syndrome of vital exhaustion and depression is a necessary or sufficient condition for the onset of myocardial infarction or sudden death. The same applies to chest pain, palpitations and dyspnea. But given the somatic predispositions, the described mental status may facilitate their appearance or shorten the way to the occurrence of the disease. These influences may go through direct neurohormonal avenues which may lead to small necroses in the myocardium, to spasms of the coronary arteries and/or to arrhythmias, or in a less direct way, by influencing those harmful habits which increase the levels of the somatic risk factors.

REFERENCES

Alonzo, A. (1975). Prodromata of myocardial infarction and sudden death. *Circulation, 52,* 1056–1062.

Appels, A. (1979). Psychological prodromata of myocardial infarction. *Journal of Psychosomatic Research, 23,* 405–421.

Appels, A., Pool, J., Kazemier, M., & van der Does, E. (1979). Psychische prodromata van het hartinfarct. *Ned. Tijdschr. Psychol., 34,* 213–223.

Dembroski, T. (Ed.), (1978). *The coronary prone behavior pattern.* New York: Springer.

Eyer, J. (1977). Prosperity as a cause of death. *International Journal of Health Services, 7,* 125–150.

Falger, P. (1987). Life changes in middle adulthood, coronary prone behavior and vital exhaustion-depression. In C. D. Spielberger, I. G. Sarason, & P. Defares (Eds.), *Stress and anxiety* (Vol. 11, pp. 151–161). Washington, D.C.: Hemisphere.

Glass, D. C. (1977). *Behavior patterns, stress and coronary disease.* Hillsdale, N.J.: Erlbaum Associates.

Kuller, L. (1979). Sudden death in atherosclerotic heart disease: The case for preventive medicine. *American Journal of Cardiology, 34,* 213–223.

Marmot, M. G., & Syme, S. L. (1976). Acculturation and coronary heart disease in Japanese Americans. *American Journal of Epidemiology, 104,* 225–247.

Rissanen, V. (1978). Promonitory symptoms and stress factors preceding sudden death from ischaemic heart disease. *Acta Medica Scandinavica, 204,* 389–396.

Russek, H. (1960). Emotional stress and coronary heart disease in American physicians. *American Journal of Medical Science, 240,* 711–721.

Suls, J., Gastorf, J. W., & Witenberg, S. H. (1979). Life events, psychological distress and the Type A coronary prone behavior pattern. *Journal of Psychosomatic Research, 23,* 315–319.

Verhagen, F., Nass, C., Appels, A., van Bastelaer, A., & Winnubst, J. (1980). A cross-validation of the A/B Typology in the Nederlands. *Psychotherapy and Psychosomatics.*

12

Life Changes in Middle Adulthood, Coronary-Prone Behavior, and Vital Exhaustion: Some Retrospective Findings

Paul R. J. Falger
University of Limburg

The contributions of psychosocial risk factors to the development of coronary heart disease (CHD) have been investigated by various research paradigms. The best developed approach involves the assessment of an overt behavioral disposition toward coronary-proneness, embodied in the Type A coronary-prone behavior pattern (CPBP) (Dembroski, Weiss, Shields, Haynes, & Feinleib, 1978). The relationship between stressful life changes (SLC) and imminent myocardial infarction (MI), or abrupt coronary death, has also been investigated extensively (Haney, 1980). More recently the study of the crucial period immediately preceding first MI, conjectured to be characterized by specific manifestations of vital exhaustion and depression (VE & D), has drawn attention (Appels, 1987).

The Type A coronary-prone behavior pattern has been characterized as: ". . . An action-emotion complex that can be observed in any person who is aggressively involved in a chronic, incessant struggle to achieve more and more in less and less time, and is required to do so against the opposing efforts of other things or other persons, . . . stemming from a fundamental and irretrievable sense of insecurity about the intrinsic value of the personality involved" (Friedman & Rosenman, 1977). The pathogenic consequences of this CPBP in both men and women over 40 years of age have been demonstrated in a series of pioneering retrospective studies (Friedman & Rosenman, 1959; Rosenman & Friedman, 1961). In a subsequent multifactorial prospective study that also included all other somatic risk factors, the Type A CPBP was established as an independent psychosocial risk constellation (Brand, 1978).

The impact of SLC on the development of MI also has been studied in both retrospective and prospective research. In a number of "case-control" studies, it was demonstrated that male subjects who survived first MI reported a rather significant increase in SLC, as measured on a modified version of the Social Readjustment Rating Scale (Holmes & Rahe, 1967), during the last two years before their premature coronary event (Rahe, Romo, Bennett, & Siltanen, 1974; Theorell & Rahe, 1972). In one of the few longitudinal studies to date, a like relationship was established (Theorell, 1976; Theorell, Lind, & Flodérus, 1975). The significant SLC in the former retrospective studies dealt primarily with important changes in both working conditions and family situation, although in the latter prospective investigation with a substantive increase in "work load" only.

Characteristic prodromal manifestations of VE & D in relation to MI were found in several studies (Appels, Pool, Lubsen, & van der Does, 1979; Orth-Gomér, Edwards, Erhardt, Fjögren, & Theorell, 1980). This constellation of VE & D consists, among other elements, of feelings of sometimes overwhelming listlessness, an increasing loss of emotional vitality and flexibility, and an urge to withdraw from social commitments, all of which may be discerned in the psychological history of a future heart patient during the last year before his MI.

So far these research paradigms have been developed relatively independently due to rather different theoretical orientations and methodological strategies, although some apparent interconnections have been suggested (Jenkins, 1978a). The present study explored some of these interrelationships. Two specific hypotheses were investigated:

1) Persons exhibiting the Type A coronary-prone behavior pattern are exposed to more stressful life changes than Type B individuals, because the life style of a Type A person is imbued with greater activity towards achievement.

2) Persons experiencing a manifest state of vital exhaustion and depression have recently been exposed to more stressful life changes than individuals who have not experienced emotional disturbances.

These hypotheses were derived from our theoretical model for the description and subsequent explanation of the impact of SLC in middle adulthood and preceding developmental phases. This framework is grafted upon current notions in life-span developmental psychology (Falger, 1983). However, to some extent these notions can be discerned among the historical antecedents of contemporary life changes research (Antonovsky & Kats, 1967; Dohrenwend & Dohrenwend, 1974). According to this dynamic developmental model, it is postulated that the "life structure" of middle-aged males who eventually develop CHD is characterized by the occurrence of crucial crisis situations surrounding important phases in their psychosocial development, which they are unable to anticipate and/or cope with adequately. The concept of a "life structure" consisting of consecutive phases that represent psychosocial developmental tasks to be resolved is derived from several investigations (Gould, 1972; Levinson, Darrow, Klein, Levinson, & McKee, 1978; Schaie, 1977). In most of these biographical studies it is demonstrated that even the most disparate lives are governed by the same underlying order: a sequence of stable developmental phases and of transitions. Individuals will anticipate these sequences and subsequently respond to them, however, with qualitatively different coping strategies. These may vary considerably in adequacy, in some instances resulting ultimately in dysfunctional behavior. It could be conceived that the Type A CPBP may contribute decisively to such pathogenic development if a critical number of significant SLC are encountered over one or more phases of the "life structure" even when continuous psychosocial change, and thus a capacity for anticipating and coping with newly emerging SLC is the most consistent feature in life-span development (Brim & Kagan, 1980; Thomae, 1979). These SLC may be conducive to VE & D, and consequently, may accelerate imminent MI.

One of the central aspects of the pathogenic CPBP, that is the dimension of "perceived controllability" may be particularly relevant in this context. On the basis of the laboratory experiments by Glass (1977), it can be concluded that a learned and, most probably, lasting inability to respond properly to a personal environment perceived as relatively uncontrollable may account for this feature. In his series of studies on uncontrollable stress, Glass demonstrated that Type A subjects initially performed "hyperresponsively" as long as the experimental setting was perceived as controllable by adequate action. Defective controlling behavior, however, will be engendered as soon as the uncontrollable nature of the stimuli becomes apparent. According to a recently formulated cognitive model of coping with psychological stress (Burchfield, 1979), such consistently inadequate perceptions of social situations (as can be found to some extent in the Glass experiments) should be deemed to lead to psychic exhaustion because of a failure to learn situational expectancies and appropriate responses. These aspects of both the Glass experiments and the Burchfield model do apply, then, to the discriminating situational circumstances in which the CPBP is elicited (compare Friedman & Rosenman, 1977).

METHOD

Subjects

A population sample of 136 male subjects between 39 and 41 yrs. of age participated in this cross-sectional study on the prevalence of stressful life changes in relation to the Type A coronary-prone behavior pattern, and to manifestations of vital exhaustion and depression. This sample was drawn randomly from a larger cohort of the same age of the male population of Maastricht (South-Limburg area, the Netherlands), that responded to our invitation to volunteer in completing mail questionnaires for research purposes. The study was performed during the fall of 1979.

Procedure

Each subject completed three mail questionnaires: (1) the authorized Dutch version of the Jenkins Activity Survey (JAS) for measuring the Type A coronary-prone behavior pattern, (2) the Maastricht questionnaire (MQ) on manifestations of vital exhaustion and depression, and (3) our newly developed Middle Adulthood Life Changes questionnaire (MALC).

1) The concurrent validity of the Dutch JAS-form had been established previously in a prevalence study on 258 middle-aged males (Appels, De Haes, & Schuurman, 1979). In this investigation, 36 out of the original 61 JAS-items did meet the pre-set contextual requirements for a Dutch population. From the different scoring systems that are available for the JAS, Bock's optimal scaling

procedure was used. In this study, the ultimate agreement between the obtained JAS scores and the participants' behavioral classification as based on the original Structured Interview assessment (Jenkins, 1978b; Rosenman, 1978), was 91% (Appels et al., 1979a).

2) The MQ is a self-administered questionnaire containing 58 items that will measure the prodrome of vital exhaustion and depression that is hypothesized to precede MI. In a hierarchical cluster analysis on the MQ, this prodromal complexion consisted of feelings of tiredness, helplessness, and hopelessness, loss of vitality, depression and hypochondriasis, sleep disturbances, and exhaustion (Appels et al., 1979b). In a 10-month prospective study with the MQ, it was demonstrated that 37 middle-aged men who suffered a new coronary event (including MI, and angina pectoris) within this interval reported a mean MQ score (133.4) that was almost two standard deviations elevated above the mean MQ score (98.4) obtained from 317 "healthy" middle-aged controls (Appels et al., 1979b).

3) The MALC that consists of 22 stressful life changes is being included for the first time in this type of investigation. The ten SLC items in the work and career domain were formulated on the basis of a critical analysis of the studies by Theorell et al. (1975) on SLC in middle adulthood, and subsequent MI (Falger, 1979). The twelve SLC items in the remaining family and social domain were selected from the contents of other life changes questionnaires like the Social Readjustment Rating scale (Holmes & Rahe, 1967), in so far as those do pertain explicitly to the notion of adult life crises (Riegel, 1975). These 22 SLC items are presented in Table 1, together with their frequency distributions in absolute numbers and in percentages of prevalence rates.

RESULTS

For purposes of statistical analysis, the scores on the JAS and on the MQ were dichotomized according to the following procedures:

1) The range of the scores on the JAS continuum was −25.480 to +38.150, the mean score being 9.002 (Standard Deviation 15.432). Employing the distribution characteristics of the former Dutch validity study (Appels, De Haes, & Schuurman, 1979), 70 subjects were designated as Type A and the remaining 66 as Type B. No further possible subdivisions into Type A1 and A2, or Type B3 and B4 were emphasized (Jenkins, 1978b).

2) The score range on the MQ was 56 to 124, with a mean of 78.816 (Standard Deviation: 17.001) when using an improved computational procedure as compared to the results of Appels, et al. (1979b). Given the usually rather positive skewness of the MQ distribution, the median (72.5) was employed as a dividing point. However, in most of the following computations the 32 subjects with a MQ score ≥ to one Standard Deviation above the mean (i.e., ≥ 95.817) were compared with the 32 lowest-scoring subjects on the MQ. This was primarily done in order to obtain two groups that would differ to a meaningful extent on the dimension of vital exhaustion and depression. Unlike the scores on the JAS continuum, the scores on the MQ so far discriminate towards the positive extreme of the scores range only, at least with respect to their associations with CHD, and MI (Appels et al., 1979b).

Table 1   Distribution of reported stressful life changes from the Middle
Adulthood Life Changes questionnaire

No.	Item	N^a	$\%^b$
	Family & social domain		
10	Serious illness/death of relatives	56	41.2
03	Effected considerable loan	50	36.8
06	Serious marital conflicts	45	33.1
09	Conflicts with relatives	43	31.6
11	Lost close friends	35	25.7
04	Continuous educational problems with children	34	25.0
12	Changes personal habits	33	24.3
02	Financial troubles	30	22.1
01	Moved to other house	19	13.9
08	Serioius illness/death in family	15	11.0
05	Children left home	5	3.7
07	Divorce	4	2.9
	Total	369	
	Work & career domain		
16	Working overtime	83	61.0
17	Considerable increase in job responsibility	56	41.2
13	Changes in social interactions at work	42	30.9
15	Problem with supervisor about work	41	30.2
14	Problems with subordinates about work	38	27.9
21	Considered voluntary changing to other work	32	23.6
18	Promotion to higher hierarchical level	28	20.6
19	Begun studying for improving present position	25	18.4
20	Compelled to look for other job	7	5.2
22	Retirement/inability to continue working on medical grounds	1	0.7
	Total	353	

[a]Sample size = 136 men, age 39–41.
[b]Prevalence rates.

3) On the MALC an average of six SLC was reported over the last two years, ranging from none at all to eleven. The reported numbers of SLC in both the family and social, and the work and career domains were attributed to either one of two categories: "0–3" and "3 or more" SLC. For computational operations in which a total MALC score over both domains is involved, these categories are: "0–4," and "5 or more" SLC, respectively.

4) In the first series of one-way ANOVAs, the scores on the JAS of the total population under study were broken down by total MALC scores, and by MALC scores on the family and social and work and career domains. The results are presented in Table 2.

In a second series of one-way ANOVAs, the results on the MQ of the entire sample were broken down by total MALC scores, and also by MALC scores on the family and social and work and career domains. These results are shown in Table 2.

Table 2 One-way ANOVAs on JAS, MQ, and reported stressful life changes from the Middle Adulthood Life Changes questionnaire

	SS	F[a]	P
ANOVAs on the Jenkins Activity Survey (JAS)			
JAS × total stressful life changes	3915.07	18.580	.0000
JAS × family & social stressful life changes	1471.57	6.427	.0124
JAS × work & career stressful life changes	2288.85	10.271	.0017
ANOVAs on the Maastricht Questionnaire (MQ)			
MQ × total stressful life changes	2496.23	9.155	.0030
MQ × family & social stressful life changes	1542.22	5.514	.0203
MQ × work & career stressful life changes	1632.30	5.851	.0169

SS = Sum of squares.
[a]Degrees of freedom: 1,134.

5) The striking significant differences in these ANOVAs are displayed visually in Figures 1 to 3. In Figure 1 the differences in "life changes density" between Type A and Type B subjects are presented with respect to the reported number of SLC in the family and social domain, in Figure 2 with regard to the number of SLC in the work and career domain. In Figure 3, the differences in "life changes density" with regard to both domains are presented for the 32 individuals, characterized as "emotionally exhausted and depressed," and the 32 lowest-scoring subjects on the MQ.

6) On the basis of these significant results, the data was first analyzed by a series of one-tailed χ^2-analyses in which separate MALC items in both the family and social and work and career domains would discriminate between Type A ($N = 70$) and Type B ($N = 66$) subjects.

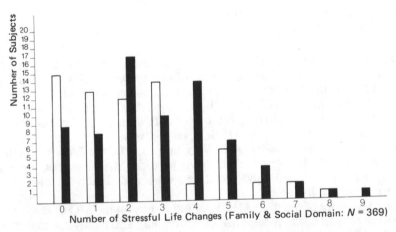

Figure 1 Life changes density of Type A vs. Type B subjects in the family & social domain: ■ = Type A ($N = 70$); □ = Type B ($N = 66$).

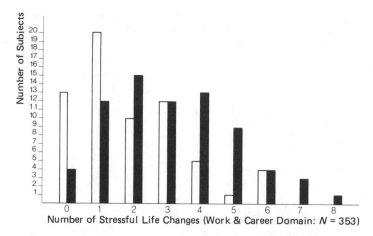

Figure 2 Life changes density of Type A vs. Type B subjects in the work & career domain: ■ = Type A (*N* = 70), □ = Type B (*N* = 66).

In the former domain, only two out of twelve SLC as measured on the MALC were reported significantly more frequent by Type A individuals. These two discriminating SLC are presented in Table 3.

In the work and career domain, however, 7 out of 10 SLC were indicated significantly more often by Type A subjects than by their Type B counterparts. These seven SLC are presented in Table 3.

7) In a second series of one-tailed χ^2-tests the data was analyzed for which separate MALC items in both domains would differentiate between individuals, characterized as "emotionally exhausted and depressed" (*N*=32) and the 32 persons without such emotional disturbances as indicated by their scoring lowest on the MQ.

In the family and social domain, 6 out of 12 SLC were reported significantly more often by "emotionally exhausted" individuals. These six discriminating items are presented in Table 3.

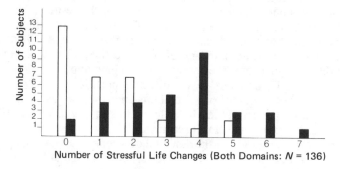

Figure 3 Life changes density of exhausted/depressed vs. non-exhausted/non-depressed subjects in both domains: ■ = Exhausted/Depressed (*N* = 32); □ = Non-Exhausted, Non-Depressed (*N* = 32).

Table 3 One-tailed χ^2-analyses on reported stressful life changes from the
Middle Adulthood Life Changes questionnaire, JAS, and MQ

No.	Item	JAS[a]	MQ[b]
	Family & social domain		
04	Continuous educational problems with children	N.S.	8.95****
06	Serious marital conflicts	8.86****	7.27****
03	Effected considerable loan	4.17**	4.66**
02	Financial troubles	N.S.	3.78*
11	Lost close friends	N.S.	3.51*
12	Changes in personal habits	N.S.	2.94*
	Work & career domain		
14	Problems with subordinates about work	12.66****	N.S.
15	Problems with supervisor about work	8.88****	N.S.
16	Working overtime	6.90****	N.S.
13	Changes in social interactions at work	5.52***	7.94****
17	Considerable increase in job responsibility	5.35**	N.S.
18	Promotion to higher hierarchical level	3.36*	N.S.
21	Considered voluntary changing to other work	3.12*	3.92**

[a] Sample size: 136 men, age 39–41.
[b] Sample size: 64 men, age 39–41.
  *Degrees of freedom: 1; $p < .050$
 **Degrees of freedom: 1; $p < .025$
***Degrees of freedom: 1; $p < .010$
****Degrees of freedom: 1; $p < .001$

In the work and career domain, only 2 out of 10 SLC were indicated as significantly more frequent by subjects characterized as "emotionally exhausted." Those two SLC are presented in Table 3.

DISCUSSION

With respect to cross-sectional research in behavioral medicine, it has been pointed out that the retrospective character of this methodological procedure may hamper to some degree the generalizability of the results (Casey, Masuda, & Holmes, 1967; Jenkins, Hurst, & Rose, 1979) in particular when MI patients are to be compared with "healthy" controls (De Faire & Theorell, 1976). However, since the prime objective of our investigation was to explore some interrelationships between the research paradigms about the Type A CPBP, SLC and VE & D, and not to identify the peculiar characteristics of the psychosocial "life structures" of MI patients and controls (as we have begun to explore in another recent study by Falger, Bressers, & Dijkstra, 1980) these findings do encourage some closer scrutiny.

Both our hypotheses about the assumed differences in "life changes density" (Figures 1–3) between Type A subjects, or "emotionally exhausted and depressed" individuals and their respective counterparts have at least fully been corroborated in general terms (Table 2), and to a considerable degree for separate SLC (Table 3). Moreover, after our investigation was finished, we came upon comparable results that were reported in some recently completed studies on these same issues. In the first of these retrospective studies (Suls, Gastorf, & Witenberg, 1979), it was demonstrated that Type A college students ($N = 63$) identified as such on the student version of the JAS (compare Glass, 1977), did report the occurrence of a substantially larger amount of SLC significantly more often than Type B students ($N = 62$). In a second cross-sectional study (Burke & Weir, 1980), it was shown that middle-aged Type A individuals ($N = 127$) characterized by their relative degree of displaying Type A behavior on the Sales' scale, indicated significantly larger prevalence rates of occupational demands, concrete SLC at work, greater interference of work with home and family life and less marital satisfaction. In a third prospective study over a 3-year period, on 517 "healthy" middle-aged subjects (Warheit, 1979), it was concluded that subjects with high SLC scores at the end of the investigation had significantly more depressive symptomatology, as compared with individuals with average SLC scores. In most instances, in our own study as well as in those latter studies, the very character of the crucial SLC that were reported may be said to be congruent with the theoretical notions underlying the constructs of the CPBP, and of VE & D.

Thus, the SLC "problems with subordinates about work," "problems with supervisor about work," "working overtime," and "considerable increase in job responsibility" that in our study were reported significantly more often by Type A subjects (Table 3), may be characterized as representing specific dimensions of "perceived controllability," as applied to the personal work and career domain. The individual high-set standards with regard to achievement at work that are preponderant in the Type A CPBP (Friedman & Rosenman, 1959; Burke & Weir, 1980) may get frustrated if adequate "control" over the work environment cannot be exerted or sustained over a substantial length of time (compare Glass, 1977). This sense of frustration might be amplified by a parallel loss of "control" in the family and social domain, as exemplified in the SLC "serious marital conflicts" and "effected considerable loan" that were reported more frequently on the MALC by Type A individuals than by their Type B counterparts (Table 3), over the last two years.

On the other hand, the SLC "changes in social interactions at work" and particularly "considered voluntary changing to other work" that figure so prominently among the significant differences in "life changes density" between subjects that are "emotionally exhausted and depressed" and individuals that are not (Table 3), could indicate a gradual withdrawal from responsibility and social interactions in the work and career domain and be exemplary of the prodome of VE & D (Appels et al., 1979b). This withdrawal might be precipitated, then, by a prolonged failure to find necessary emotional support in the family and social domain, as may be evident from the SLC "continuous educational problems with children," "serious marital conflicts," and "lost close friends" that are indicated significantly more often by the former category of subjects (Table 3). An additional burden on the "life changes density" of these individuals may be inherent in the SLC "financial troubles" and "effected considerable loan" (Table 3). An indication that the "emotionally exhausted" subject may be engaged in physical efforts to cope with this "tabulation of misery" may be evident from the SLC "changes in personal habits," that in particular describes changes in nutritional, drinking, and sleeping patterns, according to the extensive formulation of this item in the MALC.

With respect to this latter tentative conclusion it should be mentioned that a crucial distinction between the proposed "life structures" of Type A and Type B subjects has been ascribed to continuous differences in relatively high, and moderate levels of bodily energy-mobilization and expenditure (Appels, 1984; Falger et al., 1980). In coping with consecutive SLC it is assumed that the Type A individual will mobilize his physical and psychic resources with less restraint than his more placid counterpart in order to regain the perceived "balance" of his previous, self-imposed high level of performance (and probably to mask as well his possibly depressed emotional condition that may result). The Type A subject thus will expose himself to the hazards of gradual depletion of necessary energy. It is at this point that the parallel will become apparent between our contemporary industrial society, which wastes its natural resources including human beings on an unprecedented scale, and the increasingly dominant and clearly pathogenic coronary-prone behavior pattern that has been emerging over the last decades in order to meet the demands to sustain its unhampered functioning (Eyer, 1977).

REFERENCES

Antonovsky, A., & Kats, R. (1967). The life crisis history as a tool in epidemiological research. *Journal Health Social Behavior, 8,* 15–21.

Appels, A. (1987). The syndrome of vital exhaustion and depression. In C. D. Spielberger, I. G. Sarason, & P. B. Defares (Eds.), *Stress and anxiety* (Vol. 11, pp. 143–150). Washington, D.C.: Hemisphere.

Appels, A., De Haes, W., & Schuurman, J. (1979a). Een test ter meting van het "coronary-prone behavior pattern" Type A. *Nederlands Tijdschrift Psychologie, 34,* 181–188.

Appels, A., Pool, J., Lubsen, J., & van der Does, E. (1979b). Psychological prodromata of myocardial infarction. *Journal Psychomatic Research, 23,* 405–421.

Brand, R. (1978). Coronary-prone behavior as an independent risk factor for coronary heart disease. In T. Dembroski, S. Weiss, J. Shields, S. G. Haynes, & M. Feinleib (Eds.), *Coronary-prone behavior.* New York: Springer.

Brim, O., & Kagan, J. (1980). Constancy and change: A view of the issues. In O. Brim and J. Kagan (Eds.), *Constancy and change in human development.* Cambridge, Mass.: Harvard University Press.

Burchfield, S. (1979). The stress response: A new perspective. *Psychosomatic Medicine, 41,* 661–672.

Burke, R., & Weir, T. (1980). The Type A experience: Occupational and life demands, satisfaction and well being. *Journal Human Stress, 6,* 28–38.

Casey, R., Masuda, M., & Holmes, T. (1967). Quantitative study of recall of life events. *Journal Psychosomatic Research, 11,* 239–247.

De Faire, U., & Theorell, T. (1976). Life changes and myocardial infarction: How useful are life changes measurements? *Scandinavian Journal Social Medicine, 4,* 115–122.

Dembroski, T., Weiss, S., Shields, J., Haynes, S. G., & Feinleib, M. (Eds.). (1978). *Coronary-prone behavior.* New York: Springer.

Dohrenwend, B. S., & Dohrenwend, B. P. (1974). A brief historical introduction to research on stressful life events. In B. S. Dohrenwend, & B. P. Dohrenwend (Eds.), *Stressful life events: Their nature and effects.* New York: Wiley.

Eyer, J. (1977). Prosperity as a cause of death. *International Journal Health Services, 7,* 125–150.

Falger, P. (1979). Changes in "work load" as potential risk constellation for myocardial infarction: A review. *Gedrag, Tijdschrift voor Psychologie, 7,* 96–114.

Falger, P. (1983). Pathogenic life changes in middle adulthood and coronary heart disease: A life-span developmental perspective. *International Journal Aging Human Development, 16,* 7–27.

Falger, P., Bressers, I., & Dijkstra, P. (1980). Levenslooppatronen van hartinfarct-patiënten en van controlegroepen: Enkele overeenkomsten en verschillen. *Gerontologie, 11,* 240–257.

Friedman, M., & Rosenman, R. (1959). Association of specific overt behavior pattern with blood and cardiovascular findings. *Journal American Medical Association, 169,* 1286–1296.

Friedman, M., & Rosenman, R. (1977). The key cause: Type A behavior pattern. In A. Monat & R. Lazarus (Eds.), *Stress and coping.* New York: Columbia University Press.

Glass, D. (1977). *Behavior patterns, stress, and coronary disease.* Hillsdale, N.J.: Erlbaum.

Gould, R. (1972). The phases of adult life: A study in developmental psychology. *American Journal Psychiatry, 129,* 33–43.

Haney, C. (1980). Life events as precursors of coronary heart disease. *Social Science Medicine, 14,* 119–126.

Holmes, T., & Rahe, R. (1967). The social readjustment rating scale. *Journal Psychosomatic Research, 11,* 213–218.

Jenkins, C. D. (1978a). Behavioral risk factors in coronary artery disease. *Annual Review Medicine, 29,* 543–562.

Jenkins, C. D. (1978b). A comparative review of the interview and questionnaire methods in the assessment of the coronary-prone behavior pattern. In T. Dembroski, S. Weiss, J.Shields, S. Haynes, & M. Feinleib, (Eds.). *Coronary-prone behavior.* New York: Springer.

Jenkins, C., Hurst, M., & Rose, R. (1979). Life changes: Do people really remember? *Archives General Psychiatry, 36,* 379–384.

Levinson, D., Darrow, C., Klein, E., Levinson, M., & McKee, B. (1978). *The seasons of a man's life.* New York: Ballantine.

Orth-Gomér, K., Edwards, M. E., Erhardt, L., Fjögren, A., & Theorell, T. (1980). Relation between ventricular arrhythmias and psychological profile. *Acta Medica Scandinavica, 207,* 31–36.

Rahe, R., Romo, M., Bennett, L., & Siltanen, P. (1974). Recent life changes, myocardial infarction, and abrupt coronary death. *Archives Internal Medicine, 133,* 221–228.

Riegel, K. (1975). Adult life crises: A dialectical interpretation of development. In N. Datan & L. Ginsberg (Eds.), *Life-span developmental psychology: Normative life crises.* New York: Academic Press.

Rosenman, R. (1978). The interview method of assessment of the coronary-prone behavior pattern. In T. M. Dembroski, S. M. Weiss, T. W. Shields, S. G. Haynes, & M. Feinleib (Eds.), *Coronary-prone behavior.* New York: Springer.

Rosenman, R., & Friedman, M. (1961). Association of specific behavior pattern in women with blood and cardiovascular findings. *Circulation, 24,* 1173–1184.

Schaie, K. (1977). Toward a stage theory of adult cognitive development. *International Journal Aging Human Development, 8,* 129–138.

Suls, J., Gastorf, J., & Witenberg, S. (1979). Life events, psychological distress, and the Type A coronary-prone behavior pattern. *Journal Psychosomatic Research, 23,* 315–319.

Theorell, T. (1976). Selected illnesses and somatic factors in relation to two psychological stress indices: A prospective study on middle-aged construction building workers. *Journal Psychosomatic Research, 20,* 7–20.

Theorell, T., Lind, E., & Flodérus, B. (1975). The relationship of disturbing life changes and emotions to the early development of myocardial infarction and other serious illnesses. *International Journal Epidemiology, 4,* 281–293.

Theorell, T., & Rahe, R. (1972). Behavior and life satisfaction characteristics of Swedish subjects with myocardial infarction. *Journal Chronic Diseases, 25,* 139–147.

Thomae, H. (1979). The concept of development and life-span developmental psychology. In P. Baltes, & O. Brim (Eds.), *Life-span development and behavior* (Vol. 2). New York: Academic Press.

Warheit, G. (1979). Life events, coping, stress, and depressive symptomatology. *American Journal Psychiatry, 136,* 502–507.

13

Psychoneuroendocrinological Correlates of Myocardial Infarction

*P. Pancheri, M. Bellaterra, G. Reda, S. Matteoli, E. Santarelli, G. Pugliese,
S. Mosticoni, and A. Figà-Talamanca*
University of Rome

Acute myocardial infarction (AMI) constitutes an intensely stressful event, which threatens an individual's physical integrity and survival, and often decisively changes the entire life structure of the afflicted individual. Moreover, infarction produces painful sensations, as well as particularly intense alterations of the somatic coenesthesia, and generally requires hospitalization in specialized therapeutic units where the patient is exposed to deaths and the suffering of other patients affected by the same illness.

The characteristics of AMI make it possible to study, both retrospectively and prospectively, the individual reactions of predominantly middle-aged male subjects to acute stress, within a relatively homogeneous population. These are studied from three different perspectives: first, at the level of emotional reactions and the mechanisms used by patients in coping with the stressful situation; secondly, at the level of psychoneuroendocrine arousal associated with stress; and, finally, in terms of clinical correlates for these two variables.

In a previous study (Pancheri, Bellaterra, Matteoli, Cristofari, Polizzi, & Puletti, 1978) it was demonstrated that *state* and *trait* anxiety and the MMPI personality profile, on admission to a coronary care unit (CCU), were effective predictors of the short-term course of illness. Elevated state anxiety and inadequate coping mechanisms have a negative influence on patients with infarction, and are associated with complications during their period of observation with the CCU. The results of this study confirmed findings of other investigators who also observed that stressful situations occurring prior to infarction were of prognostic importance (Rahe, Romo, Bennett & Siltanen, 1974; Theorell & Rahe, 1974; Theorell & Rahe, 1975).

Stress reactions are also characterized by behavioral and psychoneuroendocrine changes which act upon the biological substratum, conditioning the organic defenses of the cardiac system (Cairncross & Barret, 1975; Greenhoot & Reichenback, 1969; Raab, 1968). In AMI, such problems have been studied primarily from the viewpoint of corticosurrenal and catecholamine reactions, but systematic analyses of the relationships between psychological-emotional and endocrine reactions are relatively few.

Immediately after infarction, the hypothalamus-pituitary-adrenal (HPA) axis is activated, resulting in marked increase of plasma cortisol values. There is also a tendency toward reduction in cortisol levels during the subsequent 72 hrs, with elevated plasma cortisol values associated with the adverse course of infarction (Bailey, Abernethy, & Beaven, 1967; De Elio, Bosh, & Santos, 1975; Logan & Murdoch, 1966; Strange, Vetter, Rowe, & Oliver, 1974). These data suggest that the initial cortisol values can be used as a prognostic indicator for the short-term evolution of illness (Chopra, Thadani, Olive, Portal, & Parkes, 1972; Klein & Palmer, 1963; Prakash, Parmley, Horwath, & Swan, 1972; Sabato, Petrozzi, Marana, Magalini, Scrascia, & Bondoli, 1976/77; Wienes, 1977).

There may also be a correlation between the intensity of the stress reaction as reflected in the arousal of the HPA axis and the complications of the infarction. However, psychometric evaluations are needed in order to clarify the role that emotions and coping mechanisms play in triggering and maintaining stress reactions. In a recent study, Freeburg and his associates (Freeburg, Brown, Holdofsky, & Howley, 1970) investigated the relation between neuroendocrine (GH and cortisol) and emotional parameters during the acute phase of AMI and its clinical course during a 2-year follow-up. This study showed that surviving patients had lower initial GH values and consumed a smaller dosage of tranquilizers than the nonsurvivors. However, Freeburg's study did not focus specifically on the emotional and personality correlates of neuroendocrine arousal.

Studies of catecholamine activation tend to indicate a concordant increase in both plasma and urinary catecholamine activity immediately after infarction, with a less rapid reduction than that found for cortisol. There is also evidence of a more negative outcome with high initial plasma catecholamine values, especially with regard to the onset of arrhythmias, but the findings are less consistent than in the case of cortisol (Jewitt, Reid, & Thomas, 1969; McDonald, Baker, Bray, McDonald, & Resticeux, 1969; Strange et al., 1974; Strange, Rowe, & Oliver, 1978; Vetter, Strange, Adams, & Oliver, 1974).

More definitive results have been obtained for plasma values of cyclic adenosine 3" 5"-monophosphate (cAMP), which is used as an index of global adrenergic activity after the onset of infarction. Immediately after infarction, cAMP values have been elevated and both initial values and subsequent changes appear to be significantly related to the clinical course of events (Platania, Liberatore, Reda, Magnatta, Spallone, Lacerna, & Lauro, 1979; Rabinowitz, Kligerman, & Parmley, 1974; Reda, Puglione, Santarelli, Ferretti, Portaleoni, Matteoli, & Lauro, in press; Strange et al., 1974). The ineffectiveness of coping mechanisms is also likely to produce complications and intense stress reactions when endocrine levels are significantly elevated.

The goal of this study was to investigate emotional and neuroendocrine reactions to stress caused by infarction. A global interpretative model will also be presented

METHOD

The experimental design consisted of both prospective and retrospective elements. The subjects were patients admitted to the CCU at the Rome

University Hospital with a diagnosis of myocardial infarction. The day after admission, hormonal rates of cortisol and cAMP were determined. By the second day after admission, a psychometric examination and standardized anamnestic investigation were completed. Hormonal values and state anxiety were measured daily for five consecutive days.

Subjects

The patient group was comprised of 24 males with acute myocardial infarction; all patients were admitted to the CCU within the 12-hr period following the onset of chest pain. The patients ranged in age from 35 to 65 years (average age, 51.95), and were from a medium-low socioeconomic level. Diabetics and patients with hypertension or pacemakers were excluded. Patients treated with alpha and beta adrenergic blockers and/or stimulating drugs and xanthine bronchial dilators during their hospital stay, or during the two previous weeks, were also excluded. A flow chart indicating the decision rules for selecting the patients is presented in Figure 1.

Diagnosis of myocardial infarction was made on the basis of clinical, electrocardiographic and laboratory data in accordance with the criteria of the New York Health Association (NYHA) (1973). During hospitalization, all patients underwent a series of clinical examinations and laboratory tests in order to establish the type and severity of infarction. The location of infarction was anterior in 14 patients and inferior in 10 others. Anterolateral and lateral infarctions are grouped with anterior infarctions: Patients classified as inferior infarctions included inferior and true posterior infarction. Besides analgesic treatment, the only other routine therapy generally practiced was that of nitrates. Emergency therapy employed in cases of cardiac failure, arrhythmias, or other complications did not produce evident effects upon the cAMP and cortisol concentrations.

PROCEDURE

At the end of the observation CCU period, the experimental group was subdivided into four subgroups, based on the presence and severity of complications observed after the initial psychoneuroendocrine evaluation. Psychometric, psychoendocrine and anamnestic profiles were established in terms of complicated and noncomplicated patient illness. During the first five days, routine practice also included daily electrocardiograms and serum enzyme determinations (CPK, GOT).

Hormonal Evaluation

In order to evaluate the metabolic responses of stress, plasma levels of cotisol and cAMP were assessed. At 8 a.m., for five consecutive days, blood samples were drawn. In order to avoid stress due to venipuncture, the needle was inserted 20 minutes before drawing the samples. As soon as it was drawn, part of the blood sample (2 cc) was put into test tubes kept under ice which contained 50 ul. of EDTA 0.5M for cAMP; for the cortisol assessment, the

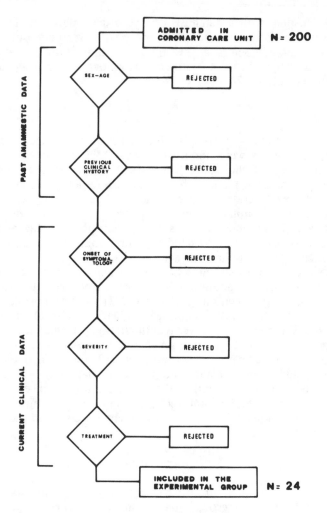

Figure 1 Decision rules for selection of AMI patients.

other part of the blood sample (3 cc) was put into test tubes without a reactive. The test tubes were immediately placed in a refrigerated centrifuge for ten min at 2000 rpm, and the plasma was then put into a deep freezer at −20 degrees centigrade. Plasma cortisol was dosed by use of the radioimmunoassay method (RIA), cAMP was dosed by means of the protein binding assay, according to Gilman (1970). For technical reasons, the dosage on cAMP was carried out in only 12 cases.

Psychometric Evaluation

Evaluation of stressful life events was carried out by means of the Life Experience Survey (LES) (Johnson & Sarason, 1978; Sarason, Johnson, &

Siegel, 1979), which consists of a list of 57 stress events. This instrument was selected because it requires the subject to rate the stressfulness of each event. In studies with patients having various illnesses, it has been found that negative life change as measured by the LES is more discriminating between various diagnostic groups than scores obtained with other similar instruments (Pancheri, DeMartino, Biondi, & Mostjconi, 1979). In this study, the LES negative change score (NCS) was used. This score is obtained by totaling all the negative scores that a subject assigns to the stressful events.

The Italian version of the LES was administered immediately after the psychiatric interview. On the second day of hospitalization, the Minnesota Multiphasic Personality Inventory (MMPI) (Dahlstrom & Welsh, 1960) was administered in the CCU.

Anxiety was assessed by means of the State-Trait Anxiety Inventory (STAI) (Spielberger, Gorsuch, & Lushene, 1970). This instrument was chosen because of its clinical validity and the relevance of the anxiety theory on which it is based for the present study. The state-trait distinction has been found to be especially useful in distinguishing between various types of psychosomatic patients (Pancheri et al., 1979). During hospitalization in the CCU, the patients were given the STAI scale each day, immediately after drawing blood for the plasma cortisol and cAMP evaluations (8 a.m.).

Experimental Subgroups

Following their release from the CCU, the patients were subdivided into four groups on the basis of the clinical data obtained during hospitalization. The following three parameters were taken into consideration:

1. Incidence of serious ventricular arrhythmias (VF and VT) or complete AV block.
2. Other arrhythmias (SVT, sinus tachycardia lasting more than two days, first and second AV block).
3. Clinical and radiological signs of pump failure.

Patients were assigned to the "complicated" group ($N = 6$) if they simultaneously presented both arrhythmias and serious pump failure. The "noncomplicated" group ($N = 9$) consisted of patients having none of the foregoing characteristics. Two groups of intermediate severity were defined by the extent of heart failure and arrhythmias. The clinical characteristics of the four groups are presented in Table 1. A score of one to four was assigned to each patient, depending on the severity of complications.

RESULTS

The regression of the LES Negative Change Scores (NCS) for time periods of 5 and 10 years prior to infarction was computed for the total group. The dependent variables in these analyses were: initial and mean postinfarction hormonal values, state and trait anxiety scores, and complication severity scores. Linear correlations were also calculated between severity scores, initial and mean STAI scores, and initial and mean cortisol values.

Table 1 Clinical characteristics of CCU patients

Subgroups	N	Complications	Severity scale
1	9	No heart failure no arrhythmias	1
2	4	Heart failure + no arrhythmias	2
3	5	Heart failure + arrhythmias + Heart failure + + no arrhythmias	3
4	6	Heart failure ≥+ + arrhythmias ≥+	4

The major analysis of intergroup differences centered on differences between the two extreme groups. In addition, the differences between the more complicated groups (3 & 4) and the relatively uncomplicated groups (1 & 2) were evaluated. Intergroup differences in NCS values over 5 and 10 years, STAI scores, MMPI single scale scores, and initial and mean cortisol and cAMP values were evaluated, using the t-tests for independent groups.

Group profiles over time for the STAI scores, and cortisol and cAMP levels were also calculated: Differences between groups were evaluated by means of two-way analyses of variance for repeated measures. In order to evaluate the relative influence of the variables that contributed to the intergroup differences, discriminant analyses were performed for those variables for which significant differences were found in the univariate analysis. These analyses were first carried out for the two extreme subgroups (Group 4 vs. Group 1), and then for discriminating between the following three subgroups: Group 4 versus Groups 3 and 2 versus Group 1.

Regression of Life Stress Events

The regression of NCS values on the dependent variables is reported in Table 2. Significant relationships for the NCS scores 5 years prior to infarction were found for both initial and mean values of cortisol and cAMP, and for severity scores. The regression of the NCS values on trait anxiety, and on initial and mean state anxiety were not statistically significant.

The regression of NCS scores for 10 years prior to infarction are also reported in Table 2. The only significant findings were for mean cortisol levels and the severity of complications. The regression of NCS on the severity scale was −.41 for 5 years and −.51 for 10 years.

The correlations of the severity scores with cortisol and STAI scores are reported in Table 3. These correlations indicate the relations between severity of infarction with the degree of subjective distress and activation of the HPA axis while the patients were in the CCU, and between individual differences in anxiety proneness and severity of infarction. Correlations between state anxiety and cortisol levels, which indicate the relation between the subjective and biological levels of distress, are also reported in Table 3. The correlation between initial and mean cortisol values and severity scores, and between trait anxiety and severity were statistically significant: The correlations between mean and initial state anxiety scores with severity and cortisol were not significant.

Intergroup Differences

MMPI Profiles

A comparison of the MMPI profiles for the extreme groups (Group 4 vs. Group 1) revealed that the Complicated group was more deviant, and that the general configuration of the profiles was similar in both groups. The mean profile for the Complications group showed 2-1-3 code type, with the T score for the D scale higher than 70 and Hs at the upper limits of the norm. The profile of the Noncomplicated group was completely within normal limits. Significant differences between these groups was found for the F scale ($p < .02$), the D scale ($p < .01$), and the Pt scale ($p < .05$). In the analysis comparing Groups 4 & 3 with Groups 2 & 1, smaller differences were found that were significant only for the F ($p < .05$) and D scales ($p < .05$). The mean profile for the complicated cases was at the upper limits of the norm, while that for the noncomplicated cases was within the normal limits.

Table 2   Regression of the NCS values on
cortisol, STAI X-1, STAI X-2, cAMP
and severity

	r	df	p
NCS (5 yrs)			
Cortisol _	.4728	22	.02
Cortisol X̄	.3681	22	.05
STAI X-1	.3052	22	n.s.
STAI X̄-1	.2589	22	n.s.
cAMP _	.8261	10	.001
cAMP X̄	.7748	10	.01
STAI X-2	.1202	22	n.s.
Severity scale	.4149	22	.05
NCS (10 yrs)			
Cortisol _	.2877	22	n.s.
Cortisol X̄	.4168	22	.05
STAI X-1	.1995	22	n.s.
STAI X̄-1	.1922	22	n.s.
cAMP _	.3867	10	n.s.
cAMP X̄	.3029	10	n.s.
STAI X-2	.2162	22	n.s.
Severity scale	.5139	22	.02

Table 3 Correlations among severity scale, STAI
X-1, STAI X-2 and between STAI X-1 and
cortisol

STAI $\underline{X}$-1	—	Severity scale	.1656	22	n.s.
STAI $\overline{X}$-1	—	Severity scale	.1724	22	n.s.
Cortisol	—	Severity scale	.4243	22	.05
Cortisol $\overline{X}$	—	Severity scale	.6570	22	.001
STAI X-2	—	Severity scale	.5239	22	.01
STAI $\overline{X}$-1	—	Cortisol $\overline{X}$	.2739	22	n.s.
STAI X-1	—	Cortisol	.3900	22	n.s.

Life Stress

In the analysis for negative life events (NCS) for both the 5- and 10-year periods, differences were significant for the extreme groups ($p < .05$) as well as for the enlarged groups ($p < .05$). The Complicated group reported more stressful events for both time periods, as can be seen in Table 4.

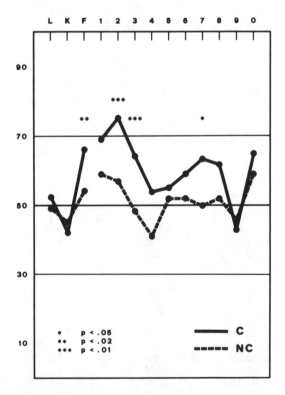

Figure 2 MMPI, groups 4 vs. 1.

State and Trait Anxiety

Both state and trait anxiety scores were more elevated for the Complicated group than for the Noncomplicated group; however, only the difference for trait anxiety was statistically significant ($p < .01$), as can be noted in Table 4.

Hormonal Values

The initial and mean values of cortisol and cAMP were more elevated in the Complicated group for both the extreme groups and the enlarged groups. However, only for the mean values of cortisol ($p < .01$) and cAMP ($p < .02$), calculated for the five measures taken on consecutive days, were these differences statistically significant, as can be seen in Table 4. Because of the small number of subjects in the extreme groups, the calculation for cAMP was based solely on the enlarged groups.

Group Profiles for Changes in State Anxiety, Cortisol and cAMP

The temporal profile for the mean STAI scores of the Complicated group (Group 4), reported in Figure 3, was consistently higher than that for the Noncomplicated group (Group 1). The ANOVA for the means obtained for

Table 4 Mean, SD, and significance of the differences between complicated and noncomplicated patients (extreme groups)

	Complicated		Noncomplicated			
	$\overline{X}$	SD	$\overline{X}$	SD	t	p
NCS-5 yrs	6.5	2.36	3.5	2.49	2.17	.05
NCS-10 yrs	20.0	14.22	5.9	1.96	2.21	.05
STAI X-1						
1	50.0	6.24	46.1	8.65	0.94	n.s.
2	49.5	7.80	46.7	8.72	0.58	n.s.
3	50.8	6.96	45.2	9.21	1.25	n.s.
4	49.3	4.06	43.5	7.54	1.79	n.s.
5	46.1	3.13	42.3	5.96	1.51	n.s.
STAI X-2	54.1	2.67	44.2	6.90	3.66	.01
Cortisol						
1	31.5	16.07	17.4	6.13	1.87	n.s.
2	28.8	11.17	14.8	3.01	2.74	.02
3	26.0	6.40	12.5	4.22	4.18	.01
4	17.2	6.84	14.4	3.33	0.83	n.s.
5	20.0	7.85	13.8	4.12	1.61	n.s.
cAMP[a]						
1	30.5	6.80	25.4	4.51	1.40	n.s.
2	27.6	11.13	21.5	6.15	1.08	n.s.
3	23.0	4.61	14.8	1.67	3.72	.01
4	23.6	2.35	14.2	5.90	3.31	.01
5	19.3	4.45	13.5	5.25	1.90	n.s.

[a]The cAMP analyses were carried out on the enlarged groups.

consecutive pairs of observations resulted in a significant F-ratio (p < .02); however, no significant differences between group means were found using t-tests for single readings (see Table 4). The analysis for the enlarged groups showed a trend similar to the findings for the extreme groups, but the differences were smaller as might be expected.

The profile of STAI scores indicated the persistence of elevated anxiety values in the Complicated group up until the fourth day. In contrast, by the second day there was a tendency toward reduction of state anxiety in the Noncomplicated group. The mean STAI State-Anxiety scores for the Complicated group taken in the CCU were significantly higher than STAI scores for the Italian male population (Pancheri, Bernabei, Bellaterra, & Tartaglione, 1976), whereas, for the Noncomplicated group, these differences were not significant. The Italian STAI normative sample was based on the responses of 370 normal subjects (165 males, 205 females). The males were chiefly military draftees plus a few college undergraduates; the females were all undergraduate college students. The age range of this normative sample was 20 to 27 years.

In the comparison of extreme and enlarged groups for cortisol, the ANOVAs indicated statistically significant differences between groups and

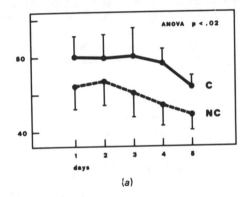

(a)

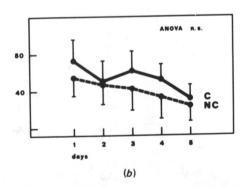

(b)

Figure 3 (a) STAI X-1, groups 4 vs. 1; (b) STAI X-1, groups 4 + 3 vs. 1 + 2.

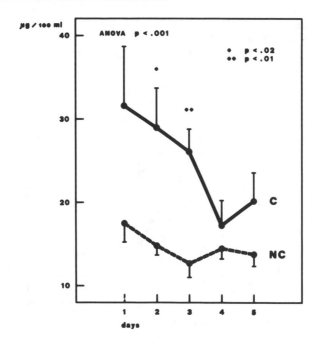

Figure 4 Cortisol, groups 4 vs. 1.

across days in both comparisons. For all five serial evaluations, the mean profile for the Complicated group was elevated in comparison with the noncomplicated group, as can be seen in Figure 4; the differences between groups were statistically significant on the second ($p < .02$) and third ($p < .01$) days for the extreme groups, and on the second, third and fifth days for the enlarged groups.

For cAMP, the ANOVA indicated significant differences between the mean profiles for the Complicated and Noncomplicated groups, but due to the reduced number of subjects, the analysis was based solely upon the enlarged groups. As can be seen in Figure 5, the mean profile for the enlarged Complicated group was consistently elevated in all the serial evaluations, with a tendency toward a reduction in cAMP values over time for both groups. The differences between groups were statistically significant on the third and fourth days ($p < .01$).

Multivariate Analysis

Four variables were selected for the stepwise discriminant analyses of differences among the groups. The 5-year NCS was selected since the largest proportional increase in negative events occurred during this period preceding infarct. Trait anxiety was selected as an index of anxiety proneness before the infarct. State anxiety and the initial cortisol level were considered to be the best

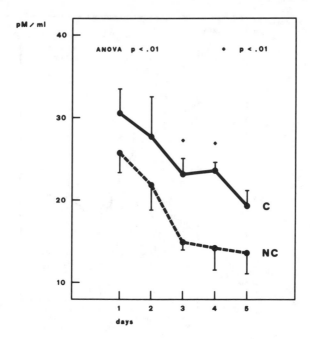

Figure 5 cAMP, groups 4 + 3 vs. 1 + 2.

indicators of acute stress immediately following infarct. The discriminant analysis carried out for these four variables resulted in practically identical findings for the extreme and three-group (Complicated, Intermediate, Noncomplicated) comparisons. Since the three-group analysis was based on the total sample, only the results for this analysis are reported in Figure 6.

The discrimination between the three groups appeared significant along the Root 1 axis, which was positively loaded by trait anxiety and negatively by the NCS-5 life events measure. The placement of the Complicated group in the discriminant space suggested strong association with high trait anxiety and a high incidence of negative life events. The Noncomplicated group was low in trait anxiety values. Moreover, the discriminant function analysis showed that the most important discriminating factor in the Complicated group was trait anxiety, while the most important factor in this analysis for the Noncomplicated group was the low incidence of NCS.

DISCUSSION

An important conclusion that can be drawn from the findings in this study is that psychometric measures of emotion are related to endocrine variables in the infarction stress situation. Elevated values of trait and state anxiety and depressive personality characteristics were positively correlated with level of endocrine arousal. The hypothalamus-pituitary-adrenal axis (HPA) and adrenergic receptors were activated in patients with greater anxiety proneness and a tendency to become depressed in stress situations.

Consistent with Spielberger's (1966, 1972, 1977) State-Trait Anxiety model, cognitive evaluation of the infarction threat appears to be influenced by anxiety proneness (trait anxiety), resulting in a more intense state anxiety reaction. We may speculate that this cognitively mediated state anxiety reaction activates the neuroendocrine system, which in its turn evokes other physiological changes.

The depressive traits observed in the MMPI profiles of patients with complications seem to reflect an inhibition in their coping mechanisms in threatening situations. Depressive emotional states typically involve basic tendencies toward passivity, negative self-evaluation, and feelings of helplessness. Such states are likely to amplify the cognitive evaluation of the infarct as highly threatening, which will enhance the psychoendocrine reaction to stress.

An especially important issue is the relation between the emotional reactions of the patients in the Complicated group in the present study and the premorbid personality traits of persons struck by infarction. Premorbid personalities of infarction patients are known to be characterized by hostility, competitiveness, ambition, dominance, and time urgency, which comprise the Type-A behavior syndrome. These traits are good predictors of both onset and the negative course of illness (Friedman & Rosenman, 1971). We may speculate that the elevated state anxiety observed in patients in the Complicated group resulted from an acute failure of coping mechanisms in a predisposed personality. This hypothesis conforms with observations by Glass (1978) that people with Type-A personality are more likely to develop feelings of resignation and helplessness behaviors when faced by uncontrollable stressors.

Another important issue concerns the effects of the stress reaction on the course of illness. According to Selye's (1973; 1974) original conceptions, stress was considered to be an adaptive and defensive mechanism that stimulated metabolism and tissues for adaptation to increased environmental demands.

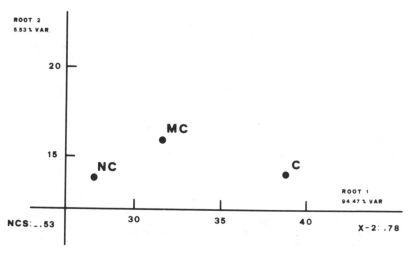

Figure 6 Discriminant analysis on the three groups (1, 2 + 3, 4).

Arousal of the hypothalamus-pituitary-adrenal axis and catecholamine activation were essential in mediating adaptation to emergency situations induced by stressors. At the clinical psychosomatic level, a problem arises when stress reactions are too intense, too prolonged in time, and disproportionate to the stimulus.

In his critique of Selye's work, Mason (1975a,b,c), has pointed out that the psychoendocrine arousal observed in stress appears to be mediated by emotional arousal at the limbic-hypothalamic level, suggesting that intense or prolonged emotional arousal can lead to excessive psychoneuroendocrine stimulation, with an increase in circulating hormones and negative consequences for tissue metabolism. The results of the present study provide additional empirical support for Mason's model, for example, a consistent relationship was observed between emotional arousal, psychoneuroendocrine response and the clinical course of infarction.

The relation between high plasma cortisol levels and the appearance of clinical complications in the present study confirmed similar observations by other investigators. Some investigators have suggested a direct relationship between cortisolemia and the severity of infarction, attaching little importance to the effects of emotional arousal for the elevation of plasma cortisol (Ceremuzynski, 1967). Consistent with this view, Melsom and his associates (Melsom, Andreanen, Melsom, Hansen, Grendahl, & Hillestead, 1976) found high cortisol levels after infarct, which were not significantly influenced by administration of Diazepam. Since a reduction of central arousal did not bring about significant reductions in plasma cortisol in this study, severity of infarct would seem to be the main factor influencing the level of serum cortisol.

Although the findings in the present study suggested that emotional reaction induced high values of cortisolemia, the possibility that strictly somatic events contributed to the observed elevations of plasma cortisol in patients with infarct complications cannot be ruled out. While enzymatic increase, an expression of the extent of the lesion, was also higher for patients

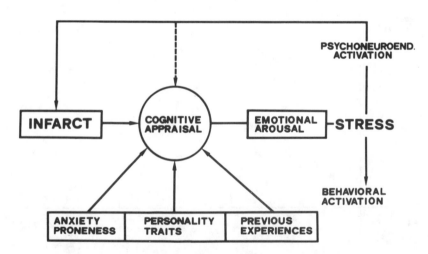

Figure 7 Psychophysiological mechanisms that link psychological to somatic data.

in the Complicated group than for the Noncomplicated group, this finding can be interpreted as evidence that more severe and extended infarction evoked more intense emotional and psychoendocrine stress reactions.

The total adrenergic activity, evaluated by means of cAMP plasma values, seemed to play an important role in the onset of arrhythmic complications. The cAMP level was consistently more elevated for the patients in the Complicated group, thus confirming the findings of other investigators (Raab, 1971). In the case of cAMP levels, there was a strong relation between modality and intensity of emotional reaction, adrenergic arousal, and the appearance of complications. It seems that catecholamine activation immediately following emotional arousal was more important than cortisol activation in inducing short-term complications. This may be due to the metabolic action of cortisol as compared with the catecholamines, which act most directly on myocardic tissue.

Although the mechanisms that influence the significant relation between number of negative events before illness and the course of illness are not clear, the results of experimental studies suggest that stressful events influence the daily excretion of catecholamines (Theorell, Lind, Karlson, & Levi, 1972). In the present study, a significant correlation was found between negative life events 5 and 10 years prior to infarction and hormonal values characteristic of stress, but these findings must be cautiously interpreted. Pancheri et al. (1979) have shown in retrospective studies that both the recall and the evaluation of previous events tends to be influenced by the patient's emotional state at the moment of evaluation. Thus, the finding in the present study of a greater incidence of negative life events in patients having more intense and more highly complicated psychoneuroendocrine reactions can be interpreted either as resulting from the effects of life events on the intensity of the stress reaction, or a consequence of anxiety experienced immediately after the onset of illness. The finding that high trait anxiety was the principle predictor of severity of infarction complication would seem to support the first alternative.

AN INTERPRETIVE MODEL

Clinical and experimental data obtained by both retrospective and prospective methods suggest that certain personality traits and mechanisms for coping with stressful life events should be considered risk factors for myocardial infarction. The results of the present study provide evidence that these same factors significantly influence the course of illness. Thus, as was found in previous studies of various psychosomatic patient groups (Pancheri et al., 1979), negative life stress events are associated with high levels of state and trait anxiety for infarct patients, and appear to influence the course of illness as reflected in the development of complications.

Theories regarding the cognitive appraisal of stressful stimuli (Lazarus, 1966; Spielberger, 1966, 1977), and Selye's and Mason's physiological concepts of stress, provide clues for the formulation of an integrated model. This model, which is presented in Figure 7, attempts to reconcile contradictory research findings, while also clarifying the psychophysiological mechanisms that link psychological to somatic data.

The cognitive appraisal of an infarction (stressor) appears to be influenced by two kinds of factors. The first consists of the premorbid personality traits that predispose an individual to experience anxiety and other negative emotions. Such personality traits accentuate cognitive evaluation of the stimulus as more threatening, especially when it is particularly intense or uncontrollable, as in the case of myocardial infarction. The second factor encompasses previous experiences and, in particular, the quantity and type of negative events that have acted on the subject. Both the event and the coping modalities for controlling emotional reactions to it influence the patient's cognitive evaluation and perception of subsequent events. Memories of failure in coping with a previous life stress event can lead a person to evaluate subsequent events as more threatening.

An infarct clearly qualifies as an intensely stressful event. It produces painful somatic sensations, forces the individual to immediately interrupt his ongoing activities, and in most cases, results in admittance to a hospital coronary unit. In addition, an infarct event is generally appraised as highly threatening because it is perceived as a grave here-and-now danger with possible dire future consequences. Along with the appraisal of the infarct as highly threatening, other characteristics intrinsic to the infarct also contribute, such as intense suffering produced by hemodynamic fluctuation and necrosis of the myocardium.

Patients' reactions to an infarct appear to be strongly influenced by their personality structure, especially anxiety proneness, and by previous experience. A high level of trait anxiety, a predisposition to react in a depressive manner when confronted with threat, a large number of previous negative life events, and inadequate coping skills seem to potentiate intense emotional arousal when a patient is confronted with the infarct event.

Emotional arousal resulting from the cognitive appraisal of an infarct event as highly threatening is manifested at the endocrine level in marked alteration in baseline values of the stress hormones, especially, cortisol and catecholamines. These hormones act on cardiac tissue already injured by the infarct, worsening the situation, and favoring the onset of complications. Direct or indirect stimulation of peripheral psychoneuroendocrine activity of the central nervous system also seems likely, with potential modification of the cognitive filter responsible for emotional arousal. Thus, the infarct event sets off a vicious chain reaction, in which intense emotional arousal evoked by cognitive appraisal produces overstimulation that contributes to infarct complications and in some cases may even result in death.

The model described above may be used to guide nonmedical therapeutic interventions for patients who are stricken by infarct. Psychotherapeutic approaches should focus on reducing the state anxiety of the infarcted patient, and at the cognitive level, to modify the patient's appraisal of the infarct event.

REFERENCES

Bailey, R. R., Abernethy, M. H., & Beaven, D. W. (1967). Adrenocortical response to the stress of an acute myocardial infarction. *Lancet, 2,* 970–973.

Cairncross, K. D., & Barret, J. R. (1975). Changes in myocardial function as a consequence of prolonged emotional stress. *Progress in Brain Research, 42,* 313–318.

Ceremuzynski, L. (1967). Clinical course of myocardial infarction and the excretion of 17 ketogenic steroids and 17 ketosteroids in urine. *Cor et Vasa, 9,* 11.

Chopra, M. P., Thadani, U., Olive, P. A., Portal, R. W., & Parkes, J. (1972). Plasma cortisol, urinary vanylmandelic acid after acute myocardial infarction. *British Heart Journal, 34,* 992–997.

Dahlstrom, W. G., & Welsh, G. S. (1960). *An MMPI handbook: A guide to use in clinical practice and research.* Minneapolis: University of Minnesota Press.

De Elio, F. G., Bosh, A. O., & Santos, M. (1975). The value of cortisol plasma levels in intensive care and coronary patients. In A. Arias (Ed.), *Recent progress in anesthesiology and resuscitation.* Amsterdam: Excerpta Medica.

Freeburg, D. R., Brown, G. M., Holdofsky, H., & Howley, T. (1970). Growth hormone and cortisol response, tranquilizer usage and their association with survival from myocardial infarction. *Psychosomatic Medicine, 40,* 462–472.

Friedman, H., & Rosenman, R. H. (1971). Type-A behavior pattern: Its association with coronary disease. *Annals of Clinical Research, 3,* 303–312.

Gilman, A. G. (1970). A protein binding assay for adenosine 3′, 5′-cyclic monophosphate. *Proceedings of the National Academy of Sciences, 67,* 305–312.

Glass, D. C. (1978). Pattern A behavior and uncontrollable stress. In T. M. Dembroski, S. H. Wein, J. H. Schields, S. G. Haynes, & H. Feinleib (Eds.), *Coronary-prone behavior.* New York: Springer-Verlag.

Greenhoot, J. H., & Reichenback, D. D. (1969). Cardiac injury subarachnoid hemorrhage: A clinical, pathological and physiological correlation. *Journal of Neurosurgery, 30,* 521–531.

Jewitt, D. E., Reid, D., & Thomas, M. (1969). Free noradrenaline and adrenaline excretion in relation to the development of cardiac arrhythmias and heart failure in patients with acute myocardial infarction. *Lancet, 1,* 635–641.

Johnson, J. H., & Sarason, I. G. (1978). Life stress, depression, anxiety: Internal-external control as a moderator variable. *Journal of Psychosomatic Research, 22,* 205–208.

Klein, A. J., & Palmer, L. A. (1963). Plasma cortisol in myocardial infarction: A correlation with shock and survival. *American Journal of Cardiology, 11,* 332–337.

Lazarus, R. S. (1966). *Psychological stress and the coping process.* New York: McGraw-Hill.

Logan, R. W., & Murdoch, W. R. (1966). Blood levels of hydrocortisone, transaminases and cholesterol after myocardial infarction. *Lancet, 2,* 521–524.

Mason, J. W. (1975a). Emotion as reflected in patterns of endocrine integration. In L. Levi (Ed.), *Emotions: Their parameters and measurement.* New York: Raven Press.

Mason, J. W. (1975b). A historical view of the stress field. *Journal of Human Stress, 1,* 6–12.

Mason, J. W. (1975c). A historical view of the stress field. *Journal of Human Stress, 1,* 22–36.

McDonald, L., Baker, C., Bray, C., McDonald, A., & Resticeux, N. (1969). Plasma catecholamines after cardiac infarction. *Lancet, 2,* 1021–1023.

Melsom, M., Andreanen, P., Melsom, H., Hansen, T., Grendahl, H., & Hillestead, L. K. (1976). Diazepam in acute myocardial infarction. Clinical effects and effects on catecholamines, free fatty acids and cortisol. *British Heart Journal, 38,* 804–810.

New York Health Association: Criteria Committee. (1973). *Nomenclature and criteria for diagnosis of the disease of the heart and great vessels.* (7th Edition). Boston: Little Brown.

Pancheri, P., Bellaterra, M., Matteoli, S., Cristofari, M., Polizzi, C., & Puletti, M. (1978). Infarct as stress agent. *Journal of Human Stress, 4,* 16–26.

Pancheri, P., Bernabei, A., Bellaterra, M., & Tartaglione, S. (1976). State and trait anxiety in Italian cardiac and dermatological patients: Clinical and cross-cultural considerations. In C. D. Spielberger, & R. Diaz-Guerrero (Eds.), *Cross-cultural anxiety.* Washington: Hemisphere.

Pancheri, P., DeMartino, V., Biondi, M., & Mosticoni, S. (1979). Life stress events and state-trait anxiety in psychiatric and psychosomatic patients. In I. G. Sarason, & C. D. Spielberger (Eds.), *Stress and anxiety* (Vol. 6). Washington: Hemisphere.

Platania, A., Liberatore, C., Reda, G., Magnatta, R., Spallone, L., Lacerna, F., & Lauro, R. (1979). Clinical course and trends in plasma cAMP levels in acute myocardial infarction. *IRCS Medical Science: Cardiovascular Systems, Clinical Biochemistry, Clinical Medicine, Haemotology, Pathology, 7,* 39.

Prakash, R., Parmley, W. W., Horwath, M., & Swan, H. J. C. (1972). Serum cortisol, free fatty acids and urinary catecholamines as indicators of complications in acute myocardial infarction. *Circulation, 45,* 736–745.

Raab, W. (1968). Correlated cardiovascular adrenergic and adrenocortical response to sensory and mental annoyances in man. *Psychosomatic Medicine, 30,* 802–818.

Raab, W. (1971). Cardiotoxic biochemical effects on emotional-environmental stressors: Fundamentals of psychocardiology. In L. Levi (Ed.), *Society, stress and disease: The psychosomatic and psychosocial diseases.* Oxford, England: Oxford University Press.

Rabinowitz, B., Kligerman, M., & Parmley, W. W. (1971). Plasma cyclic adenosine 3′, 5′-monophosphate (AMP) levels in acute myocardial infarction. *American Journal of Cardiology, 34,* 7–11.

Rahe, R. H., Romo, M., Bennett, L., & Siltanen, P. (1974). Recent life changes, myocardial infarction and abrupt coronary death studies in Helsinki. *Archives of Internal Medicine, 133,* 221–228.

Reda, G., Puglione, G., Santarelli, E., Ferretti, C., Portaleoni, P., Matteoli, S., & Lauro, R. (in press). Different trends of plasma cAMP and catecholamine levels during acute myocardial infarction (AMI): Possible scale of adrenergic receptors. *IRCS.*

Sabato, A., Petrozzi, U., Marana, E., Magalini, S. I., Scrascia, E., & Bondoli, A. (1976/77). Plasma cortisol monitoring acute myocardial infarction. *Resuscitation, 5,* 169–173.

Sarason, I. G., Johnson, J. H., & Siegel, J. M. (1979). Assessing the impact of life changes: Development of the Life Experience Survey. In I. G. Sarason, & C. D. Spielberger (Eds.), *Stress and Anxiety* (Vol. 6). Washington: Hemisphere.

Selye, H. (1973). The evolution of the stress concept. *American Scientist, 61,* 692–699.

Selye, H. (1974). *Stress without distress.* New York: Lippincott.

Spielberger, C. D. (1966). Theory and research on anxiety. In C. D. Spielberger (Ed.), *Anxiety and behavior.* New York: Academic Press.

Spielberger, C. D. (1972). Conceptual and methodological issues in anxiety research. In C. D. Spielberger (Ed.), *Anxiety: Current trends in theory and research* (Vol. 2). New York: Academic.

Spielberger, C. D. (1977). Anxiety: Theory and research. In B. B. Wolman (Ed.), *International encyclopedia of neurology, psychiatry, psychoanalysis, and psychology.*

Spielberger, C. D., Gorsuch, R. L., & Lushene, R. E. (1970). *Manual for the State-Trait Anxiety Inventory.* Palo Alto, CA: Consulting Psychologists Press.

Strange, R. C., Vetter, N., Rowe, M. J., & Oliver, M. F. (1974). Plasma cyclic AMP and total catecholamines during acute myocardial infarction in man. *European Journal of Clinical Investigation, 4,* 115–119.

Strange, R. C., Rowe, M. J., & Oliver, M. F. (1978). Lack of relation between venous plasma total catecholamine concentrations on ventricular arrhythmias after acute myocardial infarction. *British Medical Journal, 2,* 921–922.

Theorell, T., Lind, E., Karlson, C. C., & Levi, L. (1972). A longitudinal study of 21 subjects with CHD: Life changes, catecholamine excretion and related biochemical reactions. *Psychosomatic Medicine, 34,* 505–516.

Theorell, T., & Rahe, R. H. (1974). Psychosocial characteristics of subjects with myocardial infarction in Stockholm. In E. K. E. Gunderson, & R. H. Rahe (Eds.), *Life Stress and Illness.* Springfield, IL: Charles C Thomas.

Theorell, T., & Rahe, R. H. (1975). Life change events, ballistocardiography and coronary death. *Journal of Human Stress, 1,* 18–24.

Vetter, N. J., Strange, R. C., Adams, W., & Oliver, M. F. (1974). Initial metabolic and hormonal response to acute myocardial infarction. *Lancet, 1,* 284–288.

Wienes, K. (1977). Plasma cortisol, corticosterone and urea in acute myocardial infarction: Clinical and biochemical correlations. *Clinical Chimica Acta, 76,* 243–250.

IV

STRESS AND ANXIETY
IN MEDICAL
AND SURGICAL PATIENTS

14

Anxiety, Control, and Information-Seeking Behavior in Screening for Cancer

Jean Pruyn and Wim van den Heuvel
Study Center of Social Oncology, Rotterdam

Cancer is one of the most threatening diseases in western societies because of its high incidence and mortality rates (ranked second as a cause of death), and the radical forms of treatment and their side effects (hair loss, impotence, amputation, etc.). Studying the ways people cope with cancer is a major research interest of the Rotterdam Study Center of Social Oncology. In this chapter, we report the results of a study of people who were screened for colorectal cancer and found to be positive by means of tests on occult blood in the stool. Such positive test findings might be determined by further medical tests to indicate the presence of colorectal cancer. The question addressed in this research was "How do people react in such situations?"

We attempted to explain reactions to information about positive evidence of cancer in terms of concepts based primarily on social comparison theory. We also assumed that concepts like anxiety, uncertainty, and control were important in determining reactions to the threat of cancer. To explore the usefulness of these concepts, we examined data previously collected as part of a larger study on screening for colorectal cancer. We postulated that individuals who are told that they may have cancer will experience anxiety, uncertainty, and loss of control in reacting to the "stressful" situation in which they are informed about this possibility. More specifically, we were interested in how these individuals behave in order to reduce anxiety, uncertainty, and loss of control.

In many psychological theories, behavior is explained by the concept of fulfillment of needs in the situations in which people are involved. Since people act to satisfy their needs, unfulfilled needs provide motives for action. Research on cancer patients shows that they have special needs that result from strong feelings of uncertainty (Hinton, 1973; McIntosh, 1974; Trimbos & Steenkamp, 1978), anxiety (Maguire, Lee, & Berington, 1978; Wortman & Dunkel-Schetter, 1979) and loss of control (Taylor, 1979; Weisman & Sobel, 1979). Consequently, the behavior of cancer patients should reflect their efforts to reduce feelings of uncertainty, anxiety, and loss of control.

HYPOTHESES DERIVED FROM SOCIAL COMPARISON THEORY ABOUT CANCER PATIENTS

Social comparison theory offers a conceptual framework for understanding the reactions of the people in our study. The first two principles of this theory are based on the ideas of Festinger (1954):

1. There exists in the human organism a drive to evaluate one's own opinions and abilities.
2. There is a preference for using objective (nonsocial) means in these evaluations. A corollary of the second principle is that when given a range of possible persons for comparison, someone with similar ability or opinions (similars) will be chosen.

Persons who do not have an accurate appraisal of their own abilities and opinions, are at a serious disadvantage in attempting to behave adaptively. Social comparison theory assumes that the individual has a drive to reduce as much uncertainty as possible about the correctness of his or her opinions and adequacy of abilities (Goethals & Darley, 1977). Consequently, in uncertain situations most people attempt to obtain objective information to reduce their uncertainty or, if objective information is not available, they will compare themselves with similar others. Accordingly, we hypothesize:

1a. The more uncertain persons who have been informed about positive cancer tests are (positives), the more they will express a need for additional information;
1b. The more uncertain positives are, the more they will tend to compare themselves with other positives (affiliation); and,
1c. Affiliation with other positives will result in a decrease in the need for additional information.

The dimensions of social comparison theory on which people compare themselves with others can be applied not only to opinions and abilities, but also to investments, outcomes, personality characteristics, and emotions. Schachter (1959) developed the idea that emotions are evaluated by social comparison processes. His experimental research has demonstrated that persons in a condition of high fear seek the company of others (affiliation), and that individuals who are fearful prefer to affiliate with individuals at the same level of emotionality as themselves.

Under high fear, affiliation preferences may reflect the joint operation of two processes (1) need for social comparison (are my feelings normal?) and (2) need for anxiety reduction (mutual support, comfort). An extreme level of fear, however, may lead to anxiety related to an object or specific situation (state anxiety), vague or general anxiety (trait anxiety), and isolation (no need for information, no need for social comparison) in order to protect self-esteem. Sarnoff and Zimbardo (1961) showed that state anxiety was related to affiliation, whereas trait anxiety was related to nonaffiliation. Therefore, we hypothesize:

2a. Positives with high state anxiety will more often affiliate with fellow positives than positives with low state anxiety.

2b. Positives with high trait anxiety will less often affiliate with fellow positives than positives with low trait anxiety.

A high level of fear (state anxiety) may lead to isolation to protect self-esteem. The level of fear may also interact in the relation between uncertainty and need for information. Since uncertainty generally brings a need for information, this need will be felt more strongly if some anxiety is present. If high anxiety is present, however, the threat to one's self-esteem will be very strong, and the individual will try to avoid information despite his uncertainty. Therefore, we hypothesize:

3a. In situations in which positives feel relatively certain, the need for information will be stronger in individuals with moderate state anxiety than with high state anxiety.

3b. In situations in which positives feel uncertain, the need for information will be stronger in individuals with low state anxiety than high state anxiety.

In addition to the hypothesized interaction between uncertainty and state anxiety in relation to the need for information, we also suspect an interaction between uncertainty and state anxiety in relation to affiliation. The relation between high state anxiety and affiliation (Hypothesis 2a) should be even stronger in situations of uncertainty because affiliation is not only a means for reducing anxiety, but also a way of obtaining information. Therefore we hypothesize:

4. The association between high state anxiety and affiliation will be stronger in uncertain positives than in nonuncertain positives.

Information from objective sources or obtained from social comparison is important for reducing uncertainty and negative feelings like anxiety. "Uncertainty" may be defined in terms of the predictability of an outcome. Although reliable information will increase the predictability of an outcome, the availability of outcome information is not sufficient to explain the behavior of an individual in a threatening situation. Another important factor is the extent to which the individual can influence the outcome (Schulz, 1976). This "control" factor, that is, the ability to regulate or influence intended outcomes through selective responding (Baron & Rodin, 1978), may be real or only perceived. In the specific situation of the present study, we postulate that people only perceive control: They have no means for real control. However, they may believe that medical experts are able to influence the outcome.

There is evidence that persons working on cooperative tasks choose superior individuals as partners, suggesting that they expect interaction with superior others will produce the greatest gains for themselves. This is especially true for persons with low abilities (Miller & Suls, 1977). But some studies indicate that individuals will avoid superior others even when comparison with them provides useful information (Hakmiller, 1966). In the present study, we do not expect an association between control and comparison with others, because comparison (looking for comfort, etc.) will not beneficially contribute to influencing the outcome. But information, especially from professional experts, may increase the idea of control. Therefore, in this context, we hypothesize:

5. Positives with greater perceived control will need more information than positives without perceived control.

METHOD

Study Population and Data Collection

Beginning in June 1978, persons of 40 years and over in a town of 50,000 inhabitants were asked to participate in a screening program on occult blood in the stool. Over a 3-day period, the participants collected two samples out of each stool and put them on slides. These slides were sent to the doctor who was coordinating the screening program. All persons having blood in the stool (positives) were informed by this doctor. They were told that there were several possible explanations for the test being positive and that there was a relatively small chance of having a serious disease. On the other hand, the screening was introduced and referred to as a cancer-screening test.

In the second half of 1979, all persons identified as positives were asked to cooperate in this research project. Two interviews were planned. The first took place in the week after the subjects were informed of the test results and had a talk with the doctor. The second interview was held 3 months after the first one, when additional medical examinations were completed and a definitive diagnosis was known. In this study we report the results of the first interview.

Of the persons who participated in the study, the sample included 106 positives. Of these persons, six appeared to be negative, five refused to cooperate, one could not be contacted, and one had an incomplete interview. Seven persons were excluded because they did not belong to the target group of the screening: They participated in the screening on the request of other doctors because of certain complaints. Ultimately, 86 persons (52 men, 34 women) with a positive screening result (blood in stool) were interviewed. The mean age of this positive group was 55.7 yrs.

Anxiety

To assess anxiety related to a specific situation (in this case the positive test result) and general (trait) anxiety, we used Orlebeke's Dutch translation of Spielberger's *State-Trait Anxiety Inventory* (STAI: Spielberger, Gorsuch, & Lushene, 1970). The STAI Trait (T-Anxiety) scale consists of 13 anxiety-present and 7 anxiety-absent items. Although the alpha coefficient of .88 indicated strong internal consistency, we used factor analysis to explore the dimensions within the scale, especially looking for two dimensions according to the anxiety-present/anxiety-absent content of the items. Factor analysis was also employed to identify nonconsistent items and to give more information about the components underlying "trait anxiety."

On the basis of the results of a principal component analysis, it was decided to use a solution with three factors, in which 49% of the total variance was explained. In this solution, almost all of the items loaded on factor 1 (except four items), which can be interpreted as the "anxiety factor." Factor 2 was represented by the items, "I am happy," "I feel secure," and "I am content," which also had strong loadings on factor 1. This factor was interpreted as measuring the absence of trait anxiety, and can be referred to as a "happiness" factor. The third factor seemed to measure "steadiness" ("I am calm, cool and collected," "I am a steady person").

Although three factors were identified, the largest was the first—the trait-anxiety factor. However, we did not find the anxiety-present/anxiety-absent meaning of the items reflected in the factor structure. Therefore, in subsequent analysis, we used the sum of the scores for the individual items of the T-Anxiety scale. One item, "I wish I could be as happy as others seem to be," had a low communality and was not answered by 13 people. Therefore, we eliminated this item from further analysis. The STAI State (S-Anxiety) scale is composed of 10 anxiety-present and 10 anxiety-absent items; the alpha coefficient was .93. Using a principal components factor analysis, a two-factor solution was executed. Because the items, "I feel strained" and "I feel satisfied," did not have high enough loadings on either factor, these two items were excluded from further analysis. Although the two factors did not completely correspond with the formulation of the items in a positive or negative direction, we concluded that factor 1 represented anxiety absent, while factor 2 represented anxiety present. Since both factors measure the same construct (state anxiety), we used the total sum score of the remaining items of the STAI S-Anxiety Scale.

The anxiety scales were separately analyzed for men and women. The distribution of anxiety-present and anxiety-absent items in the 2-factor solution was quite different for men and women, and the answer distributions for individual items differed for the anxiety-present and anxiety-absent items. Anxiety-present items were more often scored extremely negative than extremely positive (23 vs. 9), which seems to reflect social desirability in the answer-pattern for these items.

In summary, we concluded that the STAI T-Anxiety and S-Anxiety scales were valid and reliable. However, several items from the Dutch version of the scale were excluded because they had questionable psychometric properties. In the subsequent analyses, we used the total sum scores of the T-Anxiety and S-Anxiety scales based on the reduced set of scale items.

Health Locus of Control

We defined control as the ability to regulate intended outcomes, but recognized in this study that there may only be "perceived control" related to health and disease. To measure perceived control, we used Wallston's *Multidimensional Health Locus of Control* scale (Wallston, Wallston, & DeVellis, 1978). This scale assesses the belief that health is, or is not, determined by one's own behavior. These beliefs are described in terms of three dimensions:

1. Own behavior contributes to health and sickness.
2. Factors over which a person himself has little control, but which may be controlled by powerful others.
3. Luck, chance, or fate (factors over which people have little control).

We made a translation of the A-form (18-item version) of Wallston's scale which contains three dimensions, corresponding to those noted above:

- internal health locus of control
- powerful others health locus of control
- chance health locus of control.

A scale analysis showed that the alpha-coefficient reflecting the internal consistency reliability was .77 for the 18 items. The alpha coefficient for the 3 dimensions (subscales) were (1) internal = .77; (2) powerful others = .66; and (3) chance = .65. To test the presence of these three dimensions we factor-analyzed the data, using a principal component analysis with iterations executed to check the expected theoretical components. The three-factor solution corresponded with the dimensions of Wallston et al. (1978), and accounted for 40.6% of the variance.

The items that loaded on factor 1, the "powerful others" dimension, were "Having regular contact with my physician is the best way for me to avoid illness"; "Whenever I don't feel well, I should consult a medically trained professional"; "When I recover from an illness, it's usually because other people (for example, doctors, nurses, family, friends) have been taking good care of me"; and "Regarding my health, I can only do what my doctor tells me to do."

The items that loaded on factor 2, the "chance" dimension, were "No matter what I do, if I am going to get sick, I will get sick"; "Most things that affect my health happen to me by accident"; "Luck plays a big part in determining how soon I will recover from an illness"; "My good health is largely a matter of good fortune"; "No matter what I do, I'm likely to get sick"; and "If it's meant to be, I will stay healthy."

The items that loaded on factor 3, corresponding with the "internal" dimension, were "If I get sick, it is my own behavior which determines how soon I get well again"; "I am in control of my health"; "When I get sick I am to blame"; and "Regarding my health, I can only do what my doctor tells me to do."

Four items were excluded from further analyses because of ambiguity or low communalities. These were "Health professionals control my health"; "The main thing which affects my health is what I myself do"; "If I take the right actions, I can stay healthy"; and "My family has a lot to do with my becoming sick or staying healthy."

We computed scores for each health locus of control dimension, three scores for each individual, by multiplying the raw scores on each item with the corresponding factor-score coefficient. On the basis of these results, we concluded that the *Health Locus of Control* scale consisted of three subscales that could be used to assess perceived loss of control concerning health and illness.

Uncertainty

Uncertainty was defined as not being able to predict the outcome. To measure uncertainty, we used two questions: "Were you surprised by the test result?" and "Do you have an idea why blood was found in your stool?" The interviewee could answer yes or no to both questions. Since the two questions correlated strongly, a 3-point scale was constructed:

1. Persons who were not surprised by the positive test result and had an idea why blood was found ("certain"),
2. Persons surprised by the positive test result, but who had an idea why the blood was found,
3. Persons surprised by the positive test result, who had no idea why it was found ("uncertain").

A few persons reported that they were not surprised, but had no idea why they had a positive test result. These persons plus five individuals who did not answer the question were all excluded from further analyses.

Need for Information

All persons were informed about the positive test in the same way by one doctor. A week after the doctor had explained the meaning of the positive result, the subjects were asked detailed questions about what they were told and their possible need for further information. Of the interviewed persons, 37% said they wanted further information, 63% did not.

Affiliation

The wish to compare themselves with others (affiliation) was measured by a single question: "Do you know other positives?" Of those interviewed, 29% knew other positives and 71% did not.

RESULTS

The hypothesized associations between the variables were evaluated by using 2- or 3-dimensional tabulations and zero-order and partial correlation coefficients (Pearson correlations). The tabulations for Hypotheses 1a and 1b are reported in Table 1.

Hypothesis 1a

The more uncertain positives are, the more they will express a need for information. The association between uncertainty and need for information was not significant ($\chi^2 = 2.90$; df = 1; $.05 < p < .10$). However, there was a tendency for uncertain positives to express a need for information more often than the positives who were certain.

Table 1   Uncertainty related to need for information and knowing
other positives for persons with positive test results

	Not uncertain	Uncertain	Total
Hypothesis 1a			
Need for information	28%	45%	36%
No need for information	72%	55%	64%
Total	(43)	(38)	(81)
Hypothesis 1b			
Know other positives	32%	21%	27%
Do not know other positives	68%	79%	73%
Total	(51)	(34)	(75)

Hypothesis 1b

The more uncertain positives are, the more they will tend to compare themselves (affiliate) with other positives. As can be seen in Table 1, no association was found between uncertainty and knowing other positives (χ^2 = 1.18; df = 1; n.s.). Although "uncertainty" showed a slight tendency to be related to the "need for information" and "knowing other positives," no significant association between these two variables was found in the two-dimensional analyses. Furthermore, the association between uncertainty and information did not change when the effects of knowing other positives was controlled.

Hypothesis 1c

Affiliation with other positives will result in a decrease in the need for information. This hypothesis implies that talking with other positives will result in a decrease in the need for information. As may be noted in Table 2, the subjects who know other positives and talked with them were less likely to express a "need for information" (χ^2 = 5.077; df = 1; .02 < p < .05). Thus the hypothesis was supported by the findings.

Hypothesis 2a

Positives with high state anxiety scores will more often affiliate with fellow positives than positives with low S-anxiety scores. The association between state anxiety scores and knowing other positives is presented in Table 3. This hypothesis was not supported (χ^2 = 0.24; df = 1; n.s.).

Hypothesis 2b

Positives with high trait anxiety scores will affiliate less often with fellow positives than positives with low trait anxiety scores. The Pearson correlation coefficient (r = −.16) shows that the relationship was in the expected direction, and the association approached significance (p < .06). The STAI state and trait

Table 2 Need for information for persons knowing and talking with other positives

		Need for information		
		Yes	No	Total
Hypothesis 1c				
Know other positives	Talked with them	1	13	14
	Did not talk with them	5	6	11
	Total	6	19	25

anxiety scores correlated .64 with each other ($p < .001$); the correlation between trait anxiety and affiliation was essentially the same as the multiple correlation ($r = .17$).

Hypothesis 3a

In a situation in which positives feel relatively certain ("no uncertainty"), the need for information will be stronger for persons with moderate state anxiety than for the high state-anxiety positives. The distributions of the three variables relating to this hypothesis are shown in Table 4. Although the data are consistent with this hypothesis (57% vs. 14%), because of the small numbers in each cell, a test of significance was not computed.

Hypothesis 3b

In situations in which positives feel uncertain, the need for information will be stronger in persons with low state anxiety than in positives with high state anxiety. The data reported in Table 4 tend to support this hypothesis. Of those positives who were uncertain, the respondents with high state anxiety need information less often (47%) than those with low state anxiety (62%).

Hypothesis 4

The association between high state anxiety and affiliation will be stronger in uncertainty than when a person is not uncertain. As we noted before, we did

Table 3 State anxiety and knowing other positives

	Level of state anxiety		
	Not at all/Low	Medium/High	Total
Hypothesis 2a			
Knowing other positives	29%	24%	27%
Not knowing other positives	71%	76%	73%
Total	(34)	(41)	(75)

Table 4 State anxiety and uncertainty in relation to need for information and knowing other positives among persons with positive test results

	No uncertainty State anxiety				Uncertainty State anxiety				
	Not at all	Low	Medium	High	Not at all	Low	Medium	High	Total
Hypothesis 3a									
Need for information	17%	10%	57%	14%	25%	62%	43%	47%	36%
No need for information	83%	90%	43%	86%	75%	38%	57%	53%	64%
Total	(12)	(10)	(14)	(7)	(8)	(8)	(7)	(15)	(81)
Hypothesis 4									
Do know other positives	42%	33%	38%		15%	17%	33%	25%	27%
Do not know other positives	58%	66%	62%	100%	85%	83%	67%	72%	73%
Total	(12)	(9)	(13)	(7)	(7)	(6)	(6)	(15)	(75)

not find any association between state anxiety and knowing other positives. In the uncertainty group, however, the percentages suggested an association in the predicted direction; higher state anxiety appeared to be associated with knowing other positives (25%, 33% vs. 15%, 17%), as can be noted in Table 4.

Hypothesis 5

Positives with perceived control will need more information than positives without perceived control. The need for information was found to correlate significantly with high scores on internal health locus of control ($r = .217; p < .02$), powerful others health locus of control ($r = .365; p < .001$), and chance health locus of control ($r = .173, p < .05$).

DISCUSSION

In a field study, we explored the usefulness of theoretical concepts developed in experimental laboratory studies. A major problem inherent in field studies, as contrasted with laboratory studies, is the role of confounding variables which may interact or disturb the predicted associations. Thus, weak associations may be found where stronger associations were expected. Therefore, the goals of this study were not only aimed at testing the predictive power of a theory, but were also concerned with determining if theoretical concepts from social psychology might help to understand the behavior and feelings of people in stressful situations.

Despite the fact that we used data collected for other purposes, the results appear to support and justify the use of social comparison theory, and the concepts of uncertainty, anxiety, and control, in "explaining" the reactions of people to stressful situations. There was evidence in our data that associations derived from social comparison theory helped to explain the behavior of people who may have cancer. In this context, we believe the most important findings are that

- uncertain positives more often express a need for information
- affiliation with other positives results in a decrease in the need for information
- positives with a high trait anxiety affiliate less often with fellow-positives than positives with a low trait anxiety
- uncertainty and anxiety interact with the need for information
- the need for information increases in positives with perceived control

The operationalizing of the concepts in the present study, especially the procedure for measuring affiliation in terms of "knowing other positives," requires further discussion. Although this procedure addressed a relevant question in our field study, it only referred to cognitive aspects, and affiliation also includes emotions. In future research, it would be desirable to explore both the cognitive and the emotional aspects of the dimensions of social comparison in threatening situations.

One of the best operationalized concepts in this study was "anxiety," as measured by Spielberger's *State-Trait Anxiety Inventory*. As previously noted, we found differences for men and women in the factor-structure of the STAI Trait Anxiety scale. In an analysis that was not presented in this paper, we also found a sex-related interaction between "state anxiety" and talking with others about the screening before the beginning of the study. Women who "talked before" were more anxious than those who did not; for men, there was no difference.

In the factor analysis of the STAI Trait Anxiety scale, the "anxiety-absent" and "anxiety-present" dimensions that were expected were not found. It should be noted, however, that Orlebeke's original translation of the STAI was used in the present study. A new Dutch adaptation of Spielberger's scale has been developed by van der Ploeg, Defares, and Spielberger (1980) for which the following four factors were identified: T-anxiety absent, T-anxiety present, S-anxiety absent, and S-anxiety present. These factors were essentially the same as the factors that were reported by Vagg, Spielberger, and O'Hearn (1980) for the revised English form of the STAI (Form Y) (Spielberger, 1983). The results in the study were based on measurements taken at only one point in time. In order to understand the reactions of people in threatening situations, longitudinal studies are needed. Longitudinal studies would also provide a more adequate test of social comparison theory in stressful situations.

REFERENCES

Baron, R., & Rodin, J. (1978). Personal control as a mediation of crowding. In A. Baum, J. E. Singer, & S. Vallins (Eds.), *Advances in environmental psychology*. Hillsdale, NJ: Lawrence Erlbaum.

Festinger, L. (1954). A theory of social comparison processes. *Human Relations, 7*, 117–140.

Goethals, G. R., & Darley, J. M. (1977). Social comparison theory: An attributional approach. In J. M. Suls, & R. L. Miller (Eds.), *Social comparison processes: Theoretical and empirical perspectives*. New York: Hemisphere.

Hakmiller, K. L. (1966). Threat as a determinant of downward comparison. *Journal of Experimental Social Psychology*, supplement 1, 49–54.

Hinton, J. (1973). Bearing cancer. *British Journal Medicine Psychology, 46*, 105–113.

Maguire, G. P., Lee, E. G., & Berington, D. J. (1978). Psychiatric problems in the first year after mastectomy. *British Medicine Journal, 1*, 963–965.

McIntosh, J. (1974). Processes of communication, information seeking and control associated with cancer: A selected review of literature. *Social Science Medicine, 8*, 167–187.

Miller, R. L., & Suls, J. M. (1977). Affiliation preferences as a function of attitude and ability similarity. In J. M. Suls, & R. L. Miller (Eds.), *Social comparison processes: Theoretical and empirical perspectives*. New York: Hemisphere.

Sarnoff, L., & Zimbardo, P. G. (1961). Anxiety, fear and social affiliation. *Journal of Abnormal and Social Psychology, 62*, 356–363.

Schachter, S. (1959). *The psychology of affiliation*. Stanford, CA: Stanford University Press.

Schulz, R. (1976). Some life and death consequences of perceived control. In J. S. Caroll, & J. W. Payne (Eds.), *Cognitions and social behavior* (pp. 135–154). Hillsdale, NJ: Lawrence Erlbaum.

Spielberger, C. D. (1983). *Manual for the State-Trait Anxiety Inventory (Revised)*. Palo Alto, CA: Consulting Psychologists Press.

Spielberger, C. D., Gorsuch, R. L., & Lushene, R. E. (1970). *Manual for the State-Trait Anxiety Inventory*. Palo Alto, CA: Consulting Psychologists Press.

Taylor, S. E. (1979). Hospital patient behavior: Reactance, helplessness or control? *Journal of Social Issues, 35*, 156–184.

Trimbos, C. J., & Steenkamp, W. G. (1978). *Informatie aan kankerpatiënten*. Rotterdam: Integraal Kankercentrum.

Vagg, P. R., Spielberger, C. D., & O'Hearn, T. P. (1980). Is the State-Trait Anxiety Inventory multidimensional? *Personality and Individual Differences, 1*, 207–214.

van der Ploeg, H. M., Defares, P. B., & Spielberger, C. D. (1980). Handleiding bij de Zelf-Beoordelings Vragenlijst, ZBV. Een Nederlands-talige bewerking van de Spielberger State-Trait Anxiety Inventory, STAI-DY. Lisse: Swets en Zeitlinger.

Wallston, K. A., Wallston, B., & DeVellis, R. (1978). Development of the Multidimensional Health Locus of Control (MHLC) scales. In *Health Education Monographs, 6,* 160–169.

Weisman, A. D., & Sobel, H. J. (1979). Coping with cancer through self-instruction: A hypothesis. *Journal of Human Stress, 1,* 3–8.

Wortman, C. B., & Dunkel-Schetter, C. (1979). Interpersonal relationship and cancer: A theoretical analysis. *Journal of Social Issues, 35,* 120–155.

15

Psychological Determinants
of Length of Hospitalization
in Patients with Acute Severe Asthma

A. A. Kaptein
University of Leiden

Bronchial asthma is a disease to which psychologists have historically devoted much attention. Research on the various psychological determinants in the etiology of asthma falls within the framework of psychosomatic medicine. Recent reviews on this subject can be found in Dirks (1978), Groen (1979), Knapp, Mathé, and Vachon (1976).

Although numerous studies have focused on psychological factors involved in the *onset* of asthma, there exists a paucity of research concerning the psychological factors influencing the *course* of the disease. The study reported here deals with the effects of psychological factors on length of hospitalization, one aspect of the medical outcome of the treatment of hospitalized asthma patients.

An important theoretical concept in studies about psychological factors affecting the medical outcome of disease processes is "illness behavior," defined by Mechanic (1977) as "the varying perceptions, thoughts, feelings, and acts affecting the personal and social meaning of symptoms, illness, disabilities and their consequences" (p. 79). Mechanic has stressed the meaning of the illness for the person and emphasized the importance of the ways in which a person copes with illness.

In an extension of the work of Mechanic (1977) and Lazarus (1966), Lipowski (1969; 1970) has presented a framework for a conceptualization of the ways in which people cope with the stress and challenges of disease. Three categories of determinants of coping behavior are distinguished: those inherent in the patient, the nature of the illness, and those in the environment. Based on the above-mentioned concepts, a general theoretical model can be developed

This work is part of a larger project that is supported by the Dutch Asthma Foundation, grant 78.22. The author wishes to express his appreciation to the physicians and nursing staff of the Department of Lung Diseases of the Onze Lieve Vrouwe Gasthuis, Amsterdam, The Netherlands, for their cooperation and assistance in conducting this study. The author wishes to thank Irene Rykaszewski for assistance with the preparation and translation of this paper.

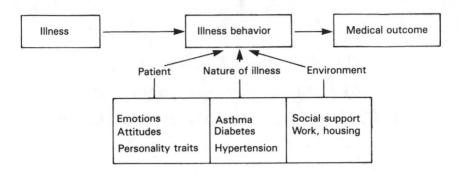

Figure 1 Theoretical model of illness behavior.

that encompasses illness, illness behavior, and the effects of illness behavior on medical outcome (Figure 1).

The results of numerous studies provide support for the validity of such a formulation. Auerbach (1973) found that surgical patients with a moderate level of state anxiety adjusted better postoperatively than patients with low or high state anxiety. Cohen and Lazarus (1973), working with a similar patient population, found significant correlations between the attitudes of avoidance and vigilance, and length of hospitalization, medical complications, and pain medication. The results of Greer, Morris, and Pettingale (1979) indicated that patients' psychological responses to the diagnosis of breast cancer were related to duration of survival. Philips and Bee (1980) found that anxious patients who underwent orthopedic surgery developed more complications, had longer hospitalization, and reported less relief from symptoms. Finally, Pilowsky, Spence, and Waddy (1979) found a high level of anxiety to be associated with a low level of adjustment to coronary artery bypass surgery.

With reference to asthma, De Araujo, van Arsdel, Holmes and Dudley (1973) reported on a group of patients with chronic asthma. They found that measures of life change and coping abilities reliably predicted the corticosteroid dosage administered. These relations were not attributable to duration of the disease or age. In a series of studies, Teiramaa (1978a, 1978b) showed that a favorable outcome in the course of asthma was related to "more extraverted tendencies and better psychosocial adaptation" (1978b, p. 121) while on the other hand "poor psychological adaptation, obsessive neurosis, immature personality and alcohol problems were associated with a static or deteriorating trend" (1978b).

Jones, Kinsman, Dirks and Wray Dahlem (1979) have recently made a significant contribution to the understanding of psychological determinants of the chronicity of asthma. The publication is a combination of extensive research in this area. In summary, two aspects of response style have been found to influence medical treatment and outcome (1) panic-fear symptomatology, a specific situational response to asthmatic distress resembling state anxiety and (2) panic-fear personality, a personality dimension that appears to be similar to trait anxiety.

METHOD

Subjects

The subjects in this study were 26 hospitalized patients who were admitted to the Department of Lung Diseases of an 800-bed hospital because of acute, severe asthma. This condition is often referred to as "status asthmaticus." It exemplifies a life-threatening medical emergency (see for further elaboration of this subject, Clark & Godfrey, 1977; Petty, 1977; Weiss, 1978).

Patients were included in the study if they were between the ages of 16 and 60 years of age, and born in The Netherlands. This group consisted of 8 men and 18 women (mean age 36.5 years, SD = 14.3). With the exception of one subject, all patients volunteered to participate in this study. The mean duration of their asthma was 9.3 years (SD = 11.4); 19 patients had allergic asthma, and 7 had nonallergic asthma. Mean length of hospitalization was 20.0 days (SD = 10.8; range 4–43 days). The severity of the asthmatic episode was judged according to the classification system of Snider (1978). The distribution in increasing severity was as follows: 5 patients with moderate asthma, 7 with severe asthma grade A, 11 with severe asthma grade B, and 3 with severe asthma grade C.

Test Measures

Asthma Symptom Checklist (ASC)

In this checklist, developed by Kinsman, Luparello, O'Banion and Spector (1973), the items reflect specific, situational symptoms that patients experience during asthmatic attacks. The version used in this study contained four dimensions: panic-fear, depression, hyperventilation, and airways obstruction.

Zelfbeoordelings Vragenlijst [ZBV, or State-Trait Anxiety Inventory (STAI)]

The STAI consists of two separate 20-item, self-report scales for measuring state anxiety and trait anxiety (Spielberger, Gorsuch, & Lushene, 1970). The version used in this study was developed by van der Ploeg, Defares, and Spielberger (1980). When filling out the state anxiety scale, patients were instructed to describe how they feel *during an asthmatic attack.*

Panic-Fear Personality Scale (PFPS)

This scale, developed by Dirks, Jones and Kinsman (1977), consists of 15 items selected from the Minnesota Multiphasic Personality Inventory (MMPI) and five filler items (Dirks, 1978). It indexes a personality dimension that appears to be similar to trait anxiety. According to Dirks, Horton, Fross, and Jones (1978), the designers of the scale, persons scoring high on this measure can be described as

fearful and emotionally labile individuals who profess to have their feelings hurt more easily than others, to feel helpless, and to give up easily in the face of difficulty. Those who score low on this scale can be described as individuals who present themselves as experiencing very little discomfort, who deny the presence of any anxiety or worry, and who claim to be unusually calm, stable and self-controlled. (p. 6)

This measure was included in the test battery to assess whether the relationship between PFPS scores and length of hospitalization found by Dirks, Kinsman, Jones, Spector, Davidson and Evans (1977) could be replicated in this population and also to study the relation between this measure and trait anxiety as measured by the STAI.

Respiratory Illness Opinion Survey (RIOS)

Attitudes towards asthma and hospitalization were measured using a questionnaire that was developed by Staudenmayer, Kinsman, and Jones (1978). Two dimensions that were expected to have the strongest relations to medical outcome were selected, namely "optimism" and "psychological stigma" (Kinsman, personal communication, 1979).

Nederlandse Persoonlijkheids Vragenlijst (NPV; Dutch Personality Inventory)

Personality traits were measured by the NPV, a widely used questionnaire in The Netherlands. Extensive validation data are available on this inventory (Luteyn, Starren, & Van Dijk, 1975). It contains 133 items measuring seven personality dimensions: neuroticism, social inadequacy, rigidity, hostility, egoism, dominance, and self esteem.

Lung Function

Every day at 12.30 hours each patient performed a "forced expiratory maneuver" on a Mijnhardt Vicatest Dry Spirometer, type VCT-2. This maneuver indexes the grade of airways obstruction. An index of severity of asthma was calculated by expressing the means of the daily forced expiratory volumes in one second (FEV_1) as a percentage of the predicted value (based on sex, height, and age).

Procedure

Each subject was tested individually on two or three occasions. Approximately 72 hours after admission to the hospital the subject was given the test battery in an office on the ward. The author introduced himself as a psychologist who was conducting research on "how people react to having asthma." In order to avoid any feelings on the part of the patient about "being mentally ill," it was explained to them that the testing was done routinely with every patient who was admitted to the hospital.

After the tests were completed, an audiotaped in-depth interview followed. The author explored feelings, attitudes, and behavior towards having asthma. Finally, the patients were informed of their scores on the tests.

RESULTS

Intercorrelations among the test score measures employed in this study are presented in Table 1. Despite high intercorrelations between various scales which measure emotional instability and anxiety, the state anxiety and trait anxiety scales of the STAI are not correlated significantly with the dependent variable. An important result concerns the significant correlations between the dependent variable, length of hospitalization, and four independent variables: panic-fear (situational anxiety), panic-fear personality, psychological stigma, and hostility. Length of hospitalization and all psychological factors were not correlated significantly with objective medical factors (duration and severity of asthma).

Patients were divided into two groups based on whether their length of hospitalization was shorter or longer than the overall mean number of days the patients stayed in the hospital (20.0 days). One tailed t-tests were performed to assess differences between these two groups. As illustrated in Table 2, the two groups differed on the following test measures: panic-fear (situational anxiety), trait anxiety, panic-fear personality, psychological stigma, neuroticism, and hostility. No differences were found between the groups on severity or duration of asthma. Patients with a hospitalization of long duration generally were more anxious, neurotic, and hostile and felt more stigmatized by their disease than patients who had a short length of hospitalization.

DISCUSSION

In general, the results of this study were consistent with similar research on illness behavior discussed above: intrapersonal and interpersonal mechanisms and processes predict length of hospitalization of asthma patients more reliably than objective indexes of severity and duration of the disease.

The finding that the panic-fear scales (both on the situation specific level and the personality trait level) correlated significantly with length of hospitalization, while the STAI scales that at face value seem to measure similar concepts did not, indicates that the STAI scales apparently tap a somewhat different aspect of anxiety.

The search for mechanisms that mediate anxiety and hostility can rather speculatively be approached from two directions. Since there are no objective criteria to use in deciding whether an asthmatic patient can be discharged safely, much latitude exists for patient and physician variables to influence this decision. On an *intra*personal level, a high level of anxiety indicates consciousness about minor symptoms of breathing difficulties, difficulties that would not be noticed or reported by a less anxious patient. The attention and concern about the symptoms on an *inter*personal level are manifested as a strong demand for attention from the physician. Hampered by the erratic character of asthma, physicians tend to adopt a conservative stance and recommend extended hospitalization. The highly hostile patients communicate overt irritation and aggression towards the physician. This type of attitude may make it difficult for the physician to maintain a professional attitude toward the patient and may result in a longer length of hospitalization.

Table 1 Correlation coefficients between length of hospitalization and psychological factors

	1.	2.	3.	4.	5.	6.	7.	8.
1. Length of hospitalization		.35*	.10	.18	.37*	.39*	.31	.47**
2. Situational anxiety			.72***	.55**	.51**	.51**	.53**	
3. State-A				.47**	.46**		.49**	
4. Trait-A					.83***	.49**	.80***	
5. Panic-fear personality						.42*	.71***	
6. Psychological stigma							.60***	.58**
7. Neuroticism								.45**
8. Hostility								

*p < .05.
**p < .01.
***p < .001.

Table 2 Mean scores of patients with short and long length of hospitalization on medical and psychological factors

	Duration of asthma	Severity of asthma	Panic-fear (Situational)	State-A	Trait-A	Panic-fear (Personality)	Psychological stigma	Neuroticism	Hostility
Short length of hospitalization (n = 17)	8.7	74.7	25.6	57.1	37.5	4.4	12.1	13.4	17.6
Long length of hospitalization (n = 9)	10.4	83.2	36.0	61.7	47.0	7.2	17.1	25.2	23.8
t (df)	-.30 (10)	-1.15 (11)	-2.66 (24)	-1.32 (13)	-2.02 (24)	-3.26 (23)	-1.93 (22)	-2.77 (24)	-2.22 (12)
p (one-tailed)	NS	NS	.01	NS	.05	.005	.05	.01	.05

203

The findings reported here support the notion that the behavior the asthma patient exhibits and the attitudes the patient has towards his illness determine to a great extent the medical outcome of the treatment. Creer (1977) has aptly indicated the direction future research should take: "the deciding factor should not be the asthma per se, however, but the person's adjustment . . . , hence, whenever possible, the primary goals must remain the delineation of how specified behavioral variables are functionally related to dependent measures of asthma" (p. 797).

REFERENCES

Auerbach, S. M. (1973). Trait-state anxiety and adjustment to surgery. *Journal of Consulting and Clinical Psychology, 40,* 264–271.

Clark, T. J. H., & Godfrey, S. (Eds.) (1977). *Asthma.* London: Chapman and Hall.

Cohen, F., & Lazarus, R. S. (1973). Active coping processes, coping dispositions and recovery from surgery. *Psychosomatic Medicine, 35,* 375–389.

Creer, T. L. (1977). Asthma: Psychologic aspects and management. In E. Middleton, C. E. Reed, & E. F. Ellis (Eds.), *Allergy: Principles and practice.* St. Louis: Mosby.

De Araujo, G., Arsdel, P. P. van, Holmes, T. H., & Dudley, D. L. (1973). Life change, coping ability and chronic intrinsic asthma. *Journal of Psychosomatic Research, 17,* 359–363.

Dirks, J. F. (1978). *The psychomaintenance of bronchial asthma: A review and preliminary theoretical integration of panic-fear research in asthma.* Unpublished doctoral dissertation, University of Denver, Denver.

Dirks, J. F., Jones, N. F., & Kinsman, R. A. (1977). Panic-fear: A personality dimension related to intractability in asthma. *Psychosomatic Medicine, 39,* 120–126.

Dirks, J. F., Kinsman, R. A., Horton, D. J., Fross, K. H., & Jones, N. F. (1978). Panic-fear in asthma: Rehospitalization following intensive long-term treatment. *Psychosomatic Medicine, 40,* 5–13.

Dirks, J. F., Kinsman, R. A., Jones, N. F., Spector, S. L., Davidson, P. T., & Evans, N. W. (1977). Panic-fear: A personality dimension related to length of hospitalization in respiratory illness. *The Journal of Asthma Research, 14,* 61–71.

Greer, S., Morris, T., & Pettingale, K. W. (1979). Psychological response to breast cancer: Effect on medical outcome. *The Lancet, 2,* 785–787.

Groen, J. J. (1979). The psychosomatic theory of bronchial asthma. *Psychotherapy and Psychosomatics, 31,* 38–48.

Jones, N. F., Kinsman, R. A., Dirks, J. F., & Wray Dahlem, N. (1979). Psychological contributions to chronicity in asthma: Patient response styles influencing medical treatment and its outcome. *Medical Care, 17,* 1103–1118.

Kinsman, R. A., Luparello, T., O'Banion, K., & Spector, S. (1973). Multidimensional analysis of the subjective symptomatology of asthma. *Psychosomatic Medicine, 35,* 250–267.

Knapp, P. H., Mathé, A. A., & Vachon, L. (1976). Psychosomatic aspects of bronchial asthma. In E. B. Weiss, & M. S. Segal (Eds.), *Bronchial asthma: Mechanisms and therapeutics.* Boston: Little, Brown.

Lazarus, R. S. (1966). *Psychological stress and the coping process.* New York: McGraw-Hill.

Lipowski, Z. J. (1969). Psychological aspects of disease. *Annals of Internal Medicine, 71,* 1197–1206.

Lipowski, Z. J. (1970). Physical illness, the individual and the coping process. *International Journal of Psychiatry in Medicine, 1,* 91–102.

Luteyn, F., Starren, J., & Van Dijk, H. (1975). *Handleiding Nederlandse Persoonlijkheidsvragenlijst.* Amsterdam: Swets & Zeitlinger.

Mechanic, D. (1977). Illness behavior, social adaptation, and the management of illness. *The Journal of Nervous and Mental Diseases, 165,* 79–87.

Petty, T. L. (1977). Status asthmaticus in adults. In E. Middleton, C. E. Reed, & E. F. Ellis (Eds.), *Allergy: Principles and practice.* St. Louis: Mosby.

Philips, B. U., & Bee, D. E. (1980). Determinants of post-operative recovery in elective orthopedic surgery. *Social Science and Medicine, 14A,* 325–330.

Pilowsky, I., Spence, N. D., and Waddy, S. L. (1979). Illness behavior and coronary artery bypass surgery. *Journal of Psychosomatic Research, 23,* 39–44.

Snider, G. L. (1978). Staging therapeutic schedules to clinical severity in status asthmaticus. In E. B. Weiss (Ed.), *Status asthmaticus.* Baltimore: University Park Press.

Spielberger, C. D., Gorsuch, R. L., & Lushene, R. E. (1970). *Manual for the State-Trait Anxiety Inventory.* Palo Alto, CA: Consulting Psychologists Press.

Staudenmayer, H., Kinsman, R. A., & Jones, N. F. (1978). Attitudes toward respiratory illness and hospitalization in asthma. *The Journal of Nervous and Mental Disorders, 166,* 624–634.

Teiramaa, E. (1978a). Psychic disturbances and duration of asthma. *Journal of Psychosomatic Research, 22,* 127–132.

Teiramaa, E. (1979b). Psychosocial and psychic factors in the course of asthma. *Journal of Psychosomatic Research, 22,* 121–125.

van der Ploeg, H. M., Defares, P. B., & Spielberger, C. D. (1980). Handleiding bij de Zelf-Beoordelings Vragenlijst, ZBV. Een Nederlands-talige bewerking van de Spielberger *State-Trait Anxiety Inventory,* STAI-DY. Lisse: Swets & Zeitlinger.

Weiss, E. B. (Ed.) (1978). *Status asthmaticus.* Baltimore: University Park Press, 1978.

16

Possible Psychological Causes of Female Infertility

J. L. M. Kremer-Nass and B. W. Frijling
University of Leiden

Doctors who are active in the field of human fertility and its problems are frequently confronted with infertility for which no medical explanation can be found. In medical practice many cases of inexplicable infertility may be linked to psychological factors, which play a role in preventing pregnancy in marriage.

The idea of the existence of psychological infertility is not new. The following quotation from W. Buchan dates from the 18th century:

> *When barrenness is suspected to proceed from affections of the mind, the person ought to be kept as easy and cheerful as possible, all disagreeable objects are to be avoided, and every effort taken to amuse and entertain the fancy. (London, 1797)*

Notice that women seem to have an exclusive right to being considered infertile because of psychological problems.

For the purpose of our research, we do not presuppose that psychological infertility exists but explore this as a possibility. Since medical knowledge of human infertility is still far from complete, involuntary infertility, which is *currently* not explainable by medical causes, may be in the future. Moreover, it appears that the opinions differ markedly on this question. To demonstrate this, we examined five frequently quoted publications and found that evidence of psychogenic infertility was noted in two studies (Adatia, 1958; Stolevic, Milosevic, Hajdukovic, & Bila, 1972), whereas it was concluded in three studies that it did not exist (Kipper, Zigler-Shani, Serr, & von Insler, 1977; Mai & Rump, 1972; Seward, Wagner, & Heinrich, 1965).

If psychosomatic infertility exists, one could define it as a psychosomatic disease. According to Weiss (1977), psychosomatic diseases have several characteristics in common:

1. The cause of the disease is related to a salient psychological characteristic of the patient.
2. The course of the disease is influenced by psychological factors.
3. There is a major symptom that is linked to a specific psychological factor.
4. The disease is functional in nature.

It is generally assumed that certain personalities are more vulnerable to psychosomatic diseases than others. A questionnaire developed by Feij (1979) explores four stable personality characteristics: extraversion, emotionalism, impulsiveness, and sensation-seeking. According to Feij, these characteristics were selected because of their broad theoretical relevance and potential application to the "diagnosis and therapy of psychosomatic complaints." Given the demonstrated validity of the Feij Self-Rating scale, a high correlation between scores on this scale and the probability of becoming pregnant would provide evidence that infertility not due to physical problems is a form of psychosomatic disease.

In our research, we observed a group of childless women who were being treated in a program of artificial insemination with the sperm of a donor, called the A.I.D. program. Most of the requests for donor-insemination came from couples of whom it was known that the women could ovulate and their husbands had been proven sterile or strongly subfertile. The goal of the A.I.D. program was to introduce good quality semen at the "optimal time."

The patients in our study were kept under observation during six insemination cycles. Although data collection was discounted after six cycles, the treatment was continued in most cases. However, this chapter presents only the results for the six cycles for which data were systematically collected. Our impression is that the results will not change significantly for subsequent cycles.

Our decision to use the A.I.D. program was determined by the fact that we considered this to be the most adequate reference group because the following four factors, which have an important influence on fertility, did not have to be accounted for: (1), the potential fertility of the woman; (2), the fertility of the man, that is, the fertility of the semen used; (3) the time of insemination; and (4) the technique of insemination. Nevertheless, in discussions of these points with experts, three questions were raised about the choice of the reference group (e.g., Blijham, Reactie, Frijling, & Nass, 1980):

1. The A.I.D. patients differ from normal populations.
2. The A.I.D. program is psychologically threatening.
3. The reactions of the husbands should have been taken into account.

In commenting on these criticisms, the following can be stated. First, the women who received the A.I.D. treatment did not differ significantly from Feij's norm population. Second, the A.I.D. patients filled in a questionnaire concerning their state anxiety immediately after the first insemination, and no relation between this variable and the probability of pregnancy was found. Finally, considering the fact that the personality traits that were measured are relatively stable, we concluded that the women's personality traits would exert their influence irrespective of the reactions or characteristics of their husbands.

PRELIMINARY RESULTS

The sample considered in this study consisted of 149 women, of whom 69 became pregnant by insemination. The scores on the Feij scale were correlated

Table 1   Pearson's product-moment
correlations between Feij's personality
characteristics and the probability of
becoming pregnant

Scale	Correlation
Extraversion	0.04
Emotionalism	0.02
Impulsiveness	0.06
Sensation-seeking	0.06

with the probability of becoming pregnant by means of Pearson product-moment coefficients. The results are presented in Table 1. None of the correlations were statistically significant.

The nonsignificant correlations found in this study provide no evidence of the existence of a relationship between the personality characteristics measured by the Feij scale and the probability of becoming pregnant for women with infertility for which no physical explanation could be detected. In further evaluating the data, we divided the sample into three separate groups on the basis of the number of psychosomatic complaints reported. Once again no significant differences were found for women reporting a large number, an average number, or a small number of symptoms. The proportion of pregnancies occurring in all three groups was essentially the same. Thus, as far as the data of our pilot study indicated, there seems to be no basis for regarding "infertility with unknown causes" as a psychosomatic disease.

CONCLUSIONS

This pilot study investigated a group of childless women who were treated in a program of artificial insemination with the sperm of a donor. The aim of the study was to investigate the effects of several personality traits on the occurrence of pregnancy. No relationships were found between extraversion, emotionalism, impulsiveness and sensation-seeking, and pregnancy. We are of the opinion, however, that it would be worthwhile to evaluate other variables more closely related to somatic functioning in future research on the contribution of psychological factors to infertility.

REFERENCES

Adatia, M.D. (1958). Psychogenic sterility. *Journal of Obstetrics and Gynecology of India, 8,* 283–290.
Blijham, H., Reactie, P., Frijling, B. W., & Nass, J. L. M. (1980). Psychogene onvruchtbaarheid. *Medisch Contact, 46,* 1420–1421.
Feij, J. A. (1979). *Temperament.* Lisse: Swets & Zeitlinger.
Kipper, D. A., Zigler-Shani, Z., Serr, D. M., & von Insler, V. (1977). Psychogenic infertility, neuroticism and the feminine role: A methodological inquiry. *Journal of Psychosomatic Research, 21,* 353–358.
Mai, F. M., & Rump, E. E. (1972). Are infertile men and women neurotic? *Australian Journal of Psychology, 24,* 83–86.
Seward, G. H., Wagner, P. S., & Heinrich, J. F. (1965). The question of psychophysiologic infertility: Some negative answers. *Psychosomatic Medicine, 27,* 533.

Stolević, E., Milosević, B., Hajduković, C., & Bila, S. (1972). Emotional moments as a possible cause of female sterility. *Psychosomatic Medicine in Obstetrics and Gynaecology,* Third International Congress, London 1971. Basel: Karger.
Weiss, J.H. (1977). The current state of the concept of a psychosomatic disorder. In Z. J. Lipowski, D. R. Lipsitt, & P. C. Whybrow (Eds.), *Psychosomatic medicine, current trends and clinical applications.* New York: Oxford University Press.

17

Anxiety and Depression in Premenstrual Syndrome

Ellen M. Goudsmit
National Association for Premenstrual Syndrome

Premenstrual Syndrome (PMS) is the term used to describe a collection of symptoms which occur during the second half of the menstrual cycle, where the symptoms are relieved by the onset of the full menstrual flow. In the majority of women these symptoms are mild, but in about 30% of all women with a natural cycle the symptoms are severe, causing considerable distress (Dalton, 1977).

Of the many symptoms that occur during the second half of the menstrual cycle, the two that seem to be the most common are anxiety or tension and depression (Moos, 1977; Rees, 1953). Golub (1976) measured anxiety, both as a state and as a trait, and depression in a group of women taken from the general population. She found that state anxiety and depression scores during the premenstrual phase were significantly higher than the intermenstrual scores. However, the premenstrual scores were far lower than those of psychiatric patients. The trait anxiety scores (which measure the predisposition of an individual to experience anxiety) were within the normal range (Spielberger, Gorsuch, & Lushene, 1970).

In a study in which the anxiety of women who experienced moderate-to-severe premenstrual symptoms was measured by the *Taylor Manifest Anxiety Scale* (TMAS), the anxiety levels of the PMS women exceeded those of a control group during the entire cycle (Halbreich & Kas, 1977). Since the TMAS measures trait anxiety, the authors concluded that high trait anxiety women were more predisposed to premenstrual symptoms.

The present study investigated levels of state and trait anxiety and depression in a group of women with PMS. The aim of the study was to determine whether women with PMS have higher state and trait anxiety and higher depression scores than a group of women who have no premenstrual symptoms. A woman was defined as suffering from PMS if she fulfilled all of the following criteria: (a) the symptoms occurred exclusively during the second half of the menstrual cycle; (b) the symptoms increased in severity as the cycle

Formerly of the University of Amsterdam, Dr. Goudsmit is now at The National Association for Premenstrual Syndrome.

progressed; (c) the symptoms were relieved by the onset of the full menstrual flow; and (d) the symptoms had been present for at least three consecutive cycles.

METHOD

Subjects

The subjects were 15 married women who had a predictable cycle which lasted between 26 and 32 days. Furthermore, all of them had already been recruited as subjects for a research study taking place at St. Thomas' Hospital, London, which investigated the effectiveness of pyridoxine as treatment for PMS. Their ages ranged from 24 to 44 years, with an average of 33.7 years. None of the women were currently taking psychotropic drugs, hormone preparations, or diuretics.

The control group consisted of 10 students and staff who were working in the hospital and who experienced no or only very mild premenstrual symptoms. Their ages ranged from 24 to 41 years, the mean being 26.7 years. None of the control subjects were taking hormonal preparations at the time of the study.

Test Instruments

The Background Information Questionnaire (BIQ)

This form was used to elicit details about age, marital status, occupation, and length of the menstrual cycle. The women were also asked to list any symptoms they experienced and to indicate which symptoms were the most troublesome and when they occurred and first became noticeable. They were also asked about their gynecological history and whether they were currently taking medicinal preparations of any kind. This information was used to assess a woman's suitability for inclusion in this study.

The Menstrual Distress Questionnaire (MDQ)

The list used in this study was a shortened version of the original Moos MDQ, devised by Clare (1977). In this version, all symptoms that did not show cyclical variation were omitted, and a number of symptoms were renamed to make them less ambiguous (e.g., lower motor coordination was renamed clumsiness). The modified MDQ has 34 items, each of which is rated on a 4-point scale. The scores obtained for each day were added up and used to confirm the diagnosis of PMS as defined above.

The State-Trait Anxiety Inventory (STAI)

The STAI, devised by Spielberger et al. (1970), consists of self-report scales that measure two distinct anxiety concepts: state and trait anxiety. State anxiety refers to a state of tension and arousal taking place at a given moment. Trait anxiety indicates the predisposition of an individual to react to stress with an increase in state anxiety.

The STAI was chosen as a measure of anxiety because it is reliable and valid and distinguishes between anxiety as a state and a trait. Moreover, because it is brief, it can be administered to subjects while they are waiting to have their blood taken. The A-State form was always given first.

The Depression Adjective Check List (DACL)

The DACL, developed by Lubin (1967), is a short self-report measure of transient depressive mood. There are four lists of adjectives, but only two of these, lists A and C (with an intercorrelation of .86), were judged suitable for use by English women. Each list was administered twice, in no particular order.

The DACL was chosen because it was easy to understand and short enough to be administered in the waiting room. In addition, it has acceptable reliability and validity data.

Procedure

The design of the study was similar to that of Golub (1976), except that each woman was tested on four rather than only two occasions. On the first occasion, which was on the 12th day of the menstrual cycle, the women were given an instruction sheet which requested carefully considered responses, and explained such terms as "mild," "moderate," and "severe," which are used in the questionnaires. The scores obtained on day 12 served as baseline measures. The other testing occasions occurred on days 18, 22 and 26 of the cycle.

The tests were administered between 10:00 a.m. and 4:00 p.m. in the consulting room of the Department of Gynecology. They were always presented in the same order, that is, STAI, DACL, MDQ. In order to minimize a carry-over effect from one occasion of measurement to the next, no feedback about performance was given. If menstruation failed to occur within 2 days of the expected date of onset, the data were discarded.

RESULTS

The data were evaluated by analyses of variance for repeated measures, except when tests of normality indicated that scores were not normally distributed, in which case a nonparametric test was used. For comparisons between days and within each group, the Wilcoxon matched-pairs test was used. For comparisons between groups on specific days, the Mann-Whitney U test was applied (Siegel, 1956). Significant differences at the .05 and .01 level of confidence are indicated by one and two asterisks, respectively, in the histograms depicted in Figures 1–3.

Menstrual Distress

A diagnosis of PMS was confirmed on the basis of MDQ scores. If the MDQ score on day 12 was lower than those on days 22 and 26, and scores on days 18, 22, and 26 showed marked increases reflecting increased menstrual distress, the woman was included in the PMS group. As Figure 1 shows, the mean MDQ score of the PMS group on day 12 was slightly higher than on day 18, but

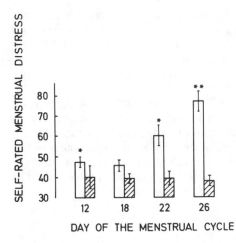

Figure 1 Means and standard errors of measurement for self-rated menstrual distress for selected days during the menstrual cycle for women with PMS and a control group. Asterisks indicate the level of significance of the difference between the means for the two groups on specified days (*p < .05; **p < .001); □ = PMS; ▨ = CONTROL.

significantly lower than on day 22 (p < .05) and day 26 (p < .01). The consistently lower MDQ scores of the control group confirmed that these women experienced little menstrual distress and showed minimal cyclical variations in menstrual distress symptoms.

State Anxiety

Of the many symptoms reported by the PMS group, tension and depression were often recorded as being the most troublesome. Figure 2 shows women with PMS reported progressively higher levels of state anxiety as the cycle progressed, whereas women in the control group showed relatively little variation in this measure. Analyses of variance (two-way ANOVAs with repeated measures on one factor) revealed significant Groups effect on one factor (p < .001) and a Groups by Time Periods interaction (p < .05).

The state-anxiety scores of the PMS group on day 18 were significantly lower than the anxiety scores on days 22 and 26 (p < .05 & .01, respectively). The scores of the PMS group on day 12 were similar to those reported by Golub (1976), in contrast to the scores on day 26 which were extremely high and far exceeded those found by Golub. The premenstrual state-anxiety scores of the PMS group also exceeded those reported in the STAI manual for psychiatric patients with anxiety neurosis (Spielberger et al., 1970). In sharp contrast, the control group recorded low state-anxiety scores throughout the cycle, although there was a significant increase between day 12 and day 22 (p < .05). Also notable was the significant decrease in the scores of the control group from day 22 to baseline levels and the similarity in the state anxiety scores of the control and patient groups on day 18.

Trait Anxiety

The trait anxiety scores of the PMS group were consistently and significantly higher than those of the control group (p < .001), as Figure 2 shows. The PMS group recorded increasingly higher trait scores from day 18 onwards, and the difference between days 18 and 26 was statistically significant (p < .05). Variation in trait anxiety scores of the PMS group during the menstrual cycle was *not* expected and raises questions about this scale as a measure of a stable personality trait. The trait anxiety scores of the PMS group in the present study were higher than those of Golub's (1976) subjects, but were lower than the scores reported in the STAI Manual for psychiatric patients suffering from anxiety or depression (Spielberger et al., 1970).

Depression

The scores for depressive mood, reported in Figure 3, were generally similar to those obtained for state anxiety. In the ANOVA for the DACL Depression scores, significant main effects were found for Groups (p < .001) and Days (p < .05), and a Groups by Days interaction (p < .01). Although there was little variability in the scores of the PMS group from day 12 to day 18, the increases in the DACL scores for this group from day 18 to day 26 was significant (p < .01). Moreover, the DACL scores of the PMS group were higher than those of the control group on all four testing days; these differences were significant on days 12, 22 and 26. The premenstrual DACL scores of the PMS group in the present study were nearly twice those recorded by Golub (1976).

In order to determine the relation between trait anxiety and the other questionnaire measures, Spearman's rank order correlation coefficients were computed for the data obtained on day 12 (baseline) and day 26 (premenstrual), (Siegel, 1956). Highly significant positive correlations of trait anxiety with MDQ scores (r_s = .65; p < .009) and depressive mood (r_s = .81,

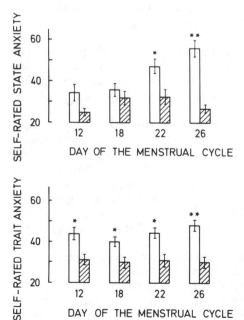

Figure 2 Means and standard errors of measurement for self-rated state and trait anxiety for selected days during the menstrual cycle for women with PMS and a control group (*p < .05; **p < .001): □ = PMS; ▨ = CONTROL.

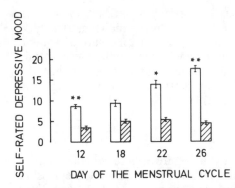

Figure 3 Means and standard errors of measurement for self-rated depressive mood for selected days during the menstrual cycle for women with PMS and a control group (*p < .05; **p < .001):☐= PMS;▨= CONTROL.

p < .001) were found on day 26, indicating that women with higher trait anxiety reported higher levels of menstrual distress and more depression during the premenstrual phase. Correlations of trait anxiety with the other measures did not reach statistical significance.

DISCUSSION

In this study, a modified version of the Moos (1977) Menstrual Distress Questionnaire was used to confirm a diagnosis of Premenstrual Syndrome (PMS). Measures of anxiety and depression were recorded by 15 women suffering from PMS on four occasions during their menstrual cycle. State anxiety and depressive mood increased markedly from day 18 onwards, and scores on day 26 exceeded those recorded by women recruited from the general population (Golub, 1976). Furthermore the premenstrual scores of women suffering from PMS were similar to those of psychiatric patients with anxiety neurosis and depression, as reported in the STAI Manual (Spielberger, et al., 1970). These findings suggest that PMS is a temporary condition related to the menstrual cycle, which becomes more distressing as the cycle progresses. The elevations in anxiety and depression scores on day 26 suggested that PMS should be considered a temporary disability which deserves treatment (Dalton, 1977) and not merely a few days of discomfort that women should be able to cope with.

Trait anxiety was measured in order to evaluate the relationship between PMS and a predisposition to suffer from anxiety. The finding that seven women in the PMS group recorded trait anxiety scores above the normal range reported in the STAI Manual (Spielberger et al., 1970) was consistent with observations by Halbreich and Kas (1977) that women with high trait anxiety are more predisposed to PMS. It cannot be concluded, however, that women suffer from PMS because they have higher levels of trait anxiety because almost half of the women in the PMS group recorded "normal" trait anxiety as well as distressing premenstrual symptoms.

The finding that women in the PMS group tended to report increasing trait anxiety as the cycle progressed was unexpected because trait anxiety is considered to be a relatively stable personality characteristic. Alternatively, it may be that the test is extremely sensitive to changes in self-concept and that as the discomfort increased, so did the way in which the women perceived themselves. This possibility is supported by the stability of the scores of the control group and by the high depression scores recorded during the premenstrual phase of the PMS group.

Although psychosocial factors may influence the premenstrual distress experienced by some women the findings of this study do not support the view that PMS is a psychogenic condition. In fact, the temporary nature of PMS and its relationship to menses suggest that hormones are involved in the etiology of this condition. The possibility that a hormonal imbalance predisposes women to experience discomfort and that psychosocial problems exacerbate the discomfort warrants further study.

The work of Haskett, Steiner, Osmun, and Carroll (1980) and the findings of this study demonstrate the importance of using a questionnaire to confirm verbal reports of PMS, and indicate the usefulness of the MDQ as a screening tool in the diagnosis of PMS. Strict definitions should be used in diagnosing PMS to ensure that there is at least one week in which no symptoms are reported. Once PMS can be successfully distinguished from Menstrual Distress, it will be fruitful to investigate whether PMS is a unitary condition as Dalton has proposed (1977), or whether it is made up of separate symptom clusters, each caused by a different hormonal abnormality, as hypothesized by Clare (1979).

Future studies should investigate the nature of Menstrual Distress as distinguished from PMS. Dalton (personal communication) and Haskett, Steiner, Osmun, and Carroll (1980) have observed that Menstrual Distress is a condition akin to PMS, but has different characteristics. Haskett et al. (1980) found that women with high MDQ scores on day 12 reported a different set of symptoms from women who had low MDQ scores on that day. Further research is needed to investigate the role of psychological and hormonal disturbances in the etiology of both PMS and menstrual distress.

REFERENCES

Clare, A. W. (1977). Psychological profiles of women complaining of premenstrual symptoms. *Current Medical Research and Opinion*, Suppl. 4, *4*, 23–28.

Clare, A. W. (1979). The treatment of premenstrual symptoms. *British Journal of Psychiatry, 135*, 576–579.

Dalton, K. (1977). *The premenstrual syndrome and progesterone therapy.* London: Heinemann Medical Books.

Golub, S. (1976). The magnitude of premenstrual anxiety and depression. *Psychosomatic Medicine, 38*, 4–12.

Halbreich, U., & Kas, D. (1977). Variations in the Taylor MAS of women with premenstrual syndrome. *Journal of Psychosomatic Research.*

Haskett, R. F., Steiner, M., Osmun, J. N., & Carroll, B. J. (1980). Severe premenstrual tension: Delineation of the syndrome. *Biological Psychiatry, 15*, 121–139.

Lubin, B. (1967). *Manual for the Depression Adjective Check Lists.* San Diego, CA: Educational and Industrial Testing Service.

Moos, R. H. (1977). *Menstrual Distress Questionnaire Manual.* Palo Alto, CA: Ecology Laboratory, Stanford University.

Rees, L. (1953). Psychosomatic aspects of the premenstrual tension syndrome. *Journal of Mental Science, 99*, 62.

Siegel, S. (1956). *Nonparametric Statistics.* Tokyo: McGraw-Hill.

Spielberger, C. D., Gorsuch, R. L., & Lushene, R. E. (1970). *State-Trait Anxiety Inventory Manual.* Palo Alto, CA: Consulting Psychologists Press.

18

Situational and Individual Determinants of State Anxiety in Surgical Patients

A. Ph. Visser
University of Limburg

Anxiety is a dominant emotional reaction of patients to illness and hospital admission (Verwoerdt, 1972). In early studies of the anxiety of surgical patients, inadequate anxiety measures were used, as was noted by Bergsma and Rullmann-Schadee (1976), Franklin (1974), and Wolfer (1973). The development of reliable and valid tests to assess anxiety, such as the *State-Trait Anxiety Inventory* (Spielberger, Gorsuch, & Lushene, 1970), has stimulated research on factors influencing the anxiety reactions of surgical patients.

Two factors affecting state anxiety have been given prominence in research on the emotional reactions of surgery patients: *anxiety dispositions* (trait anxiety) and the *psychosocial care* given to patients (Auerbach, 1973; Felton, Huss, Payne, & Srsic, 1976; Kinney, 1977; Martinez-Urrutia, 1975). In most studies, these factors were considered separately. This chapter reports the results of a study that investigated the combined influence on the state anxiety of surgical patients of trait anxiety and psychosocial care given by nurses.

EFFECTS OF TRAIT AND STATE ANXIETY AND PSYCHOSOCIAL CARE ON SURGICAL PATIENTS

Undergoing surgery does not influence the trait anxiety level of patients, as demonstrated by the absence of any pre- and postoperative differences in a number of studies (Auerbach, 1973; Martinez-Urrutia, 1975; Spielberger, Auerbach, Wadsworth, Dunn, & Taulbee, 1973). In most studies, investigators have reported a decline in state anxiety from pre- to postsurgery (Chapman & Cox, 1977; Johnson, Dabbs, & Leventhal, 1970; Kinney, 1977), which was independent of the preoperative trait-anxiety level. But this does not mean that trait anxiety has no influence on the patient's state anxiety. Patients with high

I wish to thank P. van Velthoven, W. Nijk, P. Grond, and the nurses of the wards for their cooperation in this project. I am grateful to Dr. J. Bergsma and Dr. L. van Rooijen for their valuable comments.

Formerly of The Free University, Dr. Visser is now at the University of Limburg.

preoperative trait anxiety experience stronger feelings of state anxiety, both before and after surgery, than patients with low preoperative trait anxiety. Spielberger et al. (1970) and Spielberger (1972) reported substantial positive correlations between state and trait anxiety (0.67–0.51).

In several studies of surgical patients a hospital-specific trait anxiety measure was successfully used. Martinez-Urrutia (1975) showed that fear of surgery influenced the preoperative state-anxiety level but not postoperative state anxiety, and Lucente and Fleck (1972) found a positive correlation between a Hospital Anxiety Scale and the Taylor Manifest Anxiety Scale. Thus, it appears that situation-specific trait anxiety measures are potential predictors of hospital-specific anxiety and that the latter influence preoperative state anxiety levels.

The psychosocial care given to patients prior to surgery, such as information and emotional support, also influences state anxiety. Leigh, Walker, and Janaganathan (1977) reported that providing surgical patients with a booklet on anesthesia reduced their preoperative state anxiety as compared to patients not given a booklet, and anxiety was diminished even more when a member of the anesthesia team engaged in a reassuring and informative talk with the patients. Similarly, Felton et al. (1976) observed that patients who received some kind of preoperative preparation (a folder, film, respiration exercise, etc.) showed a significantly greater decrease in the level of pre- and postoperative state anxiety than those who had no opportunity to prepare for an operation by assimilating relevant information. A number of other studies have also reported positive effects of preoperative information, instruction, and emotional support provided to patients, as reviewed by Bergsma and Rullmann-Schadee (1976), Davies-Osterkamp (1977) and Skipper and Leonard (1965).

Little attention has been given to possible interactive effects of psychosocial care and trait anxiety on the state anxiety of surgical patients. In one of the earliest studies of surgical patients, Janis (1958) observed an inverted U-shaped relationship between preoperative fear and postoperative adjustment. Patients who displayed a moderate degree of preoperative fear were less likely to develop emotional disturbances after an operation. In addition, uninformed patients displayed a lower level of preoperative anxiety. Thus, Janis' findings would lead to the prediction that preoperative emotional support would be beneficial for low-anxiety patients.

Subsequent studies have not consistently supported Janis' findings (Johnston & Carpenter, 1980). In one study, patients with strong feelings of anxiety became more anxious after a brief nonsupportive, but informative talk (Williams & Workhoven, 1975). A study by Keller (1965) also showed that brief informative interviews with patients increased their anxiety, and Kinney (1977) found that patients responded to preoperative teaching with lower state-anxiety levels, regardless of their coping style. Davies-Osterkamp (1977) related patient-counseling effectiveness to the manner in which surgical patients handled psychological preparation, and concluded from her review of relevant studies that it was not important to strive for a uniform method that was equally effective for all patients (Andrew, 1970; Langer, Janis, & Wolfer, 1975; Vernon & Bigelow, 1974).

Aims of the Study

The aim of the present study was to investigate the effects of trait anxiety *and* information supply on the state-anxiety levels of surgical patients. Three different procedures were used to provide information about ward routines and the events before and during surgery. These were a *booklet* given to the patients, *social skills training* given to ward nurses, and *preoperative talks* given to patients. In evaluating the effects of these situational factors on the patients' state anxiety, possible interactions with individual differences in trait and hospital-specific anxiety were taken into account. The following hypotheses were formulated:

1. Preoperative state anxiety of patients will be higher than their postoperative state anxiety.
2. Increasing the information supply will decrease the pre- and postoperative state anxiety of the patients.
3. Trait and hospital-specific anxiety will influence the pre- and postoperative state anxiety of the patients.

The following question was also explored: How strongly will the state anxiety of the patients be affected by their trait and hospital anxiety, as compared with the influence of the preoperative psychosocial preparation given by nurses? The effects of modifications in the information supply were also studied in terms of changes in the acquired knowledge and satisfaction of the patients (Visser, 1980a, 1980b).

METHOD

The study was conducted on two surgical wards (35 beds each) of a general hospital; each ward had its own ward sister and 12 nurses, most of them trainees. The wards are organizationally independent units within the hospital setting, but there is a common medical staff, consisting of four surgeons and three assistants. Both wards participated in an earlier communication study (Bergsma, 1976).

The present investigation was preceded by an observational study from which it was concluded that there were gaps in the systematic information supplied to patients regarding ward routines, preparation for surgery (e.g., anesthesia, operation procedures), and awakening from narcosis. After several staff meetings, it was decided to change the information given to patients about the ward routines, the operation procedures, and narcosis. The sole condition for these changes was that they should occur within the format of the existing organizational structure and working routines of the ward. An information booklet to be presented to patients on the day of admission was developed, and staff nurses from one of the wards were trained in social skills needed to conduct special preoperative informative talks with the patients of that particular ward (Visser, 1980a, 1980b).

Experimental Procedures

The patients received the information booklet on their admission to the ward. This booklet included spatial maps of the hospital and the ward, and information about the routines on the day of admission; the operation itself; narcosis, anesthesia and awakening; the psychosocial care facilities in the hospital; the names of staff members; and time schedules and hospital rules. Patients were encouraged to ask questions and express their problems.

The training of the nurses encompassed nondirective counseling techniques that were compatible with the passive role behavior of the patients in their contacts with nurses. Altogether, six nurses from one ward attended all four of the 90-min training sessions, which were held during working hours (Grond & Visser, 1979). The nurses were then trained to give preoperative and informative talks with each patient scheduled to receive surgery. These talks provided information about the forthcoming operation and gave the patients a chance to express their anxiety and worries. A check was made to determine whether the talks of 5 to 15 min each had actually taken place on the afternoon of the day prior to the operation.

The patient information booklet was introduced on both wards. The other two manipulations were limited to one ward only, which was considered the experimental ward. The ward where the previous routines were continued served as a control. In total, 185 patients participated in the study. The measurements were obtained in three different periods which constituted the three phases of the study. The first phase was carried out three months before the introduction of the booklet ($n = 51$); the second came after the booklet was introduced ($n = 49$). Both phases lasted one month each.

The third measurement period took place after the nurses' counseling training was completed and during the preoperative talks. During a period of three months, 35 patients were interviewed on the eve of the operation; 15 of them had had a preoperative talk. Similarly, 35 patients from the control ward were interviewed. This third phase took about 2 months. The total duration of the study was approximately 18 months.

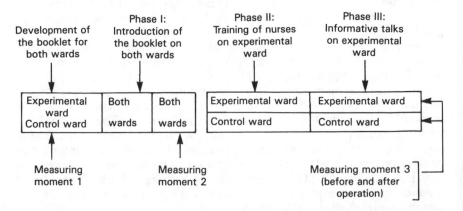

Figure 1 The three phases of the study and the measuring moments (periods) during which the questionnaires and tests were given.

The three phases and associated measuring periods are summarized in Figure 1. The time-serial design made it possible to study the effects of each experimental condition independently.

Patient Sample

The selection of the patients during the first and second measuring periods was based on two criteria: (1) Patients under the age of 16 were excluded; and (2) Patients too ill or handicapped or who were emotionally or physically unable to answer the questionnaire were excluded. The ward sisters were consulted beforehand for each case; every week a list of selected patients was submitted. Patients who were requested to participate in the investigation were not interviewed on a fixed day during their stay, but most of them (85%) were interviewed within 8 days after their operations.

In the third phase of the experiment, patients admitted to the experimental ward were randomly divided on the day of hospital admission into two groups: One group received the extra informative talk, and the other did not. During this phase the questionnaire was invariably given on the third or fourth day after the operation in order to ensure that the groups were comparable. Patients were selected for a preoperative talk on the basis of the following criteria: They were (a) scheduled for operation the next day; (b) not likely to have malignant diseases; and (c) not likely to be discharged within 1 or 2 days. Thus, the sample for the final phase was selected differently from the first two phases.

Of the available patients ($n = 358$), 52% participated in the experiment. Reasons for nonparticipation were having been already discharged (12%); having no interest or being too tired (7%); having objections to surveys (7%); not meeting all of the criteria (12%); and unknown or not recorded (10%). Thus, only 14% explicitly refused to cooperate, which was in agreement with the nonresponse rates in other Dutch patient studies.

The proportion of male (48%) and female (52%) patients was similar. The average age was 43; 30% were younger than 30; and 35% were older than 50 years. Most patients (90%) did not undergo a serious operation, as verified from the medical records. The operations were for hernia (12%), limbs (13%), gastrointestinal (11%), gallstones and appendicitis (7%), breast cancer (15%), and nonmalignant neoplasms (9%). The mean length of hospitalization was 12.6 days; 36% stayed less than one week; 29% stayed between 1 and 2 weeks. Approximately half (49%) of the patients were interviewed within 5 days; 32% one or two days before their discharge. The characteristics of the sample were comparable to those of other Dutch patient studies.

The patients independently filled in the questionnaire, which was given to them by trained psychology students. In addition to the anxiety scales, the questionnaire contained measures of satisfaction with the psychosocial care received, medical and hospital knowledge, and communication climate (attitude and behavior of doctor and nurses). The patients also answered questions on what they felt about the psychological preparation for surgery: extent and clearness of the information obtained about their operation; the visit of the anesthetist; the meaning of the information given in the booklet; and the anxiety-evoking nature of the informative talks.

State and trait anxiety were measured with a Dutch version of the STAI (Spielberger et al., 1970), which was validated in earlier research on the anxiety of dental patients (Eijkman & Orlebeke, 1975). This Dutch version of the STAI was similar to a later version developed and validated by van der Ploeg (1980). Hospital anxiety was measured with a new test consisting of 19 items, which was based on unstructured interviews with patients; some of the items were derived from the Hospital Anxiety Scale used by Lucente and Fleck (1972) and Volicer (1974). Example items are "Do you think narcosis involves great risks?"; "Are you afraid of it?"; "Do you think you might have pain after the operation?". The response alternatives were true, false, yes, or no.

The anxiety tests showed good internal consistency: The Cronbach alpha coefficients varied between .93 and .70 (mean = .82). The influence of social desirability on the anxiety tests was relatively low ($\bar{r} = -.20$). The frequency of expressing feelings towards nurses (as a state measurement) correlated significantly with the measures of hospital-specific anxiety ($r = .43$).

RESULTS

The pre- and postsurgical means for the anxiety measures are presented in Table 1 for the total sample. State anxiety was significantly higher on the eve of the operation than 3 or 4 days after, but scores on the hospital-specific anxiety measure showed no significant pre- and postoperative difference. Also, the correlation between the pre- and postsurgical measures of hospital anxiety ($r = .47; p < .001$) was higher than with state anxiety ($r = .27; p < .08$). Thus, the results demonstrated that the state-anxiety measure was sensitive to the situational influence of the presurgical condition, whereas the hospital-specific anxiety measure was not.

In the last phase of the experiment, preoperative anxiety was measured in order to ascertain the influence of the preoperative talks on state anxiety and to check whether the levels of trait anxiety and hospital-specific anxiety had changed. The results are presented in Table 2. In accordance with our expectations, the preoperative talks did not influence the trait anxiety and hospital-specific anxiety scores. Although no changes were found for patients on the experimental ward in state anxiety as a consequence of the preoperative talks, the state-anxiety level for the nontrained control ward was significantly higher than for the experimental ward (t-test: $p < .02$). Although this difference can be interpreted as an effect of the counseling training, it should

Table 1 Pre- and postoperative state and hospital anxiety levels

Anxiety scale	Before surgery ($N = 46$)	After surgery ($N = 46$)	t-test
State anxiety			
Mean	41.0	34.6	$p \leq .005$
SD	10.2	10.3	
Hospital anxiety			
Mean	24.3	24.3	NS
SD	3.4	3.7	

Table 2 Preoperative anxiety levels of patients on the experimental ward (with and without preoperative talks) and the control ward

Anxiety scale	Experimental ward		Control ward ($N = 35$)	F-test
	Preop. talk ($N = 14$)	No talk ($N = 35$)		
Trait anxiety				
Mean	36.5	36.2	36.7	NS
SD	10.4	7.1	8.6	
Hospital anxiety				
Mean	24.7	24.5	25.9	NS
SD	3.8	3.8	4.1	
State anxiety				
Mean	40.8	39.6	44.6	NS
SD	12.3	9.9	11.5	

also be noted that the nontrained ward was comprised of more female patients and more patients with a lower vocational background and higher social desirability scores (Visser, 1980b).

Psychosocial Care and Postoperative State Anxiety

The influence of the three experimental conditions on postoperative state anxiety is shown in Table 3. The total F-test showed that the patients had significantly higher state anxiety after a preoperative talk. State anxiety also seemed elevated after the introduction of the booklet on the wards. However, controlling for random sampling differences among the three conditions resulted in an almost complete disappearance of the state-anxiety differences. In the condition associated with the introduction of the booklet, the patients were interviewed sooner after their operations. The difference between the experimental group (with the booklet) and the control group (without the booklet) was found only for patients interviewed at a later stage following surgery, and just before leaving the hospital. Thus, the higher state anxiety cannot be ascribed to the booklet given to them on the day of admission.

Table 3 Postoperative state anxiety of patients in the various psychosocial care conditions

Experimental conditions	N	Mean[a]	SD
Information booklet (both wards)			
Before introduction	48	28.5	5.8
After introduction	49	32.6	9.9
(t-test, $p < .03$)			
Control ward	18	32.9	6.2
Experimental ward			
No preoperative talk	21	32.0	8.8
Preoperative talk	8	45.0	14.6
(t-test, $p < .02$)			

[a]F-test for all conditions: $F = 3.61$; $p < .03$; df = 143.

The rather high anxiety scores of the patients who received a preoperative informative talk also seem to vanish when sample characteristics are held constant. The anxiety dropped when the educational level was controlled. There was also an interaction with the number of days prior to the patients' discharge: the closer the day of discharge, the lower the level of anxiety. The experimental group, on the average, stayed in the hospital longer than the control group. The data also showed that the three psychosocial care conditions did not affect differences between pre- and postoperative hospital anxiety, but both pre- and postoperative state anxiety were higher when an informative talk with the patient had taken place prior to the operation.

The correlations between the state, trait, and hospital anxiety measures are presented in Table 4, in which it can be seen that preoperative state anxiety was most strongly correlated with preoperative hospital anxiety. This finding suggests that the patients' state anxiety on the eve of the operation was higher if they were anxious about various aspects of the operation or their stay in the hospital. Postoperative state anxiety was correlated with the patients' trait anxiety.

Since correlation between trait and hospital anxiety was $r = .45$ $(n = 42)$, partial correlations were computed in order to explain the relative influence of these factors on the pre- and postoperative state anxiety measures. The partial correlations indicated that preoperative state anxiety was more strongly influenced by hospital anxiety than by trait anxiety. Postoperative state anxiety, on the other hand, was influenced only by trait anxiety. The data also revealed that the decrease in state anxiety was the same for patients with high and low trait anxiety. However, this decrease was greater for patients with high than for those with low hospital anxiety ($\overline{X} = 9.4$ and $2.8; p < .05$).

Influence on State Anxiety of Psychosocial Care and Trait and Hospital Anxiety

The combined effects on state anxiety of the preoperative care conditions and individual differences in trait and hospital anxiety were evaluated in 4×2 factorial design analyses of variance. The scores for the hospital anxiety, trait anxiety, and total preoperative care measures were divided at the median into two groups; the fourth factor taken into account was whether or not the preoperative talk was included. The results showed a significant main effect of hospital anxiety, $F(10.3)$, $p < .01$; patients with high hospital anxiety were higher in state anxiety both before and after surgery. Moreover, postoperative state anxiety was influenced solely by the hospital anxiety, $F(4.4); p < .05$; none of the other main effects or interactions were statistically significant. The preoperative informative talk appeared to have no influence on state anxiety.

The multiple correlation of the four factors with preoperative state anxiety was .54, whereas the beta coefficient for the hospital anxiety measure alone was .46. The correlation of hospital anxiety with postoperative state anxiety was .34, with a beta coefficient for hospital anxiety of .33. Thus, hospital anxiety alone was the major predictor of patients' pre- and postoperative state anxiety scores.

Table 4 Correlations between preoperative trait and hospital anxiety and pre- and postoperative state anxiety

| | Pre- and postoperative state anxiety | | | |
| | Zero-order correlations | | Partial[a] correlations | |
Preoperative	Pre	Post	Pre	Post
Trait anxiety	.33**	.27*	.07	.22*
Hospital anxiety	.64***	.18	.34**	.11

[a]Effects of hospital and trait anxiety, respectively, have been controlled in the partial correlations for trait and hospital anxiety.
  $*.04 < p < .08.$
  $**p < .01.$
  $***p < .001.$

DISCUSSION

The findings of the present study were in general agreement with other studies of emotional reactions to surgery which found that state anxiety was higher before than after surgery (Auerbach, 1973; Johnson et al., 1970; Johnson & Carpenter, 1980; Kinney, 1977; Martinez-Urrutia, 1975; Spielberger et al., 1973). In contrast, trait-anxiety scores were essentially the same before and after surgery. Surgical patients with high hospital anxiety had higher preoperative state anxiety, and the decline in state anxiety was more marked for these patients than for patients with low hospital anxiety, as was also observed by Martinez-Urrutia (1975) for a measure of fear of surgery. The situation-specific hospital anxiety measure was a better predictor of state anxiety than the general trait-anxiety measure. Correlations among the anxiety measures suggested that preoperative hospital anxiety was an intermediary variable with reference to trait anxiety and preoperative state anxiety. These relationships are summarized in Figure 2.

The psychosocial care conditions relating to the preoperative preparation of the patients had little influence on postoperative state anxiety. Contrary to expectations, these conditions tended to be associated with higher, rather than

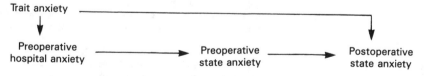

Figure 2 The influence of trait anxiety and preoperative hospital anxiety on pre- and postoperative state anxiety.

lower anxiety. Preoperative state anxiety measured on the eve of the operation was not influenced by a preparatory informative talk the previous day, nor did the psychosocial care conditions influence the other indicators of patients' psychosocial well-being, such as satisfaction and knowledge (Visser, 1980a, 1980b). The psychosocial care conditions also failed to influence the perceived "communication climate," as defined by the patients' personal evaluation of psychosocial care on admission, the medical information provided, and the preoperative preparation. As compared to the highly anxious patients, the less anxious patients seemed to perceive the psychosocial climate as more positive.

The weak effects of the psychosocial care conditions in this study contrasted with the strong influence of hospital anxiety, which was the best overall predictor of state anxiety. As in the present study, Eijkman and Orlebeke (1975) also found that a situation-specific measure of dental anxiety was a better predictor of state anxiety than individual differences in trait anxiety, but no interactions between preoperative preparation and personality traits were observed, such as those reported by Davies-Osterkamp (1977) and Janis (1958).

In future studies of psychosocial care for surgery patients, the time when the dependent variables are measured should be carefully controlled. In the present study, the measurement of preoperative state anxiety may have been too remote from the preoperative care given to the patients. This could account for why the results differed from Leigh et al. (1977), who found that a booklet on anesthetization reduced patients' state anxiety. However, it is also possible that the information booklet used in the present study was not effective in reducing state anxiety.

REFERENCES

Andrew, J. M. (1970). Recovery from surgery, with and without preparatory instruction, for three coping styles. *Journal of Personality and Social Psychology, 15,* 223–226.

Auerbach, S. M. (1973). Trait-state anxiety and adjustment to surgery. *Journal of Consulting and Clinical Psychology, 40,* 264–271.

Bergsma, J. (1976). Evaluatie van een kommunikatieprojekt in een algemeen ziekenhuis. *Mens en Onderneming, 30,* 5–22.

Bergsma, J., & Rullmann-Schadee, G. R. (1976). Onderzoek naar 'patient-centered-care.' Enkele methodologische opmerkingen. *Tijdschrift voor Sociale Geneeskunde, 54,* 40–44.

Chapman, C. R., & Cox, G. B. (1977). Determinants of anxiety in elective surgery patients. In C. D. Spielberger & I. G. Sarason (Eds.), *Stress and anxiety* (Vol. 4). Washington: Hemisphere.

Davies-Osterkamp, S. (1977). Angst und Angstbewältigung bei chirurgischen Patienten. *Medizinische Psychologie, 3,* 169–184.

Eijkman, M. A. J., & Orlebeke, J. F. (1975). De factor "angst" in de tandheelkundige situatie. *Nederlands Tijdschrift voor Tandheelkunde, 82,* 114–123.

Felton, G., Huss, K., Payne, E. A., & Srsic, K. (1976). Preoperative nursing intervention with the patient for surgery: Outcomes of three alternative approaches. *International Journal of Nursing Studies, 13,* 83–96.

Franklin, B. L. (1974). *Patient anxiety on admission to hospital.* London: R.C.N.

Grond, P. J. N., & Visser, A. Ph. (1979). Therapeutisch gedrag van verpleegkundigen en het effect van een gesprekstraining. *Tijdschrift voor Ziekenverpleging, 32,* 307–314.

Janis, J. G. (1958). *Psychological stress.* New York: Wiley.

Johnson, J. E., Dabbs, J. M., Jr., & Leventhal, H. (1970). Psychosocial factors in the welfare of surgical patients. *Nursing Research, 19,* 18–29.

Johnston, M., & Carpenter, L. (1980). Relationship between pre-operative anxiety and post-operative state. *Psychological Medicine, 10,* 361–367.

Keller, C. M. (1965). *Relationship of anxiety changes and an information giving experience.* Unpublished doctoral dissertation, New York University.

Kinney, M. R. (1977). Effects of preoperative teaching upon patients with differing modes of response to threatening stimuli. *International Journal of Nursing Studies, 14,* 49–59.

Langer, E. J., Janis, I. L., & Wolfer, J. A. (1975). Reduction of psychological stress in surgical patients. *Journal of Experimental and Social Psychology, 11,* 155–165.

Leigh, J. M., Walker, J., & Janaganathan, P. (1977). Effect of preoperative anaesthetic visit on anxiety. *British Medical Journal, 2,* 987–989.

Lucente, F. E., & Fleck, S. (1972). A study of hospitalization anxiety in 408 medical and surgical patients. *Psychosomatic Medicine, 34,* 304–307.

Martinez-Urrutia, A. (1975). Anxiety and pain in surgical patients. *Journal of Consulting and Clinical Psychology, 43,* 437–442.

Ploeg, H. M. van der. (1980). Validatie van de Zelf-Beoordelings Vragenlijst. Een Nederlandse bewerking van de Spielberger State-Trait Anxiety Inventory. *Nederlands Tijdschrift voor de Psychologie, 35,* 243–249.

Skipper, J. K., & Leonard, R. C. (1965). *Social interaction and patient care.* Philadelphia: Lippincott.

Spielberger, C. D. (Ed.). (1972). *Anxiety: Current trends in theory and research.* (Vol. 1). New York: Academic Press.

Spielberger, C.D., Auerbach, S., Wadsworth, M., Dunn, M., & Taulbee, E. (1973). Emotional reactions to surgery. *Journal of Consulting and Clinical Psychology, 40,* 33–38.

Spielberger, C. D., Gorsuch, R. L., & Lushene, R. E. (1970). *Manual for the State-Trait Anxiety Inventory.* Palo Alto, CA: Consulting Psychologists Press.

Vernon, D. T., & Bigelow, D. A. (1974). Effect of information about a potentially stressful situation on responses to stress impact. *Journal of Personality and Social Psychology, 29,* 50–59.

Verwoerdt, A. (1972). Psychopathological responses to the stress of physical illness. *Advanced Psychosomatic Medicine, 8,* 162–179.

Visser, A. Ph. (1980a). Effects of an information booklet on well-being of hospital patients. *Patient Counseling and Health Education, 2,* 51–64.

Visser, A. Ph. (1980b). De beïnvloeding van de voorlichting aan chirurgische patiënten. *Gezondheid en Samenleving, 1,* 194–221.

Volicer, B. J. (1974). Patients' perceptions of stressful events associated with hospitalization. *Nursing Research, 23,* 235–238.

Williams, J., & Workhoven, W. (1975). The psychological control of preoperative anxiety. *Psychophysiology, 12,* 50–54.

Wolfer, J. A. (1973). Definition and assessment of surgical patients' welfare and recovery. *Nursing Research, 22,* 394–401.

19

Assessed Life Stress and Experimentally Provided Social Support

Karen C. Lindner, Irwin G. Sarason, and Barbara R. Sarason
University of Washington

The literature on social support has proliferated dramatically in recent years because of a variety of informal observations and theoretical-research advances. Supervisors recognize the motivational value of supervisory interest and involvement for workers. Health professionals note the salutary effects of their attention and expressed concern on patients' well-being in recovery from illness. Psychotherapists try to provide their clients with the acceptance needed to pursue self-examination. Members of military organizations develop strong, mutually reinforcing ties with each other that contribute to their success and survival.

In addition to this type of generally informal observational data, the United States' military experience in Vietnam produced provocative evidence concerning the relationship of social support under stress to later well-being. The readjustment problems among Vietnam veterans have been unusually high; according to recent estimates 20 to 60% of these veterans report such problems (Friedman, 1981). Several causes for this high rate of poststress syndrome have been suggested. The war was a controversial one, and many members of the military felt that the public failed to display sympathy and backing for their efforts and sacrifices. Perhaps even more important was the change in military procedure in which, unlike the practice of previous wars, soldiers entered and left the Vietnam combat area as individuals, not as cohesive groups.

Thus far, most of the empirical work on social support has been directed toward two topics, social support as a stress moderator and the assessment of social support. The first concerns the relationship between social support and health where support is viewed as a moderator of stress (particularly stress experienced in the form of negative life events). Illustrative of this approach is Sarason, Sarason, Potter and Antoni's (1985) study of positive and negative life events and social support as factors in illness among Navy Submarine School students. They found that negative, but not positive, life events in the recent past were related to reports of illness. While social support by itself was not related to illness reports, the relationship between negative life events and illness was stronger among subjects with low rather than high levels of social support. The results suggest the importance of assessing both stressful life events and moderators of response to stress, such as social support, in investigating the role played by personality in illness.

The second topic has to do with the assessment of social support through the creation of scales for its measurement. Investigators have attempted to objectify theoretical ideas by construction of a number of measurement devices, mainly in the form of questionnaires that might then be used as criteria in further investigation (Henderson, Duncan-Jones, Byrne, & Scott, 1980; Sarason, Levine, Basham, & Sarason, 1983).

Several hundred articles have been published in the past few years that deal with social support (Gottlieb, 1983). Developmental and social psychological theories have stimulated much of this work. One of the most influential theorists has been John Bowlby, whose ideas concerning attachment have encouraged research into the supportive role of social relationships among both adults and children (Bowlby 1969; 1980). Spurred on by both formal and informal theories, researchers have begun to investigate in a systematic fashion a variety of aspects of social support, including how it contributes to performance, positive adjustment, and personal development and also the way it might provide a buffer against the effects of stress.

Despite the growth of interest in the topic, the tasks of empirically demonstrating social support's effects and specifying the mechanisms involved in these effects have barely begun. One of the barriers to objective research has been the lack of a reliable, general, and convenient index of social support. Some researchers have simply gathered information about subjects' confidants and acquaintances; others have focused their attention on the availability of helpful others in coping with certain work, family, and financial problems, and still others have devised questionnaires and other techniques to assess social support. These devices range from simple paper and pencil tests to detailed interview schedules.

The diversity of measures of social support is matched by the diversity of conceptualizations concerning its ingredients. However, regardless of how it is conceptualized, social support would seem to have two basic elements: (1) the number of available others to whom one can turn in time of need and (2) the degree of satisfaction with the available support. Sarason, Levine, Basham, and Sarason (1983) have constructed an instrument, the Social Support Questionnaire, that assesses these dimensions of social support. The Social Support Questionnaire (SSQ) seems to be reliable, psychometrically satisfactory instrument. Scores on the SSQ seem more strongly related to positive than negative life changes and have an inverse relationship to psychological discomfort, although this last relationship is stronger among women than men. As measured by the SSQ, social support seems to be an asset in enabling a person to persist in a task under frustrating conditions.

Until recently, most of the literature on social support has been clinical, impressionistic, and speculative. This literature has been valuable in directing attention to the relevance of social ties to personal adjustment. However, the amount of research that uses the careful controls and manipulations characteristic of experiments is insufficient. This chapter describes an experiment that deals with the behavioral and cognitive dimensions of social support. The research was stimulated by the need to specify mediational processes involved in producing the effects of social support. The time seems particularly ripe for well-controlled studies of social support because of the availability of a reliable measuring instrument. In the experiment, social support was assessed as an individual difference variable using the SSQ. Subjects differing in assessed social support performed on tasks after either receiving experimentally provided social support or a neutral condition. Thus it was possible to determine the joint effects of social support in one's life and experimental manipulations of support in particular situations.

A topic of special interest in this research was the possibility that, to some extent, specially provided support might compensate for lack of social support in the lives of some people. Demonstration of positive effects on performance of specially provided support might have significant implications for understanding how organizations function, the ability of groups of people to achieve their goals, and the process of personal development.

The experiment investigated the relationships of assessed life changes, social support, and experimentally provided social support to performance in a problem-solving situation. Life changes were included in the research design because of the possibility that social support might interact with life changes in influencing performance. While many studies have provided correlational evidence about the relationships among life changes and social support, very few investigations have examined these variables simultaneously in an experimental framework.

METHOD

Design

The study was organized as a $2 \times 2 \times 3$ experimental design with two levels of life change, two levels of assessed social support, and three levels of experimentally provided social support. Although sex of subject was not used to select subjects, sex was analyzed as a fourth ANOVA factor.

Subjects

The 113 subjects were undergraduate psychology students at the University of Washington who received credit for research participation in their psychology classes. Their levels of life changes were assessed using the Life Experiences Survey (LES) (Sarason, Johnson, & Siegel, 1978). Half of the subjects had high scores on the LES index of recent negative life changes; the remaining subjects had relatively low scores on this index. Prior to the experiment, a large group of undergraduates had been administered the LES and the SSQ. Subjects were categorized as being either low (scores of 8 or below) or high (scores of 9 or above) on the LES negative events scale. For the SSQ Satisfaction scale (SSQS), individuals with scores of 1.80 or less were designated the high-support group while those with SSQS scores of 1.81 or more were designated the low-support group.

Subjects were selected so as to fill the four cells represented by high and low LES and high and low SSQS scores. Subjects in each of these four groups were contacted by telephone and randomly assigned to experimental and control conditions until at least eight subjects were obtained for each cell of the $2 \times 2 \times 3$ matrix.

Procedure

The experimental social support intervention was a part of the instructions for performance on the problem-solving task. The task was the Means-Ends Problem-Solving test (MEPS) (Platt & Spivack, 1975), which taps the ability to define a problem, conceive of options available for action, and see the necessary means and potential obstacles that comprise a plan of action. Problems involving work situations, interpersonal relations, and emotional reactions relevant to an undergraduate population were chosen. All of the problems required subjects to write about problems involving a same-sex protagonist.

The subjects were presented with five MEPS-type problems and asked to write the middle of a story that had a beginning and end provided. For example:

> M was feeling pressured for time to meet her (his) responsibilities while both working and going to school. She (he) needed to continue to both work and go to school . . . The story ends with M feeling better about how she (he) balanced her (his) responsibilities with the time she (he) had. You begin the story with M being pressured for time.

The stories were scored using the procedure described by Platt and Spivack (1975) to assess subjects' abilities to formulate the protagonist's problem, use thinking as a step toward problem resolution, and state specific means applicable to achieving the protagonist's goals. The subjects' stories were scored by three assistants who were trained until they reached a level of 80% agreement in scoring. Pairs of scorers scored all 113 stories written about a particular problem and any differences in scoring were discussed and resolved.

The 113 subjects were administered the MEPS in small groups with subjects seated around a large table. After consent forms had been completed, the experimenter handed out MEPS story packets and read the instructions.

All subjects were told:

> We are interested in investigating how people generate solutions to problems. Today we will ask you to make up some stories. For each story you will be given the beginning of the story and how the story ends. Your job is to make up a story which connects the beginning that is given you with the ending given you. In other words, you make up the middle of the story. Do you have any questions?

Individuals who got only these instructions comprised a control condition.

The experimental social support (ESS) intervention was included as part of the instructions for the task. Subjects who received this condition were told:

> Some of you will feel uneasy about writing stories. Remember you are not the only person who feels this way. Just relax and do your best. Do you have any questions? I'll be available to you throughout your work to answer any more questions that you have. After you are done, please take your stories next door and there will be someone to debrief you and give you any more information that you should want or need.

These instructions were designed to provide subjects with reassurance and encouragement and to let them know that help was available at any point during the experimental session.

In the third experimental condition, subjects were told:

Writing stories does not bother most people. We expect you to have no trouble with the task. Just get busy and do your best. You have the instructions now. I will not be able to answer any more questions for you. After you are done, please take your stories next door and there will be someone to debrief you.

These instructions were regarded as a restricted social support condition in that subjects were not given encouragement and were not given the opportunity to seek help during the session should they feel they needed it.

Following the problem-solving task, the Cognitive Interference Questionnaire (Sarason & Stoops, 1978), was administered. It asks subjects to indicate specific kinds of task-irrelevant thoughts which might have occurred while working on a particular task. In addition, subjects filled out a brief questionnaire which asked them to rate the experimenter. They also completed rating scales describing how they felt they had performed on the MEPS.

Results

Ratings of subjects' stories were analyzed using analysis of variance for the following measures:

1. Formulation score. The degree to which the subject formulated the problem presented to the subject in the first part of the story.

2. Thinking score. The degree to which a subject described the protagonist as thinking about a problem before initiating action.

3. Initiative score. The degree to which the protagonist initiated the solution, followed up on another character's action, passively accepted a solution, or did not solve a problem.

4. Relevance score. The degree to which the protagonist's problem-solving steps were relevant to goal attainment.

For each measure, subjects' scores were summed over all stories. As a manipulation check, subjects were asked to rate their experimenter on several dimensions. Subjects who were given social support rated their experimenters as significantly more supportive $(F (2,102) = 4.038, p < .02)$ and pleasant $(F (2,102) = 3.662, p < .03)$ than did subjects in other groups.

Each analysis of variance included four factors: life changes (LES-N), social support (SSQS), sex, and experimental social support (ESS). The only significant result in the Formulation analysis was for the LESN-SSQS interaction $(F (1,88) = 7.272, p < .01)$. This interaction was caused by the fact that low LESN-high SSQS subjects emphasized problem formulation to a greater degree than did high LESN-high SSQS subjects. For low LESN subjects, high SSQS scores were also associated with higher formulation scores than was the case for low LESN-low SSQS subjects. However, this difference was not statistically significant.

Table 1   Initiative score means for groups differing in
Social Support Questionnaire satisfaction
(SSQS) scores and experimental social support
(ESS) (Ns in parentheses)

	SSQS	
ESS	High	Low
Support	9.78 (19)	12.80 (19)
Restricted·support	9.74 (21)	10.64 (17)
Control	11.63 (16)	8.70 (20)

The only significant result in the use of thinking analysis was the main effect for assessed social support (F (1,88) = 3.847, p < .05). The low SSQS group emphasized thinking as a step toward problem resolution more often than did high SSQS subjects.

There were two significant Fs in the initiative analysis. One was for SSQS × ESS (F (2,88) = 4.913, p < .01) and the other was for the four-way interaction (F (2,88) = 6.128, p < .01). Comparisons of the means involved in the SSQS × ESS interaction showed that for the control group, those with higher assessed social support has significantly higher initiative scores (p < .05) than subjects with lower assessed social support. Experimentally provided social support was associated with significantly lower initiative scores (p < .01) for high than low SSQS subjects. For low SSQS subjects, the experimental support condition was associated with the highest initiative, while for high SSQS subjects, the control condition was associated with the highest initiative scores. Table 1 presents the means for the SSQS × ESS interaction.

The relevance analysis yielded a significant 4-way interaction (F (1,88) = 4.201, p < .05). An analysis of variance was also performed on the Cognitive Interference Questionnaire, which was administered subsequent to MEPS performance. There were two significant results for the SSQS (F (1,88) = 8.79, p < .05) and Sex (F (1,88) = 7.537, p < .05) variables. Low SSQS subjects reported being distracted significantly less often (Xs = 22.74 vs. 24.14) than did high SSQS subjects. Women reported less distraction than did men (Xs = 22.32 vs. 24.73).

DISCUSSION

This research was designed to find out whether people differing in assessed social support respond differently to experimentally provided support. Our results suggest that there is a significant interaction between assessed and provided social support. Among subjects low in assessed social support, those provided with support in the experimental situation attained the highest level of problem-solving. Low SSQS subjects under the control condition had the lowest initiative scores in the entire experiment. A salutary effect on performance during the restricted support condition was not expected, yet this seems to have been the case for low SSQS subjects. In contrast, results for the high assessed social support subjects were quite clear in that the control condition was associated with the highest levels of problem solutions. Thus, support was not facilitative for subjects who reported satisfaction with regard to their social support, but was facilitative for those low in satisfaction. Surprisingly, restricted support was also facilitative for low SSQ subjects. This may have happened because, even though this condition was not supportive in the usual sense of the term, the restricted support communication did serve to structure the situation by providing information concerning how subjects might react to the story completion task by stating that most people do not have trouble with the task. This can be interpreted as reassurance or a supportive element especially if the task does not appear too demanding. In addition, the direction "just get busy" may have served to focus attention on the task and reduce interfering thoughts.

The interaction between assessed and experimentally manipulated social support provides impetus for further investigation of experimentally manipulated support, particularly with regard to definition of the specific aspects of situations that have salutary effects on performance. This interaction may have important implications for applied studies of human performance and organizational effectiveness, as well as theories of social support. Probably, the crucial ingredients in the experimental support condition used in this study was communication of empathy to the subject and the availability of help should it be needed. These two ingredients are at least potentially present in virtually every situation where people perform tasks; for example, interactions among co-acting workers.

The experimental results related to cognitive processes are also of interest. Low SSQS subjects reported devoting more thought to their problem solutions than did high SSQS subjects. The meaning of this result is not clear because the quality of the stories produced was lower. There may be important differences in thinking styles between high and low social support subjects. It is possible that low social support subjects spend considerable time thinking about problems on which they are working, perhaps to the detriment of their actual performance. This may have been particularly true for the control condition in this experiment. Too much conscious preoccupation with certain problems can have a negative effect. For example, the ability to drive a car declines with increases in the driver's preoccupation with the specific steps involved in the task. It may be that low social support individuals perceive social situations as more difficult and thus take a problem-solving approach to them rather than an intuitive approach. This idea also fits with the results discussed above in which the restricted support improved the number of positive efforts described in the stories for low SSQS, possibly by the emphasis on task orientation and reassurance. More information is needed about the relationship between social support and task-relevant and task-irrelevant cognitive activity. It would be valuable to compare individuals with different levels of assessed support in terms of their movement from thinking about problems to action concerning them.

One surprising result of this study was that those subjects high in SSQS reported more thoughts about task-irrelevant material than did those low in SSQS. It may be that the task material had less motivational quality for people who feel secure in their social relationships. They may have allowed their minds to wander because the task appeared so easy to them.

The results concerning the interaction between negative life events and satisfaction with social support are intriguing. They suggest that people low in negative life events and high in social support are more likely to formulate problems posed to them than do people high in negative life events and low in social support. One possibility suggested by this finding is that individuals who have experienced many negative life events may feel more helpless and less in control of their environment than do those whose life experiences have been relatively more positive. These results suggest the value of studying the joint effects of life changes and social support on problem-solving strategies (Miller & Lefcourt, 1983).

As suggested above, the interaction between assessed and manipulated social support may be the most significant finding of this study. Whereas experimenter-provided social support was a definite asset to the performance of low social support subjects, the opposite seemed to be the case for high SSQS subjects. Low SSQS subjects may think about tasks more than do high SSQS subjects. However, their thinking may not necessarily be followed by a high quality solution (this was true for example, of the control condition). It is possible that those low in social support think so much about what to do that the effectiveness of their performance is compromised. The possibility that under certain conditions people low in social support become "bogged down" in thinking is suggested also by Sarason, Levine, Basham, and Sarason's (1983) finding of a negative relationship between SSQ scores and the Neuroticism scale of the Eysenck Personality Inventory. The difference between emphasis on thinking about the problem and cognitive interference in the form of worries and distracting thoughts needs to be further clarified.

Supportive manipulations such as those used in this experiment may exert their influence by reducing feelings of impersonality and concerns about the availability of people on whom the individual can rely. People with low levels of social support and/or dissatisfaction with the support available to them may have relatively low levels of belief in the interest other people might have in them. The socially isolated individual is, in a sense, more on the spot than the individual who has ties with others (Jones, Kobbs, & Hockenbury, 1982). Social support manipulations may reduce perceptions of social isolation.

An important question about social support concerns whether its absence is, in a sense, inflicted upon the individual or is a function of personal attributes or lack of social skills, characteristics that either drive other people away or fail to attract them. In particular, if skills are important factors and if these can be identified rather specifically, then training strategies to help individuals alter their social interaction patterns may be a useful way of increasing social support (Sarason, Sarason, Hacker & Basham, 1985). Social skills of those differing in social support (SSQN) were recently studied in an experiment in which pairs of subjects differing in assessed social support were videotaped, first while they spent five minutes getting acquainted and then in another 5-minute period discussing how to solve a hypothetical problem about a troublesome roommate. Each subject's social skills were then rated by the experimenter on the basis of his initial contact with the subject after the role plays. Ratings were also made by both the subject and the subject's partner. Finally independent raters who viewed the videotape also made ratings of subjects' social behavior. The physical attractiveness of the subjects based on color snapshots was also rated. Each subject completed a social competence questionnaire and several problem-solving stories designed to measure social skills. These stories resembled the ones used in the present study.

Sarason, Sarason, Hacker and Basham (1985) found that subjects high in self-described social support scored higher than those low in social support on several measures of social skills. Those low in social support were described by raters as less likeable and less effective than subjects with high social support scores. Of special interest were the high correlations among the subject's appraisal of his or her own social competence, appraisals made by others, and the subject's competence as measured by knowledge of appropriate behavior in problem situations. These results clearly indicate that individuals' perceptions of their own social skills are similar to the opinions of others about their skill level. Not only did those high and low in social support elicit different responses from others and have different opinions about their own skills, but they also seemed to have different cognitions while actually in social situations. Those low in social support described themselves as uncomfortable in looking at others directly, having problems in getting people to notice them, and lacking confidence in their ability to make friends.

In Sarason, Sarason, Hacker, and Basham's study (1985), greater physical attractiveness was associated with greater satisfaction with perceived social support. This relationship was not significant for number of supports, although those high in perceived number of supports tended to be more attractive than those low in number score. Apparently, at least for same-sex interactions, physical appearance is a less important factor than social skills in promoting positive feelings about an individual. The findings of Sarason, Sarason, Hacker and Basham (1983) together with the results of the present study suggest that assessed and manipulated social support are related to social and cognitive problem solving, on the one hand, and social behavior, on the other. Low social support would seem to be a vulnerability factor in situations perceived by individuals as posing demands on them. Two important questions are: (1) Where do these vulnerabilities come from? and (2) What can be done to reduce them?

The findings of the present study suggest the possibility that some social vulnerabilities can be reduced or eliminated by specially planned interventions (Rook, 1983). There would seem to be considerable value in studying the roles of assessed and manipulated social support in situations more complex than those in the studies reported here (Argyle, 1981; Janis, 1983). For example, in certain kinds of stressful jobs, low social support people might have vulnerabilities that would suggest poor prognosis in carrying out assigned tasks. However, it may be possible to arrange situations so as to reduce the vulnerabilities. If social support is a vulnerability factor it is at least a vulnerability factor about which something can be done. Further studies involving social support assessments and manipulations could be important, both theoretically and practically.

REFERENCES

Argyle, M. (1981). The contribution of social interaction research to social skills training. In J. D. Wine & M. D. Smye (Eds.), *Social competence* (pp. 261–286). New York: Guilford Press.

Bowlby, John (1969). *Attachment and loss* (Vol. 1). New York: Basic Books.

Bowlby, John. (1980). *Attachment and loss* (Vol. 3). New York: Basic Books.

Friedman, M. J. (1981). Post-Vietnam syndrome: Recognition and management. *Psychosomatics, 22,* 931–943.

Gottlieb, B. H. (1983). Social support as a focus for integrative research in psychology. *American Psychologist, 38,* 278–943.

Henderson, S., Duncan-Jones, P., Byrne, D. G., & Scott, R. (1980). Measuring social relationships: The Interview Schedule for Social Interaction. *Psychological Medicine, 10,* 723–734.

Janis, I. L. (1983). The role of social support in adherence to stressful decisions. *American Psychologist, 38,* 143–160.

Jones, W. H., Kobbs, S. A., & Hockenbury, D. (1982). Loneliness and social skill deficits. *Journal of Personality and Social Psychology, 42,* 682–689.

Miller, R. S., & Lefcourt, H. M. (1983). Social intimacy: An important moderator of stressful life events. *American Journal of Community Psychology, 11,* 127–139.

Platt, J. J., & Spivack, G. (1975). *Manual for the Means-Ends Problem-Solving Procedure.* Philadelphia: Department of Mental Health Sciences, Hahnemann Community Mental Health/Mental Retardation Center.

Rook, K. S. (1983). *Promoting social bonding: Strategies for helping the lonely and socially isolated.* Unpublished manuscript, University of California.

Sarason, B. R., Sarason, I. G., Hacker, T. A., & Basham, R. B. (1985). Concomitants of social support: Social skills, physical attractiveness, and gender. *Journal of Personality and Social Psychology, 49,* 469–480.

Sarason, I. G., Johnson, J. H., & Siegel, J. M. (1978). Assessing the impact of life changes: Development of the Life Experiences Survey. *Journal of Consulting and Clinical Psychology, 46,* 932–946.

Sarason, I. G., Levine, H. M., Basham, R. B., & Sarason, B. R. (1983). Assessing social support: The Social Support Questionnaire. *Journal of Personality and Social Psychology, 44,* 127–344.

Sarason, I. G., Sarason, B. R., Potter, E. H., & Antoni, M. H. (1985). Life events, social support and illness. *Psychosomatic Medicine, 47*(2), 156–163.

Sarason, I. G., & Stoops, R. (1978). Test anxiety and the passage of time. *Journal of Consulting and Clinical Psychology, 46,* 102–109.

20

State Anxiety in Therapy Groups

R. D. de Jong
University of Utrecht

State anxiety may vary in intensity and fluctuate over time as a function of the stresses that impinge on an individual (Spielberger, 1966). State anxiety of participants in therapy groups is related to individual differences in anxiety proneness (trait anxiety) and characteristics of the situation and may also be due to a combination of individual and situational factors. Group leadership and the personality characteristics and behavior of the therapist, including the way of working, may be an important situational factor. Therapists differ with respect to the anxiety they tend to induce or reduce in their clients (Liebermann, Yalom, & Miles, 1973).

In investigating the effects of various situations on behavior, it is desirable to assess some measurable property of situations, for example, physical properties, or those derived from a consensus of subjective ratings (Argyle, 1976). In understanding a person's anxiety in a particular situation, his or her perception of that situation is most relevant, irrespective of whether there is a consensus about its meaning. McMichael (1978) cites research evidence indicating that supportive relationships with supervisors, co-workers, wives, and friends may function as protective buffers against the consequences of a stressor. Bowlby (1976) notes that having a trusted companion greatly reduces fear and anxiety.

The emotional support of a therapist, as reflected in caring (acceptance, friendliness), which is similar to the Rogerian concept of unconditional positive regard, can be expected to protect the client against stressors and thus reduce his or her state anxiety. Caring was one of the two factors Liebermann et al. (1973) found to be of therapeutic value in their study of encounter groups. The second benevolent group-leader factor identified by Liebermann et al. (1973), "cognitizing" (clarification, interpretation), may also correlate negatively with state anxiety because these activities help the client to cope with anxiety.

Ratings of group therapists on caring and cognitizing can reflect consensus among group members about qualities of the therapist or divergent views of individual clients. If the latter is the case, differences in client ratings can be

The research reported in this chapter was carried out in cooperation with Stichting Veluweland, Psychotherapeutic Center for the Treatment of Neuroses, Ederveen, and the Institute for Psychiatric Day Treatment, Willem Arntzhuis, Utrecht.

241

attributed to the diverse perceptions of group members or to differences in the behavior of the therapist toward individual clients. Whatever the case may be, the client's perception of a therapist has been shown to be a major factor in predicting therapeutic outcome.

In addition to the impact of situational factors on state anxiety, the personality characteristics of the client can be expected to influence outcome. According to an interactional model, personality traits may be defined in terms of individual differences in the disposition to respond with specific types of behavior to particular classes of situations (Spielberger, 1977). Social anxiety is a specific form of trait anxiety that has special relevance to differences in anxiety proneness within the context of group therapy. In group-therapy situations, it would be expected that the relation between therapists' caring and state anxiety would be stronger for clients who were high in social anxiety.

Other group members can also contribute to the anxiety of a particular client. Attraction to the group, or group cohesiveness (Liebermann et al., 1973; Yalom, 1975), may also contribute to the degree of positive feeling a client experiences in his or her relations with other group members. Thus, group cohesiveness would be expected to correlate negatively with state anxiety.

The present study investigated the effects of group and individual characteristics on state anxiety in the context of group therapy sessions. Group differences were operationalized in terms of the characteristics of the group therapist as perceived by the client and the attraction each group member feels for his or her group. A social anxiety scale was used to measure anxiety proneness. A negative relation between therapists' caring and the clients' state anxiety was predicted. This relationship was expected to be stronger for clients with greater social anxiety.

METHOD

Subjects

The subjects were 8 male and 12 female clients, ranging in age from 20 to about 40 years, who were receiving treatment in a day clinic. Complaints included anxiety, depressive affect, and problems in interpersonal relations. The clients participated in one of three treatment groups run by the clinic. Each group consisted of eight members and followed the same program. Admission to the groups was "open," that is, after one client left, the first person on the clinic waiting list was permitted to fill the vacant place in the group.

The therapeutic program included Rogerian group psychotherapy, psychodrama, music therapy, Gestalt-oriented art therapy, and psychodrama. The staff was comprised of a clinical psychologist, a psychiatrist, a social worker, and art, drama and music therapists. The sessions were led by staff members who were specialists in the particular therapeutic activity scheduled for that meeting. In addition, one staff member generally participated in each session as an observer. In this way, each client was seen over the span of 2 weeks by almost all members of the therapeutic staff. Clients who had participated in at least 14 therapeutic sessions and who were observed by at least four of the therapists were included in the study.

Procedure

At the beginning of the study, the clients completed a social anxiety scale (Willems, Tuender-de Haan, & Defares, 1973). Throughout the 10-week period of the study, group members completed a short questionnaire after each therapy session in which the client described his reaction to each treatment session. This questionnaire included:

1. A 3-item state anxiety scale. The items were selected from Oostrburg's translation of Spielberger's State-Trait Anxiety Inventory (Spielberger, Gorsuch, & Lushene, 1970) on the basis of item-remainder correlations and item content (Orlebeke, personal communication). Examples: "I feel nervous," "I am worried."

2. A 3-item group cohesiveness scale, from Yalom and Rand (1966), which was used by de Jong, Wanrooy and Koppelaar (1979) in a previous group therapy study. Examples: "I felt involved in what happened;" "In this session I participated in a way that was satisfactory to me."

3. A 4-item rating scale for describing therapists' behavior with respect to caring (positive regard, acceptance) and cognitizing (attribution of meaning, clarification). This scale was also used in a previous group therapy study (de Jong et al., 1979).

RESULTS

Reliability of the State Anxiety Measure

Cronbach's alpha coefficient was calculated for the total set of anxiety measures obtained for all subjects in the sample (1115 cases), yielding a value of .75. An alpha coefficient was also calculated for each client in order to assess to what extent the items reliably differentiated between the group sessions he or she had attended. The median value of these alpha coefficients was .65. The range, however, was large, from .10 to .95. Alpha was also calculated over persons for a sample of situations; the median alpha was .67, with a much smaller range (between .60 and .70).

The Therapist as a Situational Factor

Since five different therapists treated the same groups of clients, the therapist effect on the clients' state anxiety was examined by comparing sessions led by different therapists. This analysis was carried out for all groups combined, as well as separately for each group and each client.

The state anxiety scores were aggregated as recommended by Alker (1977). For each client, the state anxiety scores were averaged for each therapist. Kendall's coefficient of concordance (Siegel, 1956) was calculated as an index of agreement among the client's sets of state anxiety scores, averaged per

Table 1   Coefficients of concordance, (W) for
therapists as a source of variation in the
state anxiety of clients

Groups	Therapists	Clients	W	p
Combined	5	19	.076	ns
Group 1	5	5	.574	<.05
Group 2	5		.275	ns
Group 3	5	8	.134	ns

therapist. The magnitude of agreement among the clients' anxiety scores indicated the "objective" impact of the therapist factor, that is, whether therapists differed consistently with respect to the amount of state anxiety that clients experienced under their leadership.

The coefficient of concordance (W), reported in Table 1, was close to zero when the three groups were combined. When the groups were analyzed separately, however, a significant therapist effect for Group 1, but not for the other groups, indicated systematic therapist impact in only one group.

In order to evaluate individual differences between the ways clients reacted subjectively to the therapists, one-way analyses of variance were carried out, with therapists as the independent variable. For the 18 clients, only one F value was significant at the .05 level, and only three F values approached significance between the .05 and the .10 level. Obviously, such findings could be expected to occur by chance.

State Anxiety and Clients' Perceptions
of the Therapists

The clients' agreement with regard to therapists' cognitizing was significant for all three groups combined ($p < .001$), though the magnitude of W was rather modest ($W = .25$ for 19 clients, five therapists). The clients' agreement about therapists caring was low and nonsignificant. Since no consistent therapist effect on clients' state anxiety was found, the relationship between cognitizing and caring and state anxiety were analyzed in only two ways: across sessions for each client and across clients.

Pearson product-moment correlations between state anxiety and caring for each client across sessions are summarized in Table 2. For the majority of

Table 2   Correlations across sessions for individual client between
state anxiety and caring, cognitizing, and attraction to the
group

	Positive	Negative	Range of correlations
Caring	3	17	−.53 to .25
Cognitizing	8	12	−.44 to .17
Attraction to group	7	13	−.66 to .46

subjects (17 out of 20), these correlations were negative as expected. Although the number of negative correlations was larger than could be expected by chance (binomial test, $p < .001$), the magnitude of these correlations was rather modest.

The correlation of cognitizing and attraction to the group with state anxiety are also reported in Table 2. No clear relationship between state anxiety and cognitizing was found: only 12 out of 20 correlations were in the expected negative direction. There was also no evidence that state anxiety and attraction to the group covaried across sessions.

Spearman's rank order (Rho) correlation between state anxiety and caring, averaged over sessions and calculated across clients, was –.38. This correlation was statistically significant ($p < .05$) and in the expected direction, indicating that the more a client perceived the therapists as caring, the lower his or her state anxiety was likely to be. This finding seems to indicate that individuals who perceive their therapists as caring experience less anxiety than others. However, it may indicate a difference in the caring responses evoked in their therapists by various clients, or it may be due to an unknown factor that influenced both state anxiety and therapists' caring.

The Rho correlation between state anxiety and attraction to the group was –.55, indicating that the more a client feels attracted to his or her group, the less anxiety he or she is likely to experience in the group sessions. The Rho between cognitizing and state anxiety was essentially zero.

State anxiety as a reaction to the group sessions, averaged for each client, was positively and significantly correlated with social anxiety test scores as expected; the Spearman's Rho was .47 ($N = 20, p < .05$). A possible interaction between social anxiety and caring was examined by the correlation between social anxiety test scores and each client's correlation between caring and state anxiety, across sessions. Spearman's Rho was .34 ($N = 20, p < .10$), indicating a slight trend toward an interaction effect.

It may be concluded that differences among therapists did not explain fluctuations in state anxiety in the group therapy sessions. But differences among clients in anxiety-proneness (social anxiety), and, especially, in the way they perceived their therapists and other group members, were meaningfully related to state anxiety. In order to take more aspects of the group members' appraisals into account and to differentiate these from the "objective" characteristics of the group therapy situation, questionnaires and methods such as observation, interviewing, content analysis, and so forth, should be employed in future research.

REFERENCES

Alker, H. A. B. (1977). State-trait anxiety and interactional psychology. In D. Magnussen & N. S. Endler (Eds.), *Personality at the crossroads: Current issues in interactional psychology.* Hillsdale, NJ: Lawrence Erlbaum.

Argyle, M. A. (1976). Personality and social behaviour. In R. E. Harrè (Ed.), *Personality.* Oxford: Basil Blackwell.

Bowlby, J. (1976). The self-reliant personality: Some conditions that promote it. In R. E. Harrè (Ed.), *Personality,* Oxford: Basil Blackwell.

de Jong, R. D., Wanrooy, W., & Koppelaar, L. (1979). *Attraction to the group as a function of behaviour of the group therapist and client characteristics.* Presentation at the XIth International Congress of Psychotherapy, Amsterdam.

Liebermann, M. A., Yalom, I., & Miles, M. (1973). *Encounter groups: First facts.* New York: Basic Books.
McMichael, A. J. (1978). Personality, behavioral, and situational modifiers of work stressors. In C. L. Cooper & R. Payne (Eds.), *Stress at work.* Chichester: Wiley.
Siegel, S. (1956). *Non-parametric statistics.* New York: McGraw-Hill.
Spielberger, C. D. (1966). Theory and research on anxiety. In C. D. Spielberger (Ed.), *Anxiety and behavior.* New York: Academic Press.
Spielberger, C. D. (1977). State-trait anxiety and interactional psychology. In D. Magnusson & N. S. Endler (Eds.), *Personality at the crossroads: Current issues in interactional psychology.* Hillsdale, NJ: LEA.
Spielberger, C. D., Gorsuch, R. L., & Lushene, R. E. (1970). *Manual for the State-Trait Anxiety Inventory (Self-Evaluation Questionnaire).* Palo Alto, CA: Consulting Psychologists Press.
Willems, L. F. M., Tuender-de Haan, H. A., & Defares, P. B. (1973). Een schaal om sociale angst te meten. *Nederlandse Tijdschrift voor de Psychologie, 28,* 415–422.
Yalom, I. (1975). *The theory and practice of group psychotherapy.* New York: Basic Books.
Yalom, I., & Rand, K. (1966). Compatibility and cohesiveness in therapy groups. *Archives of General Psychiatry, 13,* 267–276.

Author Index

Subject Index